Malay

lonely planet

phrasebooks

and

Susan Keeney

Malay phrasebook
3rd edition – March 2008

Published by
Lonely Planet Publications Pty Ltd ABN 36 005 607 983
90 Maribyrnong St, Footscray, Victoria 3011, Australia

Lonely Planet Offices
Australia Locked Bag 1, Footscray, Victoria 3011
USA 150 Linden St, Oakland CA 94607
UK 2nd floor, 186 City Rd, London, EC1V 2NT

Cover illustration
Jungle Walk by Wendy Wright

ISBN 978 1 74059 494 3

text © Lonely Planet Publications Pty Ltd 2008
cover illustration © Lonely Planet Publications Pty Ltd 2008

10 9 8 7 6 5 4 3 2

Printed through Colorcraft Ltd, Hong Kong
Printed in China

acknowledgments

about the author

Having lived in Malaysia on and off for 16 years, Susan Keeney first started to learn Malay in the kitchens and back rooms of obscure places like Kajang and Serdang. She wound up teaching communication courses (in both Malay and English) at various universities and colleges in Malaysia. She is now teaching elementary school students (in English) in California.

from the author

Many thanks to my three children, Johan (without whom this book would never have been finished on time), Sarah and Sabrina, for their help, advice and patience while I worked on this project. I would also like to thank my one and only *guru tatabahasa*, Awang Sariyan, who was a wonderful teacher and who certainly shared my love of grammar; and most of all, my father, Bob Keeney, for all his love and support.

from the publisher

The *Malay phrasebook* was edited by first time kite-fighter Meg Worby, who learned the rules from Senior Editors, Master of Games Karin Vidstrup Monk and Chief Top Spinner Karina Coates. Quizmaster Ben Handicott proofed the book and designer Patrick Marris finished the maze of layout in record time. His layout relay team mate, champion 'Rubex cuber' Belinda Campbell, was also the creator of the beaut illustrations, and they were both encouraged from the sidelines by vocal Senior Designer Fabrice Rocher. Natasha Velleley provided the competition map and Emma Koch expertly coached the steps of the traditional 'dance of the dictionary'; medals must also go to Karin Vidstrup Monk, Sophie Putman, Ben Handicott and Karina Coates for their unbeatable expertise and assistance at the crucial stages. Tam Yewming and Kusnandar answered every question right. Publishing Manager Jim Jenkin left his competent fingerprint on the final layout and had the box seat for all the fun and games.

Special thanks to Sofie Jussof for the creation of the Sustainable Travel chapter.

CONTENTS

malay

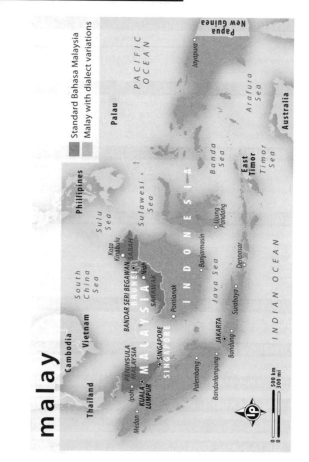

Standard Bahasa Malaysia
Malay with dialect variations

Thailand

Cambodia

Vietnam

Phillipines

Palau

PACIFIC
OCEAN

Papua
New Guinea

Jayapura

South
China
Sea

Sulu
Sea

Sulawesi
Sea

Banda
Sea

Arafura
Sea

Australia

Medan

Ipoh

PENINSULA
MALAYSIA

KUALA
LUMPUR

MALAYSIA

SINGAPORE

BANDAR SERI BEGAWAN

BRUNEI

Niah

SARAWAK

Kota
Kinabalu

SABAH

Pontianak

INDONESIA

Palembang

Bandarlampung

JAKARTA

Bandung

Surabaya

Java Sea

Banjarmasin

Ujung
Pandang

Denpasar

East
Timor

Timor
Sea

INDIAN OCEAN

0   500 km
0   300 mi

INTRODUCTION

The national language of Malaysia is Malay. Malaysians refer to it as *Bahasa Malaysia* (Language of Malaysia) or *Bahasa Melayu* (Language of the Malays). It's been the language in government and schools since the early '70s, so nearly every Malaysian speaks it, either as their first or second language.

Don't be confused by the terminology. 'Malays' are those who are racially considered Malay, usually Muslim, who also speak the language Malay. Malaysians are, of course, anyone who is a Malaysian citizen.

Malay is a member of the Western Austronesian language family and is spoken with slight variations throughout Malaysia and some parts of southern Thailand, Singapore and Brunei. In Malaysia, it's by no means the only language. Multiracial Malaysia is of course multilingual. Chinese Malaysians, who form approximately one third of the population, belong to many different dialect groups, including Cantonese, Hakka, Hokkien, Teochew and Hainanese, and many also speak Mandarin. Indian Malaysians have linguistic backgrounds in Tamil and Malayalee; other groups speak Punjabi, Gujerati and Bengali. They account for about 10% of the population.

Wherever you go in Malaysia you will see shop signs in a rainbow of languages and scripts. Malay uses the Roman alphabet, but was originally written in *jawi*, an adaptation of Arabic script created during the introduction of Islam in the 14th century. You might notice the *halal* sign in *jawi* script, which shows food is kosher for Muslims. At the crossroads of many trade routes, Malaysia's language has a potpourri of influences. In addition to Arabic (*mahkamah*, 'court'), there's Portuguese (*garfu*, 'fork'), Sanskrit (*istana*, 'palace'), Chinese (*mee*, 'noodles'), and English, (*elektrik*, 'electric').

Classical Malay was almost lost during British colonisation. It was the traders and merchants who kept the language alive during these times. 'Bazaar Malay' became a lingua franca and was the basis for the *Bahasa Melayu* we know today.

Bahasa Melayu also forms the basis for *Bahasa Indonesia*, but while Indonesian has been influenced by Dutch, Malaysian has adopted more English words, making it a dream of a language to learn for English speakers. English is Malaysia's second tongue, and is a compulsory subject in schools from the age of seven. Words such as 'clinic' and 'antibiotic' are incorporated into Malay through a change of spelling (*klinik* and *antibiotik*) and educated Malays often tend to mix languages in their daily conversations. English is commonly spoken in urban areas and it's not difficult to find someone who speaks some, even in rural areas.

While standard Malay is spoken in Kuala Lumpur, other regions of Malaysia have their own dialects that vary in pronunciation and accent. Regional accents can be strong, with variations in vocabulary. In Kelantan, *Apa khabar?*, 'How are you?' becomes *Guano demo?*. But never fear, your attempts at standard Malay will definitely be understood!

BAHASA MALAYSIA OR BAHASA MELAYU?

In this country where racial tensions still bubble under the surface of every decision, the difference between these two terms is loaded with meaning.

After the race riots of 1969 the government made many moves to address economic inequities, including a declaration that Malay should become the national language and the medium of instruction in all schools. But what to call the language?

Bahasa Malaysia, 'the language of Malaysia', was considered a unifying name, implicitly for Malaysians of all origins. In 1989 however, the members of the *Dewan Bahasa dan Pustaka* (The Hall of Language and Publishing), who are predominantly Malay, decided to change it back to *Bahasa Melayu,* 'the language of the Malays'. This move was seen by some to be a racially possessive, 'our language, not yours' move. It remains the official name.

INTRODUCTION

Bahasa Melayu is an easy language to learn to speak. The spelling is largely phonetic; tenses are simple to use and you don't have to worry about gender in grammar. This makes for fast progress and plenty of communication. You'll get a kick out of learning Malay, and remember that, even a simple *terima kasih*, te-*ree*-muh *kah*-si(h), 'thank you', will please the people you meet. *Selamat belajar*, se-*lah*-maht be-*lah*-jar, 'happy learning' and now *jumlah!* , *joom*-lah(h)! – 'let's get to it!'

MALAY & INDONESIAN

Bahasa Melayu and *Bahasa Indonesia* have only a few differences in vocabulary and pronunciation. The structure and other aspects of grammar remain the same in both languages. This means that this book could stay in your bag for travels further south, and the same goes for our *Indonesian phrasebook* – a great read – in Malaysia. The differences in vocabulary include some of the most common words:

ENGLISH	MALAY	INDONESIAN
after	*selepas*	*sesudah*
afternoon	*petang*	*sore*
beef	*daging lembu*	*daging sapi*
brother	*abang/adik*	*kakak/laki-laki*
can (as in 'I can')	*bisa*	*boleh*
car	*boleh*	*kereta*
city	*bandar*	*kota*
cold (adj)	*sejuk*	*dingin*
cute (eg, baby)	*manis/cun*	*lucu*
invite	*menjemput*	*mengundang*
Mr	*Tuan/Encik*	*Bapak*
Mrs	*Puan*	*Ibu*
office	*pejabat*	*kantor*
room	*bilik*	*kamar*
shoes	*kasut*	*sepatu*
shop	*kedai*	*toko*
toilet	*tandas/toilet*	*WC; kamar kecil*

INTRODUCTION

HOW TO USE THIS PHRASEBOOK
You *Can* Speak Another Language
It's true – anyone can speak another language. Don't worry if you haven't studied languages before, or that you studied a language at school for years and can't remember any of it. You just need to start speaking. Once you start, you'll be amazed how many prompts you'll get to help you build on those first words. You'll hear people speaking, pick up sounds from TV, catch a word or two from the local radio, see something on a billboard – all these things help to build your understanding.

Plunge In
There are a few everyday words you could learn right away. The general greeting is *Selamat pagi*, se-*lah*-maht *pah*-gee. For other hellos and goodbyes, see page 40. If you are moving though a crowd or trying to get past people it is polite to say *Maafkan saya*, mah-*ahf*-kahn *sai*-yuh, which means 'Excuse me'. For tips on civilities and body language, see page 53. Two easy words to remember are *Tidak*, *tee*-dah(k), 'No' and *Ya*, ya, 'Yes'. If you're having trouble understanding someone, just say *Saya tidak faham*, *sai*-yuh *tee*-dah(k) *fah*-hahm, 'I don't understand'. 'How much is it?' is *Berapa harganya ini?*, be-*rah*-puh *hahr*-guh-nyuh ee-nee?. If you find yourself in an emergency situation, turn to page 203 for some handy phrases.

ABBREVIATIONS USED IN THIS BOOK

adj	adjective	lit	literal translation
col	colloquial	n	noun
excl	exclusive	pl	plural
incl	inclusive	pol	polite
inf	informal	v	verb

INTRODUCTION

LEGEND

The following notation is used throughout this phrasebook:

( ) parentheses
- indicate words can be replaced with words of your choice:

> Let's meet at (6 o'clock) at ...
> *kee-*tuh ber-*te-*moo *pah-*duh   *Kita bertemu*
> *(poo-*kool e-*nahm) dee ...*   *(pukul enam) di ...*

- indicate the words are optional:

> Can you show me (on the map)?
> *to-*long *toon-*joo(k)-kahn   *Tolong tunjukkan*
> (dee *pe-*tah)?   *(di peta)?*

- indicate one of the following:
  - meaning, eg, demonstration (protest)
  - usage, eg, date (time)
  - aspect of grammar, eg, masculine (m) and feminine (f)
  - literal translation, eg, (lit: I already eat)

/ forward slash
- indicates when single words on either side of the slash are interchangeable:

> To the left/right.   ke *ki-*ree/*kah-*nahn   *Ke kiri/kanan.*
> denotes:
>   To the left.   ke *ki-*ree   *Ke kiri.*
> and   To the right.   ke *kah-*nahn   *Ke kanan.*

- indicates when single words are synonyms – or different forms of the same word (typically masculine, or feminine, singular or plural, informal or polite):

> I'm a student.   *sai-*yuh *moo-*rid/   *Saya murid/*
>   pe-*lah-*jahr   *pelajar.*
>
> I'm not a Muslim.   *sai-*yuh boo-*kahn*   *Saya bukan*
>   moos-*lee-*meen/   *Muslimin/*
>   moos-*lee-*mah(h) (m/f)   *Muslimah.*

This denotes:

I'm not a (male) Muslim.	*sai*-yuh boo-*kahn* moos-*lee*-meen (m)	*Saya bukan Muslimin.*

and

I'm not a (female) Muslim.	*sai*-yuh boo-*kahn* moos-*lee*-mah(h) (f)	*Saya bukan Muslimah.*

; semicolon
- separates two (or more) alternative words where one (or more) consists of <u>more</u> than one word:

chilli sauce	*sam*-bahl; sos *chi*-lee	*sambal; sos cili*

denotes:

chilli sauce	*sam*-bahl	*sambal*

and

chilli sauce	sos *chi*-lee	*sos cili*

- **bullet points**
- are used in the dictionary only to separate alternative words (synonyms):

painter	pe-*loo*-kis • *ahr*-tis • se-*nee*-mahn	*pelukis • artis • seniman*

If it is necessary to clarify the difference between alternatives, this is indicated in parentheses after each word.

PRONUNCIATION

Malay is a breeze to pronounce. Unlike English, Malay is spoken as it's written, in Roman script, so getting your tongue around the correct way to say things isn't difficult. The Malay alphabet is the same as the English alphabet. You can hear little seven-year-olds reciting the 'ABC' song in schools, when they are beginning their English lessons.

There are some regional differences regarding how the language is spoken in the north-east and north-west of Malaysia, but standard Malay, *Bahasa Baku,* bah-*hah*-suh *bah*-koo , is what's taught in schools and understood everywhere.

Malays will be thrilled to assist you with correct pronunciation, so be sure to ask. The following pronunciation tips will help you to speak Malay and be understood.

STRESS
Most syllables have reasonably equal stress in Malay, but a good rule of thumb is to put more emphasis on the second-last syllable.

TRANSLITERATION SYSTEM
To help you understand the relationship between the letters and their corresponding sounds, a simple phonetic transliteration has been used throughout this book. All transliterations are in purple. We use a hyphen to indicate when a new syllable begins. The syllable to be stressed is written in italics, eg, tranz-li-te-*ray*-shuhn

PRONUNCIATION

VOWELS

Malaysian vowel sounds are much more standard than in English.
The following should help you to pronounce things correctly.

a	ah	as the 'a' in 'father'
	uh	as the 'u' in 'cup'
	ai	as the 'i' in 'aisle'

Sometimes, in the words borrowed from other languages, the 'a'
sounds like 'ay' in day or the 'a' in cat – these will be transliterated
as ay and a.

e	e	as the 'e' in 'water'
	eh	as the first 'e' in 'enter'
i	ee	as the 'ee' in 'teen'
	i	as the 'i' in 'bit'
o	o	as the 'o' in 'no'
u	oo	as the 'oo' in 'zoo'
	u	as the 'u' in 'put'

Diphthongs (Vowel Combinations)

Malay has four vowel combinations.

ai	ai	as the 'ai' in 'aisle'
au	ow	as the 'ow' in 'cow'
oi	oy	as the 'oy' in 'toy'
ua	wah	as the 'wa' in 'swan'

GET TO THE POINT

Adding -*lah* to a word gives it emphasis. Put a forceful
-*lah* on the end of any phrase to really get your point
across. You can liven up the dinner table when all you
savour is *sedaplah!*, se-*dahp*-lah(h)!, (totally
delicious!), or prevent near death when you tell your
taxi driver to *Berhenti di sinilah!*, ber-*hen*-tee dee
see-nee-lah(h)!, 'Stop here!'.

CONSONANTS

Some consonants that fall at the end of a word in Malay are not pronounced as clearly as they would be in English. It's as though the speaker starts to say the letter and then swallows it. This is shown in the transliteration system by brackets, eg, boo-*soo(k)*, 'smelly'. You will see it applied in particular to h and k.

Words ending in h have some rules all of their own. An (h) indicates a breathy h sound at the end of a syllable, and a slight lengthening of the vowel sound, which can indicate a different meaning. Don't get caught out! *Dadah*, *dah*-dah(h), means 'illegal drugs' and *dada*, *dah*-duh, means 'breast'. It's not unusual for tourists ordering a nice bit of chicken in a restaurant to accidentally ask for narcotics! Ask a Malay to pronounce some of these sounds for you and see if you can hear (and repeat) the difference. Most consonants are pronounced as they are in English, and the few exceptions are listed below.

PRONUNCIATION

c	ch	as the 'ch' in 'chair'
g	g	as the 'g' in 'garlic'
gh	gh	a throaty 'g' sound, as if you are clearing your throat
h	h	always pronounced. Stressed a little more strongly than in English, as if you were sighing. This heavy pronunciation is especially evident for words of Arabic origin, when the 'h' appears between two vowels that are the same;
	(h)	at the end of a word, in brackets, a breathier, slightly prolonged version of the preceding vowel sound
k	k	as the 'k' in 'king';
	(k)	at the end of a syllable, in brackets, as a glottal stop – the sound made between the words 'uh-oh'
kh	kh	as the 'ch' in the Scottish *loch*
ny	ny	as the 'ny' in 'canyon'
ng	ng	as the 'ng' in 'singer'
r	r	always trilled clearly and distinctly
sy	sh	as the 'sh' in 'ship'

PRONUNCIATION

ABBREVIATED TALK

Many common words are abbreviated when you're speaking in a casual or intimate way. Sometimes the second syllable is used alone; sometimes a middle portion is dropped.

I (inf)	*aku/ku*	*ah*-koo/koo
you (inf)	*kamu/mu*	*kah*-moo/moo
you (inf)	*engkau/kau*	*eng*-kow/kow
near/at	*dekat/kat*	de-*kaht*/kaht
already/finished	*sudah/dah*	soo-dah(h)/dah(h)
not/isn't it?	*bukan/kan*	boo-kahn/kahn
no/not	*tidak/tak*	tee-dah(k)/tah(k)
want	*hendak/nak*	hen-dah(k)/nah(k)
this/these	*ini/ni*	ee-nee/nee
that/those	*itu/tu*	ee-too/too
a little bit	*sedikit/sikit*	se-*dee*-kit/*see*-kit
a little while	*sekejap/jap*	se-ke-*jahp*/jahp
only	*sahaja/saja*	sah-*hah*-juh/*sah*-juh

So, the question:

How long have you
been in Malaysia?

soo-dah(h) be-*rah*-puh
lah-muh *eng*-kow
de-*kaht* mah-*lay*-see-ah?

*Sudah berapa
lama engkau
dekat Malaysia?*

would become:

dah(h) be-*rah*-puh *lah*-muh
kow kaht mah-*lay*-see-ah?

*Dah berapa lama
kau kat Malaysia?*

Many aspects of Malay grammar make it an easy language to learn. Verbs don't change according to subject or tense, nouns don't have to have plural forms, and there are no gender-related rules to remember. Like any other language, there are nuances to be learned, but for the purpose of basic communication, the grammar is quite straightforward.

WORD ORDER

The structure of a Malay sentence is the same as in English: subject-verb-object.

I'm climbing the tree.
sai-yuh me-*mahn*-jaht *po*-ko(k) *Saya memanjat pokok.*
(lit: I to-climb tree)

It's not unusual in Malay for the object to be mentioned first if it's being stressed. This causes some changes in verbs, so the beginner will find it easier to simply use the subject-verb-object construction.

ARTICLES

There's no word corresponding to 'the' or 'a/an'. Instead, they're understood from the context of a sentence. Alternatively, demonstrative adjectives *ini*, 'this/these', and *itu*, 'that/those' are placed after the noun.

this book	*boo*-koo *ee*-nee	*buku ini*
		(lit: book this)
that table	*meh*-juh *ee*-too	*meja itu*
		(lit: table that)

NOUNS
Plurals

Plural forms of nouns can be indicated by doubling the noun or by the use of quantity words such as *ramai*, 'many/numerous'.

those books	*boo*-koo-*boo*-koo *ee*-too	*buku-buku itu*
		(lit: books those)
many visitors	rah-*mai* pe-*lah*-waht	*ramai pelawat*
		(lit: visitors many)

PRONOUNS
Personal Pronouns

Saya, *sai*-yuh, is the Malay equivalent of 'I' in English. Referring to yourself as *saya* is considered polite. A more informal word for 'I' is *aku*, *ah*-koo, which is often abbreviated to *ku*. However, *aku* should only be used if you know the person you're speaking to very well, and if they're of roughly the same age and status. See the next page for polite ways of addressing people.

Malay pronouns can be a bit confusing, as Malaysians will often use a person's name, family status or title instead of the pronoun 'I' or 'you'. Malaysians also sometimes use their own names or titles when referring to themselves, rather than using 'I'. It might take a while to get used to an older Malay woman referring to herself as 'Auntie'.

> *Makcik boleh buat.*
> mah(k)-chi(k) bo-*leh*(h) boo-aht

Auntie can do it.
(lit: Auntie can do)

when the sense is:

> *Saya boleh buat.*
> *sai*-yuh bo-*leh*(h) *boo*-aht

I can do it.
(lit: I can do)

Other common age-related terms which Malaysians may use instead of 'I', even if there is no real familial relationship, include:

abang	ah-*bahng*	older brother; someone slightly older than the speaker
kakak	*kah*-kah(k)	older sister; someone slightly older
adik	ah-*di*(k)	younger brother or sister; slightly younger, or any child
pakcik	*pah*(k)-chi(k)	uncle; old enough to be the speaker's uncle or father
nenek	neh-*neh*(k)	grandmother; old enough to be the speaker's grandmother
datuk	*dah*-tu(k)	grandfather; old enough to be the speaker's grandfather

The pronoun 'you' causes problems for learners of Malay, because like 'I' there are hierarchical differentiations between various forms. The safest forms of 'you' to use when you want to make sure you are being polite are:

encik	en-*chi*(k)	mister
tuan	twahn	sir
puan	pwahn	ma'am or missus
cik	chi(k)	miss

Singular Pronouns

I/me	*sai*-yuh, ah-koo	*saya, aku*
you (inf)	*kah*-moo, eng-kow ah-*wah*(k)	*kamu, engkau, awak*
you (pol)	ahn-duh, sow-*dah*-ruh	*anda, saudara*
he/she/her/him	*dee*-uh	*dia*
it	*ee*-uh	*ia*

Plural Pronouns		
we/us/our (excludes person spoken to)	kah-mee	kami
we/us/our (includes person spoken to)	kee-tuh	kita
you	ahn-duh, ah-wah(k) se-moo-uh	anda, awak semua
they/them/their	me-reh-kuh	mereka
they (inf)	dee-uh o-rahng	dia orang

Possessive Pronouns

Malay uses possessive pronouns *after* the noun. The first and second person, 'my' and 'your', as well as the third person plural, 'their', are separate words placed after the noun they modify:

my money	*doo*-it *sai*-yuh	*duit saya* (lit: money my)
your umbrella	*pai*-yung *ahn*-duh	*payung anda* (lit: umbrella your)
their car	ke-*reh*-tuh me-*reh*-kuh	*kereta mereka* (lit: car their)

In the third person singular, 'he' and 'she', the suffix -*nya* (lit: of him/her) is added to the thing that's possessed, or the word *dia*, 'his/her' is used after the noun; -*nya* can also be used in place of the plural possessive pronoun *mereka*, 'their'.

her watch	*jahm*-nyuh; jahm *dee*-uh	*jamnya; jam dia* (lit: watch-of-her; watch her)
his keys	*koon*-chee-nyuh	*kuncinya* (lit: keys-of-him)
their house	*roo*-mah(h)-nyuh	*rumahnya* (lit: house-of-their)

GRAMMAR

Relative Pronouns

The relative pronoun *yang* is used to mean 'who/which/that/the one which/that which'.

This is the book that I want to buy.
    ee-nee *boo*-koo yahng   *Ini buku yang*
    sai-yuh *mah*-hoo be-*lee*   *saya mahu beli.*
                                    (lit: this book that I want
                                     to-buy)

The man who's big is crying.
    lah-kee-*lah*-kee yahng   *Laki-laki yang*
    be-*sahr ee*-too me-*nah*-ngees *besar itu menangis.*
                                    (lit: man who big that to-cry)

ADJECTIVES

Adjectives always follow the noun they're describing.

big	be-*sahr*	*besar*
big car	ke-*reh*-tuh be-*sahr*	*kereta besar*
		(lit: car big)
clean	*ber*-si(h)	*bersih*
clean room	*bee*-li(k) *ber*-si(h)	*bilik bersih*
		(lit: room clean)

As there's no commonly used verb which means 'is/are', the above constructions can also translate as 'The car is big' and 'The room is clean'. In writing or formal speech, the verb *ialah*, ee-*ah*-lah(h), is used here.

The relative pronoun *yang*, 'which/who', is often used with an adjective, especially when you want to describe more than one thing about the noun.

the blue car with yellow tyres
    ke-*reh*-tuh *bi*-roo yahng   *kereta biru yang*
    ber-*tai*-yahr *koo*-ning   *bertayar kuning*
                                    (lit: car blue which tyre yellow)

the big, white house
    roo-mah(h) *poo*-ti(h)   *rumah putih yang besar*
    yahng be-*sahr*   (lit: house white which big)

Comparatives

The words *lebih*, 'more', and *kurang*, 'less', are used to indicate comparisons. They're placed before adjectives. The word *daripada*, 'than', appears after adjectives to form the following constructions.

lebih/kurang + adj (+ *daripada*)
(lit: more/less ... (than))

bigger	le-*bi(h)* be-*sahr*	*lebih besar*
		(lit: more big)
slower than	*koo*-rang *che*-paht	*kurang cepat*
	dah-ree-*pah*-duh	*daripada*
		(lit: less fast than)

Daripada is also used if both objects being compared are mentioned.

Mangoes are more expensive
than bananas.

mahng-guh le-*bi(h)* mah-*hahl*	*Mangga lebih mahal*
dah-ree-*pah*-duh *pee*-sahng	*daripada pisang*
	(lit: mango more
	expensive than banana)

The way you compare quality in English, eg, 'as ... as', is indicated in Malay by the prefix *se-*.

as beautiful as	se-*chahn*-ti(k)	*secantik*
		(lit: *se*-beautiful)

Superlatives

To form the adjectives that correspond to 'most ... ' or '-est' in English, the word *paling*, 'the most', is used.

noun + *paling* + adj

cheap	*moo*-rah(h)	*murah*
the cheapest	*pah*-ling moo-*rah(h)*	*paling murah*
		(lit: most cheap)
good	bah-*gus*	*bagus*
the best	*pah*-ling bah-*gus*	*paling bagus*
		(lit: most good)

ADVERBS

As in English, adverbs can appear at the beginning, at the end or within a sentence.

also	*joo*-guh/pun	*juga/pun*
always	se-*lah*-loo/	*selalu/*
	sen-tee-*ah*-suh	*sentiasa*
here	dee *see*-nee	*di sini*
immediately	*se*-ge-ruh;	*segera;*
	de-*ngahn se*-ge-ruh	*dengan segera*
in this way	be-*gee*-nee	*begini*
in that way	be-*gee*-too	*begitu*
just now	*tah*-dee	*tadi*
maybe	*moong*-kin	*mungkin*
never	*tee*-dah(k) *per*-nah(h)	*tidak pernah*
not yet	be-*lum*;	*belum;*
	be-*lum lah*-gee	*belum lagi*
often	ke-*rahp*/se-*ring*	*kerap/sering*
perhaps	*moong*-kin	*mungkin*
possibly	*moong*-kin/bo-*leh(h)*	*mungkin/boleh*
rarely	jah-*rahng*	*jarang*
really	*soong*-gu(h)/be-*gee*-too	*sungguh/begitu*
sometimes	*kah*-dahng-*kah*-dahng/	*kadang-kadang/*
	kah-dahng-*kah*-luh	*kadang-kala*
so that	soo-*pai*-yuh/*ah*-gahr	*supaya/agar*
there	dee *sah*-nuh	*di sana*
very	sah-*ngaht*	*sangat*

VERBS

Malay verbs are divided into a number of different classes, and are formed from a root word plus a suffix and/or prefix. The root word conveys the meaning, while adding suffixes and/or prefixes indicates that it's a useable verb – one you can use in a sentence. However, the bare root-word form can always be used in everyday speech and you'll still be understood.

1. The simplest type of verb stands alone and never requires a prefix. Fortunately, many of the most commonly used verbs fit into this category:

to bathe	*mahn*-dee	*mandi*
to eat	*mah*-kahn	*makan*
to go	*per*-gee	*pergi*
to laugh	ke-*tah*-wuh	*ketawa*
to sit	*doo*-du(k)	*duduk*
to sleep	*tee*-dur	*tidur*

2. The second type of verb requires the *me-* prefixes which include *meng-*, *mem-*, *men-* and *meny-* and *me-*. These are added to the root word.

me- is used with root words beginning with *l, m, n, ng, ny, r, w* or *y*. For example, the root word 'look' becomes useable: 'to look'.

look; to look	*lee*-haht/me-*lee*-haht	*lihat/melihat*
record; to record	*rah*-kahm/me-*rah*-kahm	*rakam/merakam*

meng- is used with words beginning with *g, h, k, q, a, e, i, o, u*. The *k* is dropped to make the verb.

change; to change	*gahn*-tee/	*ganti/*
	meng-*gahn*-tee	*mengganti*
pardon; to pardon	*ahm*-poon/	*ampun/*
	me-*ngahm*-poon	*mengampun*

mem- is used with words beginning with *b, v, p* or *f*. The *p* and *f* are dropped to make the verb and an *m* used instead.

buy; to buy	be-*lee*/mem-be-*lee*	*beli/membeli*
cut; to cut	*po*-tong/me-*mo*-tong	*potong/memotong*

men- is used with words beginning with *c, j, d, t,* or *z.*

search; to search	*chah*-ree/men-*chah*-ree	*cari/mencari*
climb; to climb	*dah*-kee/men-*dah*-kee	*daki/mendaki*

meny- is used with words beginning with *s.* The *s* is replaced by a *y:*

touch; to touch	*sen*-tu(h)/me-*nyen*-tu(h)	*sentuh/menyentuh*
rent; to rent	*seh*-wuh/me-*nyeh*-wuh	*sewa/menyewa*

3. The third type of verb requires the prefix *ber-* followed by the root word. For example, the root word *tanya*, 'ask', becomes *bertanya*, 'to ask'. If the root word starts with *r*, such as *renang*, 'swim', the prefix drops the *r* and the verb becomes *berenang*, 'to swim'.

walk; to walk	*jah*-lahn/ber-*jah*-lahn	*jalan/berjalan*
get ready; to get ready	se-dee-*uh*/ber-se-dee-*uh*	*sedia/bersedia*
speak; to speak	bee-*chah*-ruh/ber-bee-*chah*-ruh	*bicara/berbicara*

4. The fourth type of verb requires the prefix *me-* and the suffix *-kan*. With the addition of *-kan*, the verb must have an object.

witness; to witness	*sahk*-see/me-*nyahk*-see-kahn	*saksi/menyaksikan*
clean; to clean	ber-*si(h)*/mem-ber-*si(h)*-kahn	*bersih/membersihkan*

5. The fifth type of verb requires the prefix *me-* and the suffix *-i*. If the root word starts with *k*, it is replaced with a *g*.

enjoy; to enjoy	*nik*-maht/me-*nik*-mah-tee	*nikmat/menikmati*
love; to love	*kah*-si(h)/me-*ngah*-si-hee	*kasih/mengasihi*

Don't be too concerned about these prefixes – you'll still be understood if you use the root word in a sentence. They mainly need to be used in formal settings or when writing.

GRAMMAR

Essential Verbs

to be able (can)	bo-*leh(h)*	*boleh*
to agree	ber-se-*too*-joo	*bersetuju*
to become	men-*jah*-dee	*menjadi*
to bring	mem-*bah*-wuh	*membawa*
to come	*dah*-tahng	*datang*
to cost	ber-*hahr*-guh	*berharga*
to depart (leave)	ber-*to*-lah(k)	*bertolak*
to do	mem-*boo*-aht	*membuat*
to give	mem-*be*-ree	*memberi*
to go	per-gee	*pergi*
to know (someone)	ke-*nahl*	*kenal*
to know (how to)	*pahn*-dai/*tah*-hoo	*pandai/tahu*
to like	*soo*-kuh	*suka*
to live	*hee*-dup	*hidup*

to make	mem-*boo*-aht	*membuat*
to meet	ber-*joom*-puh	*berjumpa*
to need	per-*loo*	*perlu*
to prefer	le-*bi(h) soo*-kuh	*lebih suka*
to return	*bah*-li(k)/	*balik/*
	poo-lahng	*pulang*
to say	ber-*kah*-tuh	*berkata*
to stay	*ting*-gahl	*tinggal*
to take	me-*ngahm*-bil	*mengambil*
to understand	*fah*-hahm	*faham*
to want	*mah*-hoo/	*mahu/*
	hehn-dah(k)/	*hendak/*
	nah(k)	*nak*

Tense

Luckily for the learner of Malay, verbs don't change their form acccording to tense. The tense of a verb can be easily worked out by context or by the inclusion of a time word such as *semalam*, 'yesterday', and *nanti* or *kemudian*, 'later'.

I went swimming yesterday.
se-*mah*-lahm *sai*-yuh   *Semalam saya*
per-gee be-re-*nahng*   *pergi berenang.*
                                 (lit: yesterday I to-go to-swim)

I will eat later.
sai-yuh *mah*-kahn   *Saya makan*
ke-*moo*-dee-ahn/*nahm*-tee   *kemudian/nanti.*
                                 (lit: I to-eat later)

Another way to indicate tense is by placing certain adverbs immediately before the verb. The most common are:

already	*soo*-dah(h)	*sudah*
currently	se-*dahng*	*sedang*
have just	bah-*roo*	*baru*
not yet	be-*lum*	*belum*
still	*mah*-si(h)	*masih*
will	*ah*-kahn	*akan*

I have already eaten
sai-yuh *soo*-dah(h)   *Saya sudah*
mah-kahn   *makan.*
                                 (lit: I already eat)

TO BE

There's no direct equivalent of 'to be' in conversational Malay. The words 'is' and 'are' are implied in a sentence. In writing or formal speech, the verb *ialah*, ee-*ah*-lah(h); is used.

My name is Abu.
nah-muh *sai*-yuh   *Nama saya*
ee-*ah*-lah(h) *ah*-boo (pol)   *ialah Abu.*
                                 (lit: name I is Abu)

I am here.
sai-yuh dee *see*-nee

Saya di sini.
(lit: I in here)

That baby is hungry.
bai-yee *ee*-too *lah*-pahr

Bayi itu lapar.
(lit: baby that hungry)

To say that something does or doesn't exist, the word *ada* 'there is/ are' (lit: to-exist) can be used in a sentence with no definite subject.

Is there a night bus?
ah-duh bahs *mah*-lahm?

Ada bas malam?
(lit: to-exist bus night?)

TO HAVE

Ada can also be used to mean 'has/have'.

I have a younger brother.
sai-yuh *ah*-duh
ah-*di(k)* le-*lah*-kee

Saya ada adik lelaki.
(lit: I have younger-sibling male)

MODALS

There are other auxiliary words that can be used with a verb to indicate modality. These include *boleh*, 'can', *suka*, 'like to', *hendak/nak*, 'want to' and *tahu*, 'know how to', and they always come before the other verb.

can; be able to	bo-*leh(h)*	boleh

I can climb trees.
sai-yuh bo-*leh(h)* *pahm*-jaht
po-ko(k)

Saya boleh panjat pokok.
(lit: I can to-climb tree)

Where can I buy ...?
dee *mah*-nuh *sai*-yuh
bo-*leh(h)* be-*lee* ...?

Di mana saya boleh beli ...?
(lit: in where I can buy ...?)

like to	soo-kuh	suka

I like to eat curry.
sai-yuh *soo*-kuh *mah*-kahn   *Saya suka makan kari.*
kah-ree   (lit: I like-to to-eat curry)

I like to play soccer.
sai-yuh *soo*-kuh main   *Saya suka main bola sepak.*
bo-luh *seh*-pah(k)   (lit: I like-to to-play
    ball kick)

want to	hehm-dah(k)/nah(k)	hendak/nak

I want to dance.
sai-yuh nah(k) me-*nah*-ree   *Saya nak menari.*
    (lit: I want-to to-dance)

I don't want that one.
sai-yuh *tee*-dah(k)   *Saya tidak hendak yang itu.*
hehm-dah(k) yahng *ee*-too   (lit: I no want-to which/
    that that)

must; have to	hah-*roos*/ mes-tee	harus/mesti

What time do I have to be at
the airport?
poo-kool be-*rah*-puh *sai*-yuh   *Pukul berapa saya harus ada*
hah-roos *ah*-duh dee   *di lapangan terbang?*
lah-*pahng*-ahn *ter*-bahng?   (lit: hour how-much I
    have-to to-exist in
    field-fly?)

may/might/can	bo-leh(h)	boleh

May I speak to ...?
bo-*leh(h)* *sai*-yuh   *Boleh saya*
ber-*chah*-kahp de-*ngahm* ...?   *bercakap dengan ...?*
    (lit: can I to-speak with ...?)

May I take photos?
bo-*leh(h)* *sai*-yuh *ahm*-bil   *Boleh saya ambil gambar?*
gahm-bahr?   (lit: can I to-take photo?)

GRAMMAR

know how to	*tah*-hoo	*tahu*

I know how to swim.
   sai-yuh *tah*-hoo be-re-*nahng*   *Saya tahu berenang.*
   (lit: I know-how-to to-swim)

IMPERATIVES

If you're asking, insisting or demanding that someone does something, don't use the prefix on the verb.

   Look!   te-*ngo(k)!*   *Tengok!*

To make a more polite command, add *silakan*, 'please', before the verb, in the context of offering someone something. *Tolong*, 'please' or 'help', is used when you're asking for something you need.

Please sit down.
   see-*lah*-kahn *doo*-du(k)   *Silakan duduk.*
   (lit: please sit)

Please be quiet.
   to-long *sen*-yahp   *Tolong senyap.*
   (lit: please/help quiet)

QUESTIONS

As in English, a question can be indicated simply by raising the intonation of your voice at the end of a sentence. Other ways to form questions include ending a sentence or a word with *-kah*.

Where did he go?
   dee *mah*-nuh-kah(h)   *Di manakah*
   dee-uh *per*-gee?   *dia pergi?*
   (lit: in where-*kah* he to-go?)

Do you like spicy food?
   ah-wah(k) *soo*-kuh   *Awak suka*
   mah-kah-nan   *makanan*
   pe-*dahs*-kah(h)?   *pedaskah?*
   (lit: you like-to food hot-*kah*?)

GRAMMAR

Another option is starting a sentence with *adakah* (lit: is it that ...?).

Is the soup hot?
    ah-duh-kah(h) soop *ee*-nee
    pah-nahs?

                Adakah sup ini panas?
                (lit: is-it-that soup this hot?)

Or you can try adding *tak*, 'no', to the end of a question:

Is it spicy or not?
    pe-*dahs* tah(k)?

                Pedas, tak?
                (lit: spicy, no?)

Finally, with nouns and adverbs, add *kan* (short for *bukan*, meaning 'not') to the end of the sentence.

We're going tomorrow, right?
    kee-tuh *per*-gee *eh*-so(k)
    kahn?

                Kita pergi esok, kan?
                (lit: we-(incl) to-go
                    tomorrow, not?)

YOU AND I

In the cities, you'll hear Malay conversations sprinkled with the English pronouns 'I' and 'you'.

You *pergi mana*?	you *per*-gee *mah*-nuh?
(lit: you go where?)	Where are you going?
I *tak pergi mana-mana*.	I *tah(k) per*-gee *mah*-nuh-
(lit: I no go anywhere)	*mah*-nuh
	I'm not going anywhere.

Speaking English carries a certain degree of status; it implies you're educated. It's possible Malaysians also use English pronouns because of the hierarchy inherent in their own language: the use of the English 'I' and 'you' lets the speaker converse on a more equal footing.

GRAMMAR

QUESTION WORDS

You can add a question word at the beginning or end of a sentence:

What?   *Apa?*

What's your name?
Apa nama kamu?
ah-puh *nah*-muh *kah*-moo?
(lit: what name you?)

Who?   *Siapakah?*

Who are they?
Siapakah mereka?
see-*ah*-puh-kah(h) me-*reh*-kuh?
(lit: who they?)

Where?   *Di mana?*

Where's the post office?
Di mana pejabat pos?
dee *mah*-nuh pe-*jah*-baht pos?
(lit: in where post office?)

When?   *Bilakah?*

When does the bus depart for Ipoh?
Bilakah bas akan berangkat ke Ipoh?
bee-luh-kah(h) bahs *ah*-kahn be-*rang*-kaht ke *ee*-po(h)?
(lit: when bus will depart to Ipoh?)

Why?   *Kenapa?*

Why is the food so oily?
Kenapa makanan ini terlalu berminyak?
ke-*nah*-puh *mah*-kah-nahn *ee*-nee ter-*lah*-loo
ber-*min*-yah(k)?
(lit: why food this too-much oily?)

Which?   *Yang mana?*

Which is your book?
Yang mana buku anda?
yahng *mah*-nuh *boo*-koo *ahn*-duh?
(lit: which book you?)

How?   *Berapa?*

How much does a bus ticket to Melaka cost?
Berapa harga tiket bas ke Melaka?
be-*rah*-puh *hahr*-guh tee-*keht* bas ke me-*lah*-kuh?
(lit: how-much price ticket bus to Melaka?)

ANSWERS

Malaysians commonly answer questions concerning availability or possession with *ada*, 'have'/'to exist', or *tidak ada*, 'don't have'/ 'no to-exist'.

Do you have Western food?	*ah*-duh *mah*-kah-nahn *bah*-raht tah(k)?	*Ada makanan Barat, tak?* (lit: have food west, no?)
Yes.	*ah*-duh	*Ada.* (lit: have)
No.	*tee*-dah(k) *ah*-duh	*Tidak ada.* (lit: no have)

NEGATIVES

Three words are used to express the negative: *tidak*, 'no', *bukan*, 'not', and *jangan*, 'don't'. *Bukan* is used with nouns.

Not me.	boo-*kahn* sai-yuh	*Bukan saya.* (lit: not me)
Not that shirt.	boo-*kahn* bah-joo ee-too	*Bukan baju itu.* (lit: not shirt that)

Both *tidak* and *jangan* are used in relation to verbs; *tidak* is also used with adjectives.

I don't want to.
sai-yuh *tee*-dah(k) *mah*-hoo
Saya tidak mahu.
(lit: I no want)

Do not enter.
jah-*ngahn mah*-su(k)
Jangan masuk.
(lit: don't enter)

My car is not red.
ke-*reh*-tuh *sai*-yuh *tee*-dah(k) *meh*-rah(h)
Kereta saya tidak merah.
(lit: car my no red)

GRAMMAR

CLASSIFIERS

When you use a number with a noun in Malay you must use a
counter word (classifier) between the number and the noun. This
classifier describes the category of thing you're counting. This also
occurs in English all the time, when we talk about *slices* of toast or
pairs of pants, although we don't call them classifiers. There are
about 40 classifiers in Malay – too many to list – so here are the
most common ones.

orang   for people
>   There are three women in that house.

>   *ah*-duh *tee*-guh *o*-rahng   *Ada tiga orang*
>   pe-*rem*-pwahn *dah*-lahm   *perempuan dalam*
>   *roo*-mah(h) *ee*-too   *rumah itu.*
>   (lit: have three *orang* woman
>   inside house that)

ekor   for other living things
>   I saw six fish.

>   *sai*-yuh *nahm*-pah(k)   *Saya nampak*
>   e-*nahm* eh-kor *ee*-kahn   *enam ekor ikan.*
>   (lit: I see six *ekor* fish)

batang   for stick-like objects (eg, cigarettes, trees)
>   He bought two cigarettes.

>   *dee*-uh be-*lee* *doo*-uh   *Dia beli dua*
>   *bah*-tahng *ro*-ko(k)   *batang rokok.*
>   (lit: he buy two *batang*
>   cigarette)

biji   for small, easily moved objects (eg, fruit, eggs)
>   I ate one durian.

>   *sai*-yuh *mah*-kahn   *Saya makan*
>   *sah*-too *bee*-jee *doo*-ree-ahn   *satu biji durian.*
>   (lit: I to-eat one *biji* durian)

buah   for bulky objects and natural features (eg, houses, rivers)
>   I bought two houses.

>   *sai*-yuh be-*lee* *doo*-uh   *Saya beli dua*
>   *boo*-ah(h) *roo*-mah(h)   *buah rumah.*
>   (lit: I buy two *buah* house)

PREPOSITIONS

about	*ten*-tahng/ me-*nge*-nah-ee	tentang/ mengenai
after	se-le-*pahs*	selepas
at (place)	dee	di
at (time)	*pah*-duh; *pah*-duh *poo*-kool *wahk*-too; jahm	pada; pada pukul; waktu; jam
between	dee ahn-*tah*-ruh	di antara
during	se-*mah*-suh	semasa
for	*oon*-tu(k)	untuk
for (time)	se-*lah*-muh	selama
if	*kah*-low	kalau
in	dee; dee dah-*lahm*	di; di dalam
inside	dah-*lahm*; dee dah-*lahm*	dalam; di dalam

from (place & time)	*dah*-ree	dari
to/forward (place)	ke	ke
from (people)	dah-ree-*pah*-duh	daripada
to (people)	ke-*pah*-duh	kepada
on (time/person)	*pah*-duh	pada
on (place)	dee	di
since	se-*jahk*	sejak
through	me-*lah*-loo-ee	melalui
until	*sahm*-pai/ se-*hing*-guh	sampai/ sehingga
with	de-ngahn	dengan
without	*tahn*-puh	tanpa
by	o-*leh(h)*	oleh

Prepositions are used in the same way as English, eg:

I want rice with chilli sauce.

sai-yuh *mah*-hoo
nah-see de-*ngahm* sahm-bahl

*Saya mahu
nasi dengan sambal.*
(lit: I to-want rice with
chilli-sauce)

She waited for three hours.

dee-uh *toong*-goo se-*lah*-muh
tee-guh jahm

*Dia tunggu selama
tiga jam.*
(lit: she wait for three hour)

CONJUNCTIONS

and	dahn	dan
because	se-*bahb*/	sebab/
	ke-*rah*-nuh	kerana
but	te-*tah*-pee	tetapi
or	ah-*tow*	atau
so that	soo-*pai*-yuh	supaya
(together) with	*ser*-tuh	serta
as if	se-o-lah(h)-o-lah(h)	seolah-olah

I want to eat because I am hungry.

sai-yuh nah(k) *mah*-kahn
se-*bahb sai*-yuh *lah*-pahr

*Saya nak makan
sebab saya lapar.*
(lit: I want-to to-eat
because I hungry)

PERKENALAN

MEETING PEOPLE

Malaysians are very interested in meeting foreigners, and they'll be happy if you even attempt to speak their language. *Lepak*, *leh*-pah(k), 'hanging out' is a national pastime and since chatting to a stranger is considered normal, you'll have plenty of opportunity to practise.

First conversations tend to include questions about family, nationality, and whether you like spicy food. People will often question what you're doing, or where you're going. The 32nd person who asks *Berasal dari mana?*, ber-*ah*-sahl *dah*-ree *mah*-nuh?, 'Where are you from?' may think they're the first, so go with the flow and try asking a few questions of your own.

YOU SHOULD KNOW

ANDA PATUT TAHU

Yes.	yah	*Ya.*
No.	*tee*-dah(k)	*Tidak.*
Excuse me.	mah-*ahf*	*Maaf.*
Hello.	*heh*-lo	*Helo.*

Goodbye. (if you're staying)
se-*lah*-maht *jah*-lahn   *Selamat jalan.*

Goodbye. (if you're leaving)
se-*lah*-maht *ting*-gahl   *Selamat tinggal.*

Please sit down.
see-*lah*-kahn *doo*-du(k)   *Silakan duduk.*

Thank you (very much).
te-*ree*-muh *kah*-si(h)   *Terima kasih (banyak-*
(*bah*-nyah(k)-*bah*-nyah(k))   *banyak).*

You're welcome.
sah-muh-*sah*-muh   *Sama-sama.*

Excuse me; Sorry.
mah-*ahf*; *min*-tuh mah-*ahf*   *Maaf; Minta maaf.*

May I?; Do you mind?
> bo-*leh(h)*?   *Boleh?*

That's fine; No problem.
> bo-*leh(h)*; tah(k) *ah*-puh   *Boleh; Tak apa.*

What did you say?
> *ah*-puh-*dee*-uh?   *Apadia?*

I'm (very) sorry. (apology)
> (*min*-tuh) mah-*ahf*   *(Minta) Maaf.*

There are two Malay words for 'please'. Use *tolong*, *to*-long, 'help', if making a request or asking someone to do something for you.

Please open the window.
> *to*-long *boo*-kah *ting*-kahp   *Tolong buka tingkap.*

Or, if you're offering something to somebody, use the word *silakan*, see-*lah*-kahn (lit: be-my-guest).

GREETINGS & GOODBYES   UCAPAN SELAMAT

Malay greetings can range from a 'Hey, you!' to a lengthy and formal exchange. Not to worry, since there are across-the-board greetings that are fine to use almost anywhere. The word *selamat*, se-*lah*-maht, comes from the Arabic word *salam*, meaning 'peace'. Putting this word together with 'morning' or 'evening' means something like 'Have a nice morning/evening'.

As in English, Malay greetings are based on the time of day – and also on routine or prayer times. While you may think the day's just begun, the person you're speaking to may have already been to market and prepared lunch.

Good morning. (sunrise – 10 am)
> se-*lah*-maht *pah*-gee   *Selamat pagi.*

Before 10 is the best time to be out and about, watching kids in starched uniforms off to school, people carrying produce to market, or drivers digging into a bowl of *bubur ayam*, *boo*-bur *ai*-yahm, 'chicken porridge.'

Good day. (10 am – 4 pm)
   se-*lah*-maht te-ngah-*hah*-ree   *Selamat tengahari.*
   By this time the heat and the traffic have really kicked in.

Good afternoon. (4 – sunset)
   se-*lah*-maht pe-*tahng*   *Selamat petang.*
   The sun is beyond the danger zone and children's kites are
   filling the sky, or the punctual tropical downpour has begun.

Good night. (goodbye at night – a farewell)
   se-*lah*-maht *mah*-lahm   *Selamat malam.*

There's not really a term for good evening – instead you can just say
hello as you would in English (also used as an informal greeting
between friends):

Hello.   *heh*-lo   *Helo*

See you later.
   joom-pah *lah*-gee *nahn*-tee   *Jumpa lagi nanti.*
I'm going home now.
   sai-yuh *bah*-li(k) *doo*-loo   *Saya balik dulu.*
Bye. (pronounced as in English)   *Bye.*

FORMS OF ADDRESS   KATA SAPAAN

It's a good idea to use 'Sir' or 'Ma'am' when talking to someone
older or deserving of respect.

Mrs; Ma'am	pwahn	*Puan*
Mr	en-*chi(k)*	*Encik*
Sir	twahn	*Tuan*
Miss	chi(k)	*Cik*

GIVE PEACE A CHANCE

You'll often hear Muslims use the Arabic greeting
assalamualaikum 'peace be on you' to which the
response is *waalaikumsalam* 'and on you be peace'.
However, it's considered offensive for non-Muslims to use
this greeting, or to answer it. Just say: *Saya bukan
Muslimin/Muslimah,* sai-yuh boo-*kahn* moos-*lee*-meen/
moos-*lee*-mah(h), 'I'm not a Muslim'. (m/f)

MEETING PEOPLE

FIRST ENCOUNTERS

PERTEMUAN PERTAMA

What's your name?
  see-*ah*-puh *nah*-muh *ahn*-duh?   *Siapa nama anda?*

My name's ...
  nah-muh *sai*-yuh ...   *Nama saya ...*

I'd like to introduce ...
to you.
  sai-yuh nah(k)   *Saya nak*
  mem-per-ke-*nahl*-kahn ...   *memperkenalkan ...*
  ke-*pah*-duh *ahn*-duh   *kepada anda.*

I'm pleased to meet you.
  sai-yuh gem-*bi*-ruh ber-*te*-moo   *Saya gembira bertemu*
  de-*ngahn* *ahm*-duh   *dengan anda.*

MAKING CONVERSATION   **PERBUALAN**

Greetings aside, many people will launch straight into the guts of
a conversation. Don't be surprised if you're quickly quizzed on
topics 'Are you married?', 'Are your teeth real?' If you're asked
'How much money do you make?' you can just answer *cukup*,
choo-kup, 'enough' with a smile. Common starters include:

How are you?; How's it going?
  ah-puh *khah*-bahr?   *Apa khabar?*
Fine. And you?
  khah-bahr bai(k).   *Khabar baik.*
  ah-puh *khah*-bahr?   *Apa khabar?*
Where are you going?
  nah(k) ke *mah*-nuh?   *Nak ke mana?*

Asked most often as an ice-breaker, the response *jalan-jalan*,
jah-lahn-*jah*-lahn, 'travelling around', is perfect. Other easy
answers include:

To (Petaling Jaya).
  ke (pe-*tah*-ling *jah*-yuh)   *Ke (Petaling Jaya).*
Out and about.
  mah-kahn *ah*-ngin   *Makan angin.*
        (lit: eating the breeze)

MEETING PEOPLE

Some of the things people will want to know about you are:

How long have you been in Malaysia?
soo-dah(h) be-*rah*-puh *lah*-muh   *Sudah berapa lama di*
dee mah-*lay*-see-ah?   *Malaysia?*

I've been here for two weeks.
sai-yuh *soo*-dah(h) *doo*-uh   *Saya sudah dua minggu*
ming-goo dee *see*-nee   *di sini.*

How long will you be in Malaysia?
be-*rah*-puh *lah*-muh *ahn*-duh   *Berapa lama anda di*
dee mah-*lay*-see-ah?   *Malaysia?*

I'll be in Malaysia for (one month).
sai-yuh *ah*-kahn ber-*ah*-duh   *Saya akan berada di*
dee mah-*lay*-see-ah se-*lah*-muh   *Malaysia selama*
(se-*boo*-lahn)   *(sebulan).*

Where have you been so far?
soo-dah(h) ke *mah*-nuh?   *Sudah ke mana?*

I've been to Penang and Ipoh.
sai-yuh *soo*-dah(h) ke pee-*nahng*   *Saya sudah ke Penang*
dan *ee*-po(h)   *dan Ipoh.*

Have you been to Mersing?
soo-dah(h) ke *mer*-sing?   *Sudah ke Mersing?*

Not yet.
be-*lum*   *Belum.*

Yes, I have.
soo-dah(h)   *Sudah.*

Are you here on holiday?
ahn-duh *choo*-tee dee *see*-nee?   *Anda cuti di sini?*

I'm here ...	*sai*-yuh ...	*Saya ...*
for a holiday	ber-*choo*-tee	*bercuti*
on business	ber-*ker*-juh	*bekerja*
to study	be-*lah*-jahr	*belajar*

How long are you here for?
be-*rah*-puh *lah*-muh *ahn*-duh   *Berapa lama anda di sini?*
dee *see*-nee?

MEETING PEOPLE

I'm/We're here for ... weeks/days.

sai-yuh/kah-mee dee
see-nee se-lah-muh
... ming-goo/hah-ree

Saya/Kami di
sini selama
... minggu/hari.

Do you like it here?

ah-duh-kah(h) ahn-duh
soo-kuh dee see-nee?

Adakah anda
suka di sini?

I/We like it here very much.

sai-yuh/kah-mee sah-ngaht
soo-kuh dee see-nee

Saya/Kami sangat
suka di sini.

Can you eat spicy food?

bo-leh(h) mah-kahn
mah-kah-nahn pe-dahs?

Boleh makan
makanan pedas?

I (don't) like spicy food.

sai-yuh (tah(k)) soo-kuh
mah-kah-nahn pe-dahs

Saya (tak) suka
makanan pedas.

USEFUL WORDS & PHRASES

Sure.	be-*tul*	*Betul.*
It's OK.	tah(k) *ah*-puh	*Tak apa.*
Are you ready?	soo-dah(h) see-*ahp*?	*Sudah siap?*
Just a minute.	se-*ben*-tahr/	*Sebentar/*
	se-ke-*jahp*	*Sekejap.*
Wait!	*toong*-goo!	*Tunggu!*
Look!	*lee*-haht!	*Lihat!*
Listen!	de-*ngahr*-lah(h)!	*Dengarlah!*
I'm ready.	*sai*-yuh see-*ahp*	*Saya siap.*
Slow down!	per-lah-*hahn* see-*kit*!	*Perlahan sikit!*
Hurry up!	che-*paht* see-*kit*!	*Cepat sikit!*
Go away!	per-*gee*-lah(h)!	*Pergilah!*
Watch out!	ber-*hah*-ti-*hah*-ti!	*Berhati-hati!*
It's (not) possible.	*(tee*-dah(k)/tah(k))	*(Tidak/Tak)*
	bo-*leh(h)*	*Boleh.*

I forgot.	*sai*-yuh *loo*-puh	Saya lupa.
It's (not)	*(tee*-dah(k)/tah(k))	(Tidak/Tak)
important.	pen-*ting*	Penting.
It doesn't matter.	tah(k) *ah*-puh	Tak apa.
Let's go!	*joom*-lah(h)!	Jumlah!

What are you doing?
    ahm-duh *boo*-aht *ah*-puh?   Anda buat apa?

Are you waiting too?
    ahm-duh me-*noong*-goo   Anda menunggu juga?
    joo-guh?

Do you live here?
    ahm-duh *ting*-gahl dee   Anda tinggal di sini?
    see-nee?

What's your opinion about ...?
    ah-puh-kah(h)   Apakah pendapat anda
    pen-*dah*-paht   tentang ...?
    ahm-duh *ten*-tahng ...?

It's hot!
    pah-nahs kahn!   Panas, kan!

Beautiful, isn't it!
    chahm-ti(k) boo-*kahn*!   Cantik, bukan!

That's strange!
    pe-*li(k)*-nyuh!   Peliknya!

That's funny! (amusing)
    lah-*wah(k)*-nyuh!   Lawaknya!

MEETING PEOPLE

LEAN ON ME

Physical contact between the same sex is considered normal in Malaysia. You'll see boys hanging out with their arms around each other's shoulders, and women holding hands with their close friends or relatives.

NATIONALITIES   KEBANGSAAN

In Malay, you'll find that many names of countries are similar to the English names, but pronounced slightly differently.

Where are you from?

ahm-duh ber-*ah*-sahl *dah*-ree   Anda berasal dari mana?
mah-nuh?

I'm from ...   *sai*-yuh ber-*ah*-sahl   Saya berasal
                dah-ree ...   dari ...

Australia	*	*Australia*
Canada	*	*Kanada*
England	*ing*-ge-ris	*Inggeris*
Europe	e-*ro*-pah(h)	*Eropah*
India	*	*India*
Ireland	*	*Ireland*
Japan	*jeh*-poon	*Jepun*
New Zealand	*	*New Zealand*
Scotland	*	*Scotland*
the USA	*	*Amerika*
Wales	*	*Wales*

(* as in English)

I'm ...	*sai*-yuh *o*-rahng ...	Saya orang ...
Australian	*	*Australia*
Dutch	be-*lahn*-duh	*Belanda*
English	*ing*-ge-ris	*Inggeris*

I live in a/the ...	*sai*-yuh *ting*-gahl dee ...	Saya tinggal di ...
city	*bahn*-dahr	*bandar*
countryside	loo-*ahr bahn*-dahr	*luar bandar*
seaside	*pahm*-tai	*pantai*
suburbs of ...	*ping*-geer	*pinggir*
	bahn-dahr ...	*bandar ...*
village	*kahm*-pung	*kampung*

CULTURAL DIFFERENCES
PERBEZAAN KEBUDAYAAN

How do you do this in your country?
bah-gai-*mah*-nuh ee-nee dee-*boo*-aht dee ne-*gah*-ruh *ahn*-duh?

Bagaimana ini dibuat di negara anda?

Is this a local or national custom?
ah-daht ee-nee *ah*-daht dah-*eh*-rah(h) ah-*tow ah*-daht nah-see-*o*-nahl?

Adat ini adat daerah atau adat nasional?

I don't want to offend you.
sai-yuh tah(k) nah(k) me-*nying*-goong pe-*rah*-sah-ahn *ahn*-duh

Saya tak nak menyinggung perasaan anda.

I'm sorry, it's not the custom in my country.
mah-*ahf, ah*-daht ee-nee tah(k) bee-*ah*-suh dee ne-*gah*-ruh *sai*-yuh

Maaf, adat ini tak biasa di negara saya.

I don't mind watching, but I'd prefer not to participate.
sai-yuh le-*bi(h)* se-nahng me-*non*-ton dah-ree-*pah*-duh me-*lee*-baht-kahn *di*-ree

Saya lebih senang menonton daripada melibatkan diri.

AGE
UMUR

It's not off-limits to ask someone's age in Malaysia, so expect it often. One response could be *Cuba teka, choo*-buh *teh*-kuh, 'Guess!'

How old are you?	be-*rah*-puh oo-moor *ahn*-duh?	*Berapa umur anda?*
I'm ... years old.	oo-moor *sai*-yuh ... *tah*-hoon	*Umur saya ... tahun.*
20	*doo*-uh *poo*-lu(h)	*dua puluh*
35	*tee*-gah *poo*-lu(h) *lee*-muh	*tiga puluh lima*

(See Numbers & Amounts on page 199 for your age.)

MEETING PEOPLE

OCCUPATIONS

PEKERJAAN

What's your occupation?
ah-puh pe-*ker*-jah-ahn *ahm*-duh? *Apa pekerjaan anda?*

What do you do?
ahn-duh ber-*ker*-jah se-*bah*-gai *Anda bekerja sebagai*
ah-puh? *apa?*

I'm (a/an) ...	*sai*-yuh ...	*Saya ...*
artist	*ahr*-tees	*artis*
businessperson	pe-nee-*ah*-gah	*peniaga*
chef	*too*-kahng *mah*-sah(k)	*tukang masak*
doctor	*dok*-tor	*doktor*
engineer	joo-*roo*-te-rah	*jurutera*
factory worker	pe-*ker*-jah *kee*-lahng	*pekerja kilang*
farmer	pe-*tah*-nee	*petani*
journalist	wahr-*tah*-wahn	*wartawan*
lawyer	pe-*gwahm*	*peguam*
lecturer (university)	pen-*shah*-rah(h)	*pensyarah*
mechanic	me-*kan*-ik	*mekanik*
musician	pe-*main*	*pemain*
	moo-zi(k)	*muzik*
nurse	joo-roo-*rah*-waht	*jururawat*
office worker	pe-*gah*-wai	*pegawai*
retired	pe-*sah*-ruh	*pesara*
scientist	*sain*-tees	*saintis*
secretary	joo-roo-*taip*	*jurutaip*
student (school)	*moo*-rid/pe-*lah*-jahr	*murid/pelajar*
student (uni)	pe-*lah*-jahr	*pelajar*
teacher (school)	*goo*-roo/*chi*(k)-goo	*guru/cikgu*
unemployed	pe-*ngahng*-goor	*penganggur*
waiter	pe-*lai*-ahn	*pelayan*
writer	pe-*noo*-lees	*penulis*

MEETING PEOPLE

What are you studying?	*ahm*-duh be-*lah*-jahr *ah*-puh?	Anda belajar apa?
I'm studying ...	*sai*-yuh be-*lah*-jahr ...	Saya belajar ...
art	ke-se-*nee*-ahn	kesenian
business	per-nee-ah-*gah*-ahn	perniagaan
engineering	ke-*joo*-te-rah-ahn	kejuteraan
languages	bah-*hah*-suh	bahasa
law	*oon*-dahng-*oon*-dahng	undang-undang
literature	sahs-*ter*-ah	sastera
Malay	bah-*hah*-suh me-*lah*-yoo	Bahasa Melayu
medicine	per-*oo*-bah-tahn	perubatan
science	sains	sains
teaching	pen-*gah*-jahr-ahn	pengajaran

RELIGION   AGAMA

Most Malays are Muslim; Malaysians of other backgrounds may also be Muslim, Christian, Hindu or Buddhist. Religion is considered essential in everyone's life, and you'll maintain better relations by claiming to have one, or by saying your parents belong to one.

What's your religion?	*ahm*-duh ber-ah-*gah*-muh *ah*-puh?	Anda beragama apa?
My religion is ...	ah-*gah*-muh *sai*-yuh ...	Agama saya ...
Buddhist	*boo*-duh	Buda
Catholic	*kah*-to-lik	Katolik
Christian	*kris*-ti-ahn	Kristian
Hindu	*hin*-doo	Hindu
Jewish	yah-*hoo*-dee	Yahudi
Muslim	*is*-lahm	Islam
Protestant	*pro*-tes-tahn	Protestan

I'm ... but not practising.
sai-yuh ber-ah-*gah*-muh ...   Saya beragama ...
tah-pee jah-*rahng* ke ge-*reh*-jah   tapi jarang ke gereja.

My parents are ...
  ee-boo *bah*-puh *sai*-yuh
  ber-ah-*gah*-muh ...

*Ibu bapa saya
beragama ...*

I think I believe in God.
  sai-yuh *rah*-suh *sai*-yuh
  per-*chah*-yuh ke-*pah*-duh
  too-hahn

*Saya rasa saya
percaya kepada
Tuhan.*

I'm not religious.
  sai-yuh *tee*-dah(k)
  ber-ah-*gah*-muh

*Saya tidak
beragama.*

TABLE MANNERS

You may offer to help prepare food or clean up, but as a guest, your host will insist you sit and do nothing:

'Don't bother yourself.'
  jah-ngahn *soo*-sah(h)-*soo*-sah(h)
  Jangan susah-susah.

If the host asks you what you'd like to eat or drink, you may reply with the same phrase. When you get to the table, you'll hear:

'Please drink/eat.'
  see-luh *mee*-num/*mah*-kahn
  Sila minum/makan.

Decline an offer when it's first made – this is good manners. Then go for it!

I believe in destiny/fate.

    sai-yuh per-*chah*-yuh
    ke-*pah*-duh *tah(k)*-dir

Saya percaya
kepada takdir.

I'm interested in astrology/philosophy.

    sai-yuh ter-*tah*-ri(k) ke-*pah*-duh
    ahs-tro-*lo*-gee/*fahl*-sah-fah(h)

Saya tertarik kepada
astrologi/falsafah.

I'm an atheist.

    sai-yuh *ay*-thee-is

Saya atheis.

I'm agnostic.

    sai-yuh ahg-*nos*-tik

Saya agnostik.

THE SISTERHOOD

Considering that the official religion of Malaysia is Islam, women in general have a great deal of freedom and rights. There's a strong female presence in the working world, both in government – several cabinet ministers are women – and the private sector.

Civil laws generally cover all Malaysians, except in the area of family law, in which Muslims must follow *Syariah* court rulings. These laws are discriminatory against women, and many are working towards addressing these inequities. For example, it is very easy for a Muslim man to divorce his wife: he simply says, "I divorce you." A woman, on the other hand, must go through the *Syariah* courts to get a divorce.

Since 1979, many Malay women have made the personal decision to wear clothing that covers their whole body, except for their face and hands. Women travelling in Malaysia will need to have a think about what is appropriate in a Muslim country. Wearing short skirts, skimpy shorts or beach gear in public will only reinforce negative stereotypes and may be seen to encourage harassment. Covering up more than you usually would, and even covering your head with a scarf in rural areas or on the east coast, will help.

BODY LANGUAGE   BAHASA BADAN

A growing number of Malays feel that handshaking, or any casual physical contact between the sexes is inappropriate and against the teachings of Islam. Particularly in the more conservative northern states, or in rural areas, it's better to smile instead when meeting someone of the opposite sex. If they extend their hand, then by all means, shake it! Handshaking is otherwise widely accepted: a gentle brush of the palms rather than a knuckle-crusher is what you should aim for. It's appropriate to shake hands when being introduced, when visiting somebody in their home, or when you haven't seen someone for a while.

Touching someone's head is generally considered rude. If someone is sitting on the floor in a home, stepping over their legs is not the thing to do either. Walk around their legs, no matter how inconvenient it is. It's also considered polite to bow your body slightly and extend your right arm straight downwards towards the floor when crossing the path of someone who's seated, or when interrupting people. At the same time you can say *maaf*, mah-*ahf*, 'excuse me'.

TAKE IT EASY

The general pace of life in Malaysia may seem slower than in some other countries. Indeed, most Malaysians seem to take things at an easier pace, and considering the climate and the effort needed to get around, slowing down and chilling out is probably a wise decision – as if you need any encouragement!

MEETING PEOPLE

FEELINGS		**PERASAAN**
I'm ...	*sai*-yuh ...	*Saya* ...
Are you ...?	*ah*-duh-kah(h)	*Adakah anda ...?*
	ahn-duh ... ?	
afraid	tah-*kut*	*takut*
angry	*mah*-rah(h)	*marah*
bored	*bo*-sahn	*bosan*
cold	se-*joo(k)*	*sejuk*
disgusted	men-*yahm*-pah(h)	*menyampah*
full	ken-*yahng*	*kenyang*
grateful	ber-*shoo*-koor	*bersyukur*
happy	gem-*bee*-ruh	*gembira*
hot	*pah*-nahs	*panas*
hungry	*lah*-pahr	*lapar*
in a hurry	ter-*ge*-suh-*ge*-suh	*tergesa-gesa*
keen	ber-*soong*-guh	*bersungguh-*
	soong-guh	*sungguh*
alright (content)	pwahs	*puas*
sad	se-*di(h)*	*sedih*
sick	*sah*-kit	*sakit*
sleepy	meng-*ahn*-to(k)	*mengantuk*
snobbish	som-*bong*	*sombong*
sorry (condolence)	*ta(k)*-zee-ah(h)	*takziah*
sorry (regret)	me-nye-*sahl*	*menyesal*
thirsty	hows	*haus*
tired	le-*ti(h)*	*letih*
well	bai(k)	*baik*
worried	*bim*-bahng	*bimbang*

MEETING PEOPLE

HEART-WARMING

You'll find that many people, especially the Malays, follow the handshake with a touch of the heart, a habit worth forming. In cases where respect is called for, such as when a young child greets an elder, the child will kiss the elder's hand and then sometimes touch it to their own forehead.

BREAKING THE LANGUAGE BARRIER

MENGATASI KESUKARAN BAHASA

Do you speak English?
ah-duh-kah(h) *ahn*-duh
ber-bah-*hah*-suh *ing*-ge-ris?

Adakah anda berbahasa Inggeris?

Yes./No.
yah/tah(k) bo-*leh(h)*

Ya./Tak boleh.

I can only speak a little Malay.
sai-yuh *hahm*-yuh
ber-bah-*hah*-suh me-*lah*-yoo
se-*dee*-kit *sah*-juh

Saya hanya berbahasa Melayu sedikit saja.

Does any one here speak English?
ah-*duh* o-rahng yahng
ber-bah-*hah*-suh *ing*-ge-ris
dee *see*-nee?

Ada orang yang berbahasa Inggeris di sini?

Do you understand?
ah-duh-kah(h) *ahn*-duh
fah-hahm?

Adakah anda faham?

I (don't) understand.
sai-yuh (tah(k)) *fah*-hahm

Saya (tak) faham.

How do you say ... in Malay?
mah-chahm *mah*-nuh
chah-kahp ... dah-*lahm*
bah-*hah*-suh me-*lah*-yoo?

Macam mana cakap ... dalam Bahasa Melayu?

What's this called?
ah-puh nee?

Apa ni?

What does this mean?
ah-puh *mah(k)*-sud-nyuh?

Apa maksudnya?

Please speak slowly.
to-long *chah*-kahp
per-*lah*-hahn *see*-kit

Tolong cacap perlahan sikit.

Please write that word down for me.
to-long *too*-lis-kahn
per-kah-*tah*-ahn *ee*-too
oon-tu(k) *sai*-yuh

Tolong tuliskan perkataan itu untuk saya.

MEETING PEOPLE

Please repeat that.
    to-long oo-*lah*-ngee   *Tolong ulangi.*

Please translate for me.
    to-long ter-je-*mah(h)*-kahn   *Tolong terjemahkan*
    oon-tu(k) *sai*-yuh   *untuk saya.*

STAYING IN TOUCH   MEMBUAT JANJI

Where are you staying?
    ahn-duh *doo*-du(k) dee   *Anda duduk di mana?*
    mah-nuh?

What's your address?
    ah-puh-kah(h) *ah*-lah-maht   *Apakah alamat anda?*
    ahn-duh?

I'm staying at ...
    sai-yuh *doo*-du(k) dee ...   *Saya duduk di ...*

Can we meet again?
    bo-*leh(h)*-kah(h) *kee*-tuh   *Bolehkah kita*
    ber-*joom*-puh *lah*-gee?   *berjumpa lagi?*

Let's meet at (6 o'clock) at ...
    kee-tuh ber-*te*-moo *pah*-duh   *Kita bertemu*
    (*poo*-kool e-*nahm*) dee ...   *(pukul enam) di ...*

Come to my house any time.
    dah-tahng ke *roo*-mah(h)   *Datang ke rumah*
    sai-yuh *bee*-luh-*bee*-luh   *saya bila-bila*
    sah-juh   *saja.*

NO MEANS NO

Malaysians have a variety of ways of avoiding a direct answer, especially when it's a negative one. If you feel uncomfortable answering a particular question try some of the following (a smile works too!):

I don't know.	*sai*-yuh tah(k) *tah*-hoo	*Saya tak tahu.*
I'm busy.	*sai*-yuh *see*-bu(k)	*Saya sibuk.*
It's not appropriate.	*ee*-nee tah(k) se-*swai*	*Ini tak sesuai.*

HOMESTAYS

Hospitality on a formal level is the norm when you're invited into a Malaysian home. If you stay in a rural or small town setting, you'll probably be treated like a star! Don't be surprised to see the neighbourhood children peering in a door or window to gawk at the *orang asing*, o-rahng ah-sing, 'foreigner'.

It's good to bring a small gift *buah tangan*, boo-ah(h) tah-ngahn, (lit: fruit hand): a bag of fruit such as oranges or apples, or a small souvenir from your country. It's considered polite to greet and shake hands with every adult present – remember to wait for the hand extended from the opposite sex – and sometimes the children, too. Bringing photos of your home or family, or a map of your country, is a good idea.

Savoury and sweet cakes and tidbits are common fare in Malaysian homes. If they're not to your liking, just take a few bites. It's considered rude to refuse to eat or drink what is served. If you're unable to eat certain things, it's best to tell your host or hostess early.

I'm sorry, I can't eat wheat flour;
I have an allergy.

    mah-*ahf*, *sai*-yuh tah(k) bo-*leh(h)*   *Maaf, saya tak boleh*
    mah-kahn te-*pong gahm*-doom   *makan tepong gandum,*
    se-*bahh sai*-yuh ah-duh ah-ler-jee   *sebab saya ada alergi.*

(the English word 'allergy' is also widely understood)

I have diabetes so I can't have sugar.

    sai-yuh ah-duh dai-ah-*bee*-tees   *Saya ada diabetes,*
    jah-dee tah(k) bo-*leh(h)*   *jadi tak boleh*
    mah-kahn *goo*-luh   *makan gula.*

Sorry, I've just eaten.

    mah-*ahf sai*-yuh bah-*roo*   *Maaf, saya baru*
    mah-kahn   *makan.*

When you feel it's time to go, say *Saya nak balik dulu,* sai-yuh nah(k) bah-*li(k)* doo-loo, 'I'm going home first'. The family will undoubtedly urge you to stay, but take your leave with *Terima kasih banyak-banyak!*, te-*ree*-muh *kah*-si(h) *bah*-nyah(k)-*bah*-nyah(k), 'thanks very, very much'.

JALAN-JALAN
GETTING AROUND

Kuala Lumpur's public transport system has undergone massive changes in the last 10 years, with the introduction of the LRT (light rapid transit), improved roadways and commuter trains. Travelling in other parts of the country requires a little more patience, and even in Kuala Lumpur a heavy downpour can bring things to a stop! Buses, trains and taxis are available throughout most of the country. Road maps of the cities can be found at hotels, bookstores and newsagents.

FINDING YOUR WAY
CARI JALAN

Excuse me.	mah-*ahf*	*Maaf.*
I'm lost.	*sai*-yuh ter-se-*saht*	*Saya tersesat.*

Where's the ...?	dee *mah*-nuh ...?	*Di mana ...?*
airport	lah-*pahng*-ahn	*lapangan*
	ter-bahng	*terbang*
intercity	*steh*-sehn bahs	*stesen bas*
bus station	*bahn*-dahr	*bandar*
road to (Raub)	*jah*-lahn ke (rowb)	*jalan ke (Raub)*
train station	*steh*-sehn	*stesen keretapi*
	ke-reh-tuh-*ah*-pee	

What time does	... ber-*to*-lah(k)/*tee*-buh	*... bertolak/tiba*
the ... leave/arrive?	*poo*-kool be-*rah*-puh?	*pukul berapa?*
(inter) city bus	bahs *bahm*-dahr	*Bas bandar*
plane	*kah*-pahl *ter*-bahng	*Kapal terbang*
ship	*kah*-pahl	*Kapal*
train	ke-reh-tuh-*ah*-pee	*Keretapi*

How can I get to ...?
    mah-chahm *mah*-nuh   *Macam mana*
    sai-yuh bo-*leh*(h) *per*-gee ke ...?   *saya boleh pergi ke ...?*
Is it near/far?
    de-*kaht*-kah(h)/*jow*(h)-kah(h)?   *Dekatkah/Jauhkah?*

GETTING AROUND

Can we walk there?
bo-leh(h) jah-lahn kah-kee tah(k) ke sah-nuh?
Boleh jalan kaki
tak ke sana?

Can you show me (on the map)?
to-long toon-joo(k)-kahn (dee peh-tuh)?
Tolong tunjukkan
(di peta)?

Are there other means of getting there?
ah-duh chah-ruh lain ke sah-nuh?
Ada cara
lain ke sana?

What street is this?
jah-lahn ee-nee jah-lahn ah-puh?
Jalan ini
jalan apa?

What ... is this?	*ee-nee ... ah-puh?*	*Ini ... apa?*
city	*bahm-dahr*	*bandar*
village	*kahm-pong*	*kampung*

DIRECTIONS   ARAHAN

(Go) Straight ahead!	*(jah-lahn) te-roos!*	*(Jalan) Terus!*
To the left/right.	ke *ki-ree/kah-nahn.*	Ke kiri/kanan.

Turn left/right at the ...	*beh-lo(k) ki-ree/ kah-nahn dee ...*	Belok kiri/ kanan di ...
corner	*sim-pahng*	*simpang*
intersection	*sim-pahng*	*simpang*
next corner	*sim-pahng yang ber-ee-koot-nyuh*	*simpang yang berikutnya*
T-junction	*sim-pahng tee*	*simpang T*
traffic lights	*lahm-poo ee-shah-raht*	*lampu isyarat*

behind	dee be-lah-*kahng*	*di belakang*
far	jow(h)	*jauh*
in front of	dee de-*pahn*	*di depan*
next to	se-be-*lah(h)*	*sebelah*
opposite	ber-lah-*wah*-nahn	*berlawanan*
near	de-*kaht*	*dekat*

north	oo-*tah*-ruh	*utara*
south	se-*lah*-tahn	*selatan*
east	*tee*-mur	*timur*
west	*bah*-raht	*barat*

ADDRESSES   ALAMAT

Common words that make up Malaysian addresses include:

jalan raya	a bigger road, like a dual carriageway
jalan	road
lorong	smaller road
pesiaran	even smaller road
lebuh raya	a highway
taman	garden, as in 'Serenity Gardens' housing estate
kampong	village

Malaysian city and town addresses look similar to this:

> Ali Abubakar
> 204, Jalan Air Hitam
> Taman Mewah
> 44300 Serdang, Selangor

This means Ali Abubakar lives at number 204, Air Hitam Street (*Jalan*), Mewah Gardens (*Taman*), a housing area, in the town/city of Serdang in the state of Selangor, postcode 44300.

Addresses in rural areas may look something like this:

> Aishah Mohamed
> Lt 1445, Kampung Mangga
> Kubang Kerian, Kota Baru
> Kelantan

Lt means lot number, *kampung* means village. *Kubang Kerian* in this case is the name of a larger village area and *Kota Baru* is the name of the *daerah*, 'county', and *Kelantan* is the state.

GETTING AROUND

BUYING TICKETS

MEMBELI TIKET

Ticket prices are usually posted on noticeboards for ferry, LRT, bus and train travel. Commuter and LRT tickets can be bought from ticket machines or from employees at the stations. Fares on public transport are not negotiable.

How much does it cost to go to ...?
    be-*rah*-puh *hahr*-guh-nyuh   *Berapa harganya*
    oon-tu(k) ke ...?   *untuk ke ...?*

How much is it from Johor to Ipoh?
    be-*rah*-puh *hahr*-guh tee-*keht*   *Berapa harga tiket*
    dah-ree jo-hor ke *ee*-po(h)?   *dari Johor ke Ipoh?*

Where can I buy a ticket?
    tee-*keht* dee-*joo*-ahl   *Tiket dijual*
    dee *mah*-nuh?   *di mana?*

We want to go to ...
    kah-mee nah(k) ke ...   *Kami nak ke ...*

Do I need to book?
    ah-duh-kah(h) *hah*-roos peh-*sahn*?   *Adakah harus pesan?*

I'd like to book a seat to ...
    sai-yuh nah(k) me-*me*-sahn   *Saya nak memesan*
    tem-*paht* doo-du(k) ke ...   *tempat duduk ke ...*

I'd like (a) ...	*sai*-yuh nah(k) ...	*Saya nak ...*
one-way ticket	tee-*keht* se-*hah*-luh	*tiket sehala*
return ticket	tee-*keht* per-gee-*bah*-li(k)	*tiket pergi-balik*
two tickets	*doo*-ah tee-*keht*	*dua tiket*
student's fare	*hahr*-guh pe-*lah*-jahr	*harga pelajar*

1st class	ke-*lahs* per-*tah*-muh	*kelas pertama*
2nd class	ke-*lahs* ke-*doo*-ah/	*kelas kedua/*
	bis-nis	*bisnis*
economy class	ke-*lahs* ee-ko-*no*-mee	*kelas ekonomi*
child's/pensioner's fare	*hahr*-guh ah-*nah(k)*/ pe-*sah*-ruh	*harga anak/pesara*

What about my change?
    doo-it *bah*-li(k) *mah*-nuh?   *Duit balik mana?*

confirmation	kon-fir-*mah*-see	*konfirmasi*
destination	de-sti-*nah*-see	*destinasi*
seat	tem-*paht doo*-du(k)	*tempat duduk*
ticket	tee-*keht* ·	*tiket*
ticket counter	*kowm*-ter tee-*keht*	*kaunter tiket*
timetable	ja-*doo*-al	*jadual*

AIR   PENERBANGAN

Malaysian Airlines (MAS) and Pelangi Air offer services within the country to most locations. Both airlines have a good safety record.

Is there a flight to Penang on (Monday)?
    ah-duh-kah(h)
    pe-ner-*bah*-ngahn ke
    pe-*nahng pah*-duh
    (*hah*-ree ees-nin)?
    Adakah
    penerbangan ke
    Penang pada
    (hari Isnin)?

What time is the flight to
Penang on (Monday)?
    poo-kool be-*rah*-puh
    pe-ner-*bahng*-ahn
    ber-*to*-lah(k) ke pe-*nahng*
    pah-duh (*hah*-ree ees-nin)?
    Pukul berapa
    penerbangan
    bertolak ke Penang
    pada (hari Isnin)?

What time do I have to be at
the airport?
    poo-kool be-*rah*-puh
    sai-yuh hah-roos *ah*-duh dee
    lah-*pahng*-ahn *ter*-bahng?
    Pukul berapa
    saya harus ada di
    lapangan terbang?

When's the next flight to ...?
    bee-luh pe-ner-*bahng*-ahn
    ke ... yahng se-te-*roos*-nyuh?
    Bila penerbangan
    ke ... yang seterusnya?

I'd like to reconfirm my ticket to Perlis.
    sai-yuh nah(k) me-mas-*tee*-kahn
    tee-*keht sai*-yuh ke *per*-lees
    Saya nak memastikan
    tiket saya ke Perlis.

How long does the flight take?
    per-jah-lah-*nahn*-nya
    be-*rah*-puh lah-muh?
    Perjalanannya
    berapa lama?

Where's the baggage claim?
    bah-*gah*-see dee *mah*-nuh?
    Bagasi di mana?

GETTING AROUND

Customs   Kastam

Customs officers are generally friendly (unless you're a smuggler) and are impressed if you greet them in Malay and make an attempt to speak the language.

I have nothing to declare.
  bah-*rahng sai*-yuh *tee*-dah(k)
  per-*loo* dee-lah-*por*-kahn

*Barang saya tidak
perlu dilaporkan.*

I have something to declare.
  sai-yuh *ah*-duh bah-*rahng*
  yahng per-*loo* dee-lah-*por*-kahn

*Saya ada barang
yang perlu dilaporkan.*

Do I have to declare this?
  ah-duh-kah(h) *sai*-yuh per-*loo*
  me-lah-*por*-kahn *ee*-nee?

*Adakah saya perlu
melaporkan ini?*

This is all my luggage.
  ee-nee se-*moo*-uh
  bah-*rahng sai*-yuh

Ini semua barang saya.

I didn't know I had to declare it.
  sai-yuh *tee*-dah(k) *tah*-hoo
  bah-*rahng ee*-nee *hah*-roos
  dee-lah-*por*-kahn.

*Saya tidak tahu
barang ini harus
dilaporkan.*

aeroplane	*kah*-pahl *ter*-bahng	*kapal terbang*
airport	lah-*pahng*-ahn *ter*-bahng	*lapangan terbang*

<table>
<tr><td colspan="2" align="center">SIGNS</td></tr>
<tr><td>BARANG HILANG</td><td>LOST PROPERTY</td></tr>
<tr><td>PERTOLAKAN</td><td>DEPARTURES</td></tr>
<tr><td>KETIBAAN</td><td>ARRIVALS</td></tr>
<tr><td>PENDAFTARAN</td><td>CHECK-IN</td></tr>
<tr><td>IMIGRASI</td><td>PASSPORT CONTROL</td></tr>
</table>

BUS   BAS

Malaysia's buses are usually fast, economical and comfortable. Local and city buses can be hailed at bus stops, which usually are well signposted. You may need to make reservations for long distance buses, especially around festive times. In rural areas buses tend to be older and without air-con. For sightseeing and really experiencing local life, these are ideal. Just pay your fare to the conductor or driver.

Most city buses have complete air-con. Check when you purchase your tickets by asking: *Bas ini ada air-con tak?*, bahs *ee*-nee *ah*-duh *air*-con tah(k)?, 'Does this bus have air-con or not?'. Long distance buses have toilets and usually stop to let passengers off for meals; some will also combine a meal-stop with a prayer-stop for the Muslim passengers.

Which bus goes to ...?
   bahs yahng *mah*-nuh   *Bas yang mana*
   nahk ke ...?   *nak ke ...?*
Does this bus go to ...?
   bahs *ee*-nee *per*-gee ke ...? *Bas ini pergi ke ...?*
Do buses come often?
   bahs *ee*-nee *dah*-tahng   *Bas ini datang*
   se-*lah*-loo kahn?   *selalu, kan?*
Often./Rarely.
   se-*lah*-loo/*jah*-rahng   *Selalu./Jarang.*
Where do I get the bus for ...?
   bahs ke ... dee *mah*-nuh?   *Bas ke ... di mana?*

What time's	*poo*-kool be-*rah*-puh	*Pukul berapa*
the ... bus (to ...)?	bahs ... (ke ...)?	*bas ... (ke ...)?*
first	per-*tah*-muh	*pertama*
last	ter-*ah*-khir	*terakhir*
next	ber-ee-*koot*-nyuh	*berikutnya*

Will the bus stop at a restaurant?
   bahs *ee*-nee ber-*hen*-tee   *Bas ini berhenti*
   dee *res*-to-rahn?   *di restoran?*

GETTING AROUND

Could you let me know when
we arrive at ...?
  to-long ber-ee-*tah*-hoo
  sai-yuh *bee*-luh *kee*-tuh
  soo-dah(h) *sahm*-pai dee ...?

*Tolong beritahu
saya bila kita
sudah sampai di ...?*

Where are we now?
  kee-tuh *mah*-nuh
  se-*kah*-rahng?

*Kita mana
sekarang?*

I want to get off.
  sai-yah nah(k) *too*-roon

Saya nak turun.

TRAIN   KERETAPI

Train travel in Malaysia is fun, cheap, easy and trains are generally
on time. Express trains only stop at the main stations, but some
of the local services, especially on the east coast, offer a colourful
experience, stopping in small towns and even in the jungle to let
passengers off.

I want to go by express train to ...
  sai-yuh nah(k) nai(k)
  ke-reh-tuh-*ah*-pee
  ehk-sprehs ke ...

*Saya nak naik
keretapi
ekspres ke ...*

Which platform does the train
leave from?
  dah-ree *lahn*-dah-sahn
  mah-nuh ke-reh-tuh-*ah*-pee
  ber-*ahng*-kaht?

*Dari landasan
mana keretapi
berangkat?*

Where do I need to change trains?
  sai-yuh ber-*too*-kahr
  ke-reh-tuh-*ah*-pee dee *mah*-nuh?

*Saya bertukar
keretapi di mana?*

Does this train stop at Kuala Pilah?
  ah-duh-kah(h) ke-reh-tuh-*ah*-pee
  ee-nee ber-*hen*-tee dee
  kwah-luh *pee*-lah(h)?

*Adakah keretapi
ini berhenti di
Kuala Pilah?*

Can I get off at Kuala Pilah?
  bo-*leh*(h) *sai*-yuh *too*-roon
  dee *kwah*-luh *pee*-lah(h)?

*Boleh saya turun
di Kuala Pilah?*

Is this seat free?
ke-*roo*-see *ee*-nee
ko-song-kah(h)?   *Kerusi ini kosongkah?*

This seat's taken.
soo-dah(h) *ah*-duh *o*-rahng   *Sudah ada orang.*

Would you mind if I open
the window?
bo-*leh(h)* *sai*-yuh   *Boleh saya*
boo-kuh *ting*-kahp?   *buka tingkap?*

What's ... station?	*ah*-puh *nah*-muh-nyuh	*Apa namanya*
	steh-sehn ...?	*stesen ...?*
this	*ee*-nee	*ini*
the next	yahng	*yang*
	ber-ee-*koot*-nyuh	*berikutnya*

Do I need to change trains?
ah-duh-kah(h) *sai*-yuh
hah-*roos* ber-*too*-kahr
ke-reh-tuh-*ah*-pee?   *Adakah saya*
                                       harus bertukar
                                       keretapi?

You must change at ...
ahn-dah hah-roos   *Anda harus bertukar di ...*
ber-*too*-kahr dee ...

I want to get off at ...
sai-yuh nah(k) *too*-roon dee ...   *Saya nak turun di ...*

How long will it be delayed?
be-*rah*-puh *lahm*-baht-nyuh?   *Berapa lambatnya?*

THEY MAY SAY ...

ke-reh-tuh-*ah*-pee ee-nee/ee-too ...	This/That train is ...
dee-bah-*tahl*-kahn	cancelled
lahm-baht	delayed/late
te-*paht*	on time

GETTING AROUND

TAXI TEKSI

Taxis in most big cities now operate with meters – if not, it's best to sort out the fare before getting in! Long distance taxis are a convenient way to get around, and still cheap. These taxis take up to four passengers, and will often wait around to find the full number bound for the same destination. You can pay a little more and have the whole vehicle to yourself.

Is this taxi available?
tehk-see *ee*-nee *ko*-song-kah(h)? *Teksi ini kosongkah?*
Please use the meter.
to-long *pah*-kai *mee*-ter *Tolong pakai meter.*
How much is the fare?
be-*rah*-puh *hahr*-guh *Berapa harga*
per-jah-*lah*-nahn? *perjalanan?*

Please take me	*to*-long *hahn*-tahr	*Tolong hantar*
to ...	*sai*-yuh ke ...	*saya ke ...*
this address	*ah*-lah-maht *ee*-nee	*alamat ini*
the airport	lah-*pahng*-ahn *ter*-bahng	*lapangan terbang*

Instructions Arahan

Here's fine, thanks.
ber-*hen*-tee dee *Berhenti di*
see-nee *sah*-juh *sini saja.*
The next street, please.
jah-lahn ber-ee-*koot*-nyuh *Jalan berikutnya.*

FINDING YOUR RELIGION

Be forewarned, the drivers of long distance taxis often drive at high speeds. Malaysian drivers will overtake almost anywhere, and the motto in the cities seems to be 'if there's a space, fill it'. There aren't as many accidents as you might imagine, so just close your eyes and hang on.

The next street (to the left/right).
jah-lahn (dee se-be-*lah(h)* ki-reel*kah*-nahn)	*Jalan (di sebelah kiril kanan)*
yahng ber-ee-*koot*-nyuh	*yang berikutnya.*

Continue/Straight on!	te-*roos*-kahn!	*Teruskan!*
Please slow down.	per-lah-*hahm*-kahn se-*dee*-kit	*Perlahankan sedikit.*
Please hurry.	to-long che-*paht* se-*dee*-kit	*Tolong cepat sedikit.*
Stop here!	ber-*hen*-tee dee *see*-nee!	*Berhenti di sini!*
Stop at the corner.	ber-*hen*-tee dee *soo*-dut ee-too	*Berhenti di sudut itu*
Please wait here.	to-long *toong*-goo dee *see*-nee	*Tolong tunggu di sini.*

I'll be right back.
sai-yuh *ah*-kahn kem-*bah*-lee se-ke-*jahp lah*-gee	*Saya akan kembali sekejap lagi.*

BOAT BOT/KAPAL

Some isolated areas in Sabah and Sarawak can only be reached by small river boats. Ferries are commonly used to reach islands off the coast. Some local operators are lax about observing safety rules; if you think a boat is overloaded or otherwise unsafe, don't board it. Speedboat ferries are faster but the journey can be rough.

THEY MAY SAY ...

soo-dah(h) pe-*nu(h)*
It's full.

tah(k) *ah*-duh ke-*roo*-see *lah*-gee
There aren't any seats.

eh-so(k) *ah*-duh ko-song/tem-*paht* doo-du(k)
There are seats for tomorrow.

boat	bot/*kah*-pahl/ *sahm*-pahn	*bot/kapal/* *sampan*
cabin	*bee*-li(k)	*bilik*
dock	*jeh*-tee	*jeti*
harbour/port	pe-lah-*boo*-hahn	*pelabuhan*
river	*soo*-ngai	*sungai*
sail	*lai*-yahr	*layar*
sea	lowt	*laut*

Where does the boat leave from?
  kah-pahl *ee*-too
  ber-*ahng*-kaht dee *mah*-nuh?   *Kapal itu*
                                        berangkat di mana?
What time does the boat arrive at ...?
  poo-kool be-*rah*-puh
  kah-pahl *ee*-too *tee*-buh dee ...?   *Pukul berapa*
                                        kapal itu tiba di ...?

CAR   KERETA

Car hire is possible throughout Malaysia; you can also hire a driver,
although this is much more expensive. Most petrol stations are
self-service. Look for a *layanan-penuh*, lai-*yah*-nahn-pe-*nu(h)*, sign
if you want your car filled for you.

Where can I hire a car?
  dee *mah*-nuh *sai*-yuh
  bo-*leh(h)* men-*yeh*-wuh   *Di mana saya*
  ke-*reh*-tuh?   *boleh menyewa*
                                        kereta?
How much is it daily/weekly?
  be-rah-*puh*-kah(h) *hahr*-guh   *Berapakah harga*
  seh-*wah*-nyuh *oon*-tu(k)   *sewanya untuk*
  se-*hah*-ree/se-*ming*-goo?   *sehari/seminggu?*
Does that include insurance?
  ah-duh-kah(h) *hahr*-guh-nyuh   *Adakah harganya*
  ter-*mah*-su(k) in-soo-*rahns*-kah(h)?   *termasuk insuranskah?*
Can we get a driver?
  bo-*leh(h)*-kah(h) *kah*-mee   *Bolehkah kami*
  men-*dah*-paht pe-*mahn*-doo?   *mendapat pemandu?*

Where's the next petrol station?
   steh-sehn *min*-yah(k)
   ber-ee-*koot*-nyuh dee *mah*-nuh?

Stesen minyak berikutnya di mana?

I want ... litres of petrol.
   sai-yuh nah(k) ...
   lee-ter *min*-yah(k)

Saya nak ... liter minyak.

Please fill up the tank.
   to-long pe-*nu(h)*-kahn
   tahng-kee

Tolong penuhkan tangki.

Please check the ...   *to*-long pe-*rik*-suh ...   *Tolong periksa ...*
   oil   *min*-yahk *hee*-tahm   *minyak hitam*
   tyre pressure   te-*kahn*-an *tai*-yahr   *tekanan tayar*
   water   air   *air*

Is this the road to ...?
   ee-nee-kah(h) *jah*-lahn ke ...?

Inikah jalan ke ...?

Can I park here?
   bo-*leh(h) leh*-tah(k)
   ke-*reh*-tuh dee *see*-nee?

Boleh letak kereta di sini?

How much does it cost to park here?
   be-*rah*-puh *hahr*-guh
   me-*leh*-tah(k) ke-*reh*-tuh
   dee *see*-nee?

Berapa harga meletak kereta di sini?

ROAD SIGNS

BERI JALAN	GIVE WAY
DILARANG ...	NO ...
MASUK	ENTRY
LETAK KERETA	PARKING
JALAN TOL	TOLLWAY
KERJA RAYA	ROADWORKS
SEHALA	ONE WAY
TEMPAT	CAR PARK

GETTING AROUND

air	oo-*dah*-ruh	*udara*
automatic	oh-toh-*mah*-tik	*otomatik*
battery	bah-*te*-ree	*bateri*
brakes	brehk	*brek*
car	ke-*reh*-tuh	*kereta*
clutch	klahch	*klac*
driver	pe-*mahn*-doo	*pemandu*
drivers licence	*leh*-sen me-*mahn*-doo	*lesen memandu*
engine	*ehn*-jin	*enjin*
garage	*gah*-rahj	*garaj*
horn	hon	*hon*
indicator	pe-*noon*-joo(k)	*penunjuk*
lights	*lahm*-poo	*lampu*
main road	*jah*-lahn *rai*-yuh/ oo-*tah*-muh	*jalan raya/utama*
oil	*min*-yah(k) *hee*-tahm	*minyak hitam*
petrol (gas)	*min*-yah(k)/*peh*-trol	*minyak/petrol*
diesel	*dee*-sel	*disel*
premium	pre-*mee*-um *tahm*-puh	*premium tanpa*
unleaded	*ploom*-boom	*plumbum*
unleaded	*tahm*-puh *ploom*-boom	*tanpa plumbum*
puncture	ke-bo-*cho*-rahn	*kebocoran*
radiator	rah-dee-*ah*-tor	*radiator*
roadmap	*peh*-tuh *jah*-lahn	*peta jalan*
seatbelt	*tah*-lee *ping*-gahng	*tali pinggang*
	ke-*reh*-dahr	*keledar*
self-service	*lai*-yahn *dir*-ree	*layan diri*
speed limit	hahd *lah*-joo	*had laju*
tyres	*tai*-yahr	*tayar*
windscreen	*kah*-chuh de-*pahm*	*kaca depan*
distance	*jah*-rah(k)	*jarak*
length of time	*lah*-muh	*lama*

Car Problems

Masalah Kereta

We need a mechanic.
kah-mee me-mer-*loo*-kahn
me-*ka*-nik.

*Kami memerlukan
mekanik.*

What make is it?
ke-*reh*-tuh je-*nis*
ah-puh ee-*nee*?

*Kereta jenis
apa ini?*

Our car broke down at ...
ke-*reh*-tuh *kah*-mee
ro-sah(k) dee ...

*Kereta kami
rosak di ...*

The car isn't working.
ke-*reh*-tuh ee-nee *ro*-sah(k)

Kereta ini rosak.

The engine's dead.
ehn-jin *mah*-tee

Enjin mati.

The engine is overheating.
ehn-jin ter-*lah*-loo *pah*-nahs.

Enjin terlalu panas.

I've run out of petrol
min-yah(k) *soo*-dah(h) *hah*-bees

Minyak sudah habis.

A COUNTRY MILE ...

With traffic jams in bigger cities, confusing signs in smaller towns, and some poor maintenance on out-of-the-way roads, you might be better off asking 'how long' rather than 'how far' your destination is!

How long (time/distance)
is the journey?
be-*rah*-puh (lah-*muh*/jow(h))
ber-*jah*-lah-nahn ee-nee?

*Berapa (lama/jauh)
perjalanan ini?*

It's 50km away.
jah-*rah*(k)-nyah lee-*mah*
poo-lu(h) ki-lo-*mee*-ter

*Jaraknya lima
puluh kilometer.*

The trip takes two hours.
per-*jah*-lah-nahn ee-nee
me-*ngahm*-bil *doo*-uh jahm

*Perjalanan ini
mengambil dua jam.*

The battery's flat.
bah-*ter*-ee *ee*-nee *mah*-tee

Bateri ini mati.

The radiator's leaking.
rah-dee-*ah*-tor *bo*-chor

Radiator bocor.

I have a flat tyre.
tai-yahr-nyuh *kem*-pis

Tayarnya kempis.

I've lost my car keys.
koon-chee ke-*reh*-tuh
sai-yuh *hee*-lahng

*Kunci kereta
saya hilang.*

BICYCLE   BASIKAL

Bike hire is becoming popular throughout the region and is a
great way to get around resort areas. Serious cyclists will need to
buy or bring their own bikes.

Where can I hire a bicycle?
dee *mah*-nuh *sai*-yuh bo-*leh(h)*
me-*nyeh*-wuh bah-*see*-kahl?

*Di mana saya boleh
menyewa basikal?*

I have a flat tyre.
tai-yahr *sai*-yuh *kem*-pis

Tayar saya kempis.

How much is it ...?	be-*rah*-puh *hahr*-guh-nyuh ...?	*Berapa harganya ...?*
per hour	*oon*-tu(k) se-*jahm*	*untuk sejam*
until (3 o'clock)	*sahm*-pai (*poo*-kool *tee*-guh)	*sampai (pukul tiga)*
the day	*oon*-tu(k) se-*hah*-ree	*untuk sehari*

bike	bah-*see*-kahl	*basikal*
brakes	brayk	*brek*
to cycle	ber-bah-*see*-kahl	*berbasikal*
gears	*gee*-gee	*gigi*
handlebars	*gah*-gahng bah-*see*-kahl	*gagang basikal*
helmet	*to*-pee ke-*leh*-dahr	*topi keledar*
inner tube	*tee*-oob dah-*lah*-mahn	*tiub dalaman*
lights	*lahm*-poo	*lampu*
lock	*koon*-chee	*kunci*
pump	pahm	*pam*
puncture	ke-bo-*cho*-rahn	*kebocoran*
saddle	ke-*roo*-see	*kerusi*
wheel	*ro*-duh	*roda*

GETTING AROUND

LOCAL TRANSPORT

KENDARAAN TEMPATAN

Beca, *beh*-chuh, bicycle-rickshaws, used to be found in many towns and cities across the nation, but these days they are only common in some northern towns.

Wait!	toong-*goo*!	*Tunggu!*
I want to get off!	*sai*-yuh nah(k) *too*-roon!	*Saya nak turun!*
Careful!	ber-*hah*-ti-*hah*-ti	*Berhati-hati*
	see-kit!	*sikit!*
Danger!	bah-*hai*-yuh!	*Bahaya!*
Stop!	ber-*hen*-tee!	*Berhenti!*

BABY YOU CAN GUARD MY CAR

When you park on the streets in larger towns and cities, you may be helped into your parking space by a smiling character, madly waving his arms. He is a *jaga kereta* boy, *jah*-guh ke-*reh*-tuh (lit: guard car). Although some cities have tried to eradicate this freelance job, it is best to give him a small amount of money, one or two *ringgit*, for helping you. You can pay up before leaving the car, or say 'Guard my car well', *Jaga kereta saya baik-baik*, *jah*-guh ke-*reh*-tuh *sai*-yuh bai(k)-bai(k), and pay when you come back.

ACCOMMODATION
PENGINAPAN

Accommodation choices in Malaysia run from cheap as chips to very expensive, from no-frills *rumah tumpangan*, *roo*-mah(h) toom-*pahng*-ahn, to government-run 'rest houses', *rumah rihat*, *roo*-mah(h) ree-haht, to 5-star hotels. Guest houses, which can be little huts or dorm-like accommodation, are available at beach centres and in major tourist cities. Homestays are still possible in some towns.

FINDING ACCOMMODATION
MENCARI PENGINAPAN

I'm looking for a ...	*sai*-yuh men-*chah*-ree ...	*Saya mencari ...*
camping ground	tem-*paht*	*tempat*
	per-kheh-*mah*-hahn	*perkhemahan*
guesthouse	*roo*-mah(h) te-*tah*-moo	*rumah tetamu*
upmarket hotel	*ho*-tehl *meh*-wah(h)	*hotel mewah*

Where's a ... hotel?	*ho*-tehl yahng ... dee *mah*-nuh?	*Hotel yang ... di mana?*
cheap	ter-moo-*rah*	*termurah*
clean	*ber*-si(h)	*bersih*
good	bah-*gus*	*bagus*
nearby	de-*kaht*	*dekat*

I've already found a hotel.
sai-yuh *soo*-dah(h) *joom*-puh se-*boo*-ah(h) *ho*-tehl

Saya sudah jumpa sebuah hotel.

Please take me to the ... hotel.
to-long *hahn*-tahr *sai*-yuh ke *ho*-tehl ...

Tolong hantar saya ke hotel ...

ACCOMMODATION

What's the address?
ah-puh-kah(h) *ah*-lah-maht-nyuh?   *Apakah alamatnya?*

Could you write down the
address, please?
to-long too-*lis*-kahn   *Tolong tuliskan*
ah-lah-*maht* ee-too   *alamat itu?*

The hotel is near the ...	*ho*-tehl-nyuh de-*kaht* ...	*Hotelnya dekat ...*
alley	lo-*rong*	*lorong*
beach	*pahn*-tai	*pantai*
shop	ke-*dai*	*kedai*
street	*jah*-lahn	*jalan*
town square	*dah*-tah-rahn	*dataran*

BOOKING AHEAD   MEMBUAT TEMPAHAN

Can I book a room?
bo-*leh(h)* mem-*boo*-aht   *Boleh membuat*
tem-*pah*-hahn *bee*-li(k)?   *tempahan bilik?*

My name's ...
nah-muh *sai*-yuh ...   *Nama saya ...*

For (three) nights.
se-*lah*-muh *(tee*-guh) *mah*-lahm   *Selama (tiga) malam.*

How much for ...?	be-*rah*-puh *hahr*-gah-nyuh ...?	*Berapa harganya ...?*
one night	*oon*-tu(k) *sah*-too *mah*-lahm	*untuk satu malam*
a week	*oon*-tu(k) se-*ming*-goo	*untuk seminggu*
two people	*oon*-tu(k) *doo*-uh *o*-rahng	*untuk dua orang*

I'll/We'll be arriving ...	*sai*-yuh/ *kah*-mee ah-*kahm* tee-buh ...	*Saya/Kami akan tiba ...*
on the (3rd)	*pah*-duh *(tee*-guh hah-ree-*bu*-lahn)	*pada (tiga haribulan)*
later tonight	*mah*-lahm ee-nee *nahm*-tee	*malam ini nanti*

CHECKING IN   MENDAFTARKAN DIRI

No matter how long you're staying, you may be able to arrange a *diskaun*, dis-kown, 'discount'. An easy way to get cheaper room rates is to exclaim *Mahalnya!*, mah-*hal*-nyuh!, 'So expensive!' in mock horror, and act like you're going elsewhere. See what offer comes up then, but be sure you look at the room before you decide to take it.

I'd like a room for ...	sai-yuh men-chah-ree bee-li(k) oon-tu(k) ...	Saya mencari bilik untuk ...
one person	se-o-rahng	seorang
two people	doo-uh o-rahng	dua orang
I'd like a room with a ...	sai-yuh men-chah-ree bee-li(k) yahng mem-poon-yah-ee ...	Saya mencari bilik yang mempunyai ...
bathroom	bee-li(k) air	bilik air
fan	kee-pahs	kipas
shower	tem-paht mahn-dee	tempat mandi
TV	tee vee	TV
window	ting-kahp	tingkap
I'm going to stay for (one) ...	sai-yuh ah-kahn ber-mah-lahm se-lah-muh (sah-too) ...	Saya akan bermalam selama (satu) ...
day	hah-ree	hari
week	ming-goo	minggu

I'd like to share a dorm.
  sai-yuh nah(k) ber-kong-see bee-li(k) hos-tehl

Saya nak berkongsi bilik hostel.

Is there a room available?
  ah-duh bee-li(k) yahng ko-song?

Ada bilik yang kosong?

Can I see the room?
  bo-leh(h) sai-yuh me-lee-haht bee-li(k) ee-too?

Boleh saya melihat bilik itu?

ACCOMMODATION

ACCOMMODATION

Is there a discount for ...?   *ah*-duh *dis*-kown *oon*-tu(k) ...?   Ada diskaun untuk ...?
  children   *ah*-nah(k)   anak
  students   pe-*lah*-jahr   pelajar

I'm not sure how long I'm staying.
  sai-yuh be-*lum tah*-hoo
  be-*rah*-puh *la*-muh *sai*-yuh
  ah-kahn ber-*mah*-lahm
  dee *see*-nee
    Saya belum tahu
    berapa lama saya
    akan bermalam
    di sini.

I (don't) like this room.
  sai-yuh (tah(k)) *soo*-kuh
  bee-li(k) *ee*-nee
    Saya (tak) suka
    bilik ini.

Do you have a better room?
  ah-duh *bee*-li(k) yahng
  le-*bi(h)* bai(k)?
    Ada bilik yang
    lebih baik?

Do you have a room with ..?   *ah*-duh tah(k) *bee*-li(k) yahng *ah*-duh ...?   Ada tak bilik yang ada ...?
  two beds   *doo*-uh *kah*-til   dua katil
  a double bed   *kah*-til be-*sahr*   katil besar

Where's the bathroom?
  bee-li(k) *mahm*-dee
  dee *mah*-nuh?
    Bilik mandi
    di mana?

Is there hot water all day?
  ah-duh-kah(h) air *pah*-nahs
  se-*pahm*-jahng *hah*-ree?
    Adakah air panas
    sepanjang hari?

Is breakfast included?
  mah-kahn *pah*-gee
  ter-*mah*-su(k)-kah(h)?
    Makan pagi
    termasukkah?

This room's fine.
  bee-li(k) *ee*-nee se-*swai*
    Bilik ini sesuai.

Paying

How much does it cost per day?
be-*rah*-puh *hahr*-guh-nyuh
oon-tu(k) se-*hah*-ree?

What's the daily rate?
be-*rah*-puh *hahr*-guh
hah-ree-*ahn*-nyuh?

Does the price include breakfast/tax?
hahr-guh-nyuh ter-*mah*-su(k)
sah-rah-pahn-kah(h)/
choo-kai-kah(h)?

Do you allow children?
bo-*leh*(h) *sai*-yuh
bah-wah ah-*nah*(k)?

Is there an extra charge for children?
ah-duh *hahr*-guh tahm-*bah*-hahn
oon-tu(k) ah-*nah*(k)?

Can I pay by ...?	bo-*leh(h) bai*-yahr de-*ngahm ...?*	
credit card	kahd *kreh*-dit	
travellers cheque	chehk pe-*lahm*-chong	

Pembayaran

*Berapa harganya
untuk sehari?*

*Berapa harga
hariannya?*

*Harganya termasuk
sarapankah/
cukaikah?*

*Boleh saya
bawa anak?*

*Ada harga tambahan
untuk anak?*

*Boleh bayar
dengan ...?*
kad kredit
cek pelancong

ACCOMMODATION

THEY MAY SAY ...	
soo-dah(h) pe-*nu(h)*	We're full.
be-*rah*-puh *lah*-muh?	For how long?
be-*rah*-puh *mah*-lahm/o-rahng?	How many nights/people?
ter-*mah*-su(k) teh(h)/*ko*-pee	It includes tea/coffee.
bai-*yahr doo*-loo	Please pay now.
bai-*yahr* ke-*moo*-dee-ahn	Pay later.

ACCOMMODATION

REQUESTS & COMPLAINTS

Do you have a safe where I can leave my valuables?
ah-duh pe-*tee* keh-bahl
oon-tu(k) men-*yim*-pahn
bah-rahng ber-*hahr*-guh?

Could I have a receipt for them?
ah-duh *reh*-seet
oon-tu(k) me-*reh*-kuh?

Where can I wash my clothes?
dee *mah*-nuh *sai*-yuh
bo-*leh(h)* men-*choo*-chee
pah-kai-ahn?

Do you have a laundry service?
ah-duh *ser*-vis *choo*-chee
pah-kai-ahn?

When will they be ready?
bee-luh *see*-ahp?

Can I use the telephone?
bo-*leh(h)* *pah*-kai
teh-*leh*-fon tah(k)?

There are mosquitoes.
ah-duh *nyah*-mu(k)-lah(h)

PERMINTAAN & ADUAN

Ada peti kebal
untuk menyimpan
barang berharga?

Ada resit untuk mereka?

Di mana saya
boleh mencuci
pakaian?

Ada servis cuci
pakaian?

Bila siap?

Boleh pakai telefon tak?

Ada nyamuklah.

Do you have (a) ...?	*ah*-duh ...?	*Ada ...?*
insect repellant	*oo*-baht *nyah*-mu(k)	*ubat nyamuk*
mosquito net	ke-*lahm*-boo	*kelambu*

I need another ...	*sai*-yuh me-mer-*loo*-kahn *lah*-gee *sah*-too ...	*Saya memerlukan lagi satu ...*
blanket	se-*lee*-moot	*selimut*
pillow	*bahn*-tahl	*bantal*
pillowcase	sah-*rong bahn*-tahl	*sarung bantal*
sheet	*chah*-dahr	*cadar*
towel	too-*ah*-lah	*tuala*

Please change it/them.
to-long *too*-kahr-kahn *ee*-nee

Tolong tukarkan ini.

Please clean my room.
to-long *ber*-si(h)-kahn
bee-li(k) *sai*-yuh

Tolong bersihkan bilik saya.

Excuse me, I have a problem.
mah-*ahf*, ah-duh mah-*sah*-lah(h)

Maaf, ada masalah.

The (window) is broken.
(ting-kahp) *ee*-too ro-*sah(k)*

(Tingkap) itu rosak.

I can't open/ close the ...	*sai*-yuh tah(k) bo-*leh(h)* *boo*-kuh/too-*tup* ...
door	*peen*-too
window	*ting-kahp*

Saya tak boleh buka/tutup ...
pintu
tingkap

I can't lock the door.
sai-yuh *tee*-dah(k)
bo-*leh(h)* *koon*-chee *pin*-too

Saya tidak boleh kunci pintu.

I've locked myself out.
koon-chee *sai*-yuh
ter-*ting*-gahl *dah*-lahm *bee*-li(k)

Kunci saya tertinggal dalam bilik.

Can you get it fixed?
bo-*leh(h)* *bai*-kee tah(k)?

Boleh baiki tak?

The room is too ...	*bee*-li(k) *ee*-nee ter-*lah*-loo ...	*Bilik ini terlalu ...*
cold	se-*joo(k)*	*sejuk*
dark	ge-*lahp*	*gelap*
hot	*pah*-nahs	*panas*
noisy	bee-*sing*	*bising*
smelly	boo-*soo(k)*	*busuk*

ACCOMMODATION

candle	*li*-leen	*lilin*
chair	ke-*roo*-see	*kerusi*
door	*pin*-too	*pintu*
electricity	eh-*lehk*-trik	*elektrik*
key	*koon*-chee	*kunci*
lamp	*lahm*-poo	*lampu*
lock	*koon*-chee	*kunci*
mattress	tee-*lahm*	*tilam*
mosquito coil	*oo*-baht *nyah*-mu(k)	*ubat nyamuk*
quiet	sen-*yahp*	*senyap*
roof	*ah*-tahp; *boom*-boong	*atap; bumbung*
soap	*sah*-bon	*sabun*
toilet paper	*ti*-soo; *ti*-soo *tahm*-dahs	*tisu; tisu tandas*
towel	*twah*-lah	*tuala*
to wake	*bah*-ngoon	*bangun*
wardrobe	ahl-*mah*-ree	*almari*
... water	air ...	*air ...*
drinking	*mee*-num	*minum*
hot	*pah*-nahs	*panas*

TIME AFTER TIME

Malaysians divide up their day this way:

morning (from dawn until noon)
  pah-gee   *pagi*

midday (from noon until about three o'clock)
  te-ngah-*hah*-ree   *tengahari*

afternoon/evening (from about three o'clock until sunset)
  pe-*tahng*   *petang*

night (from sunset until dawn)
  mah-lahm   *malam*

CHECKING OUT

MENINGGALKAN HOTEL

I'm leaving today.
sai-yuh ber-*ahng*-kaht
hah-ree *ee*-nee

Saya berangkat hari ini.

Please prepare my/our bill.
to-long se-*dee*-ah-kahn
bil *sai*-yuh/*kah*-mee

*Tolong sediakan
bil saya/kami.*

There's a mistake in the bill.
bil *ee*-nee *sah*-lah(h)

Bil ini salah.

Please call me a taxi.
to-long *pahng*-gil-kahn *tehk*-see

Tolong panggilkan teksi.

Can I leave my	bo-*leh(h)* tah(k)	*Boleh tak*
things here	*sai*-yuh *sim*-pahn	*saya simpan*
until ...?	*bah*-rahng dee	*barang di*
	see-nee *sahm*-pai ...?	*sini sampai ...?*
this afternoon	te-ngah-*hah*-ree/	*tengahari/*
	pe-*tahng* *ee*-nee	*petang ini*
this evening	pe-*tahng* *ee*-nee	*petang ini*
tonight	*mah*-lahm	*malam*

ACCOMMODATION

LONGER STAYS

**PENGINAPAN JANGKA
PANJANG**

Some guesthouses offer cheaper rates for longer stays. Also look into homestays, available in Kota Baru, Kuala Lumpur and Johor Baru.

to rent	me-*nyeh*-wuh	*menyewa*

Is there a room available?
ah-duh *bee*-li(k) *ko*-song?

Ada bilik kosong?

I'm looking for a room near the beach/city-centre.
sai-yuh *chah*-ree *bee*-li(k)
de-*kaht* *pan*-tai/
poo-saht *bahn*-dahr

*Saya cari bilik
dekat pantai/
pusat bandar.*

I want to rent a room/house for
(three) months.

sai-yuh nah(k) me-*nyeh*-wuh
bee-li(k)/*roo*-mah(h)
se-*lah*-muh *(tee*-guh) *bu*-lahn

*Saya nak menyewa
bilik/rumah
selama (tiga) bulan.*

How much per month?

be-*rah*-puh *hahr*-guh-nyuh
oon-tu(k) se-*bu*-lahn?

*Berapa harganya
untuk sebulan?*

DI BANDAR   AROUND TOWN

The atmosphere on the streets of Malaysia is action-packed. People are out and about from early morning long into the night. Shops are usually open until 9 or 10pm, restaurants much later, and roadside stalls later still. Night markets, *pasar malam*, *pah-sahr mah-lahm*, are a must for the visitor who wants a taste of the Malaysian way of life.

AROUND TOWN

LOOKING FOR ...

English	Pronunciation	MENCARI ...
How far is a/an/ the ...?	be-*rah*-puh jow(h) ...?	*Berapa jauh ...?*
I'm going to a/an/ the ...	*sai*-yuh *per*-gee ke ...	*Saya pergi ke ...*
I'm looking for a/an/the ...	*sai*-yuh men-*chah*-ree ...	*Saya mencari ...*
bank	bank	*bank*
barber shop	ke-*dai goon*-ting *rahm*-boot	*kedai gunting rambut*
consulate	*kon*-soo-laht	*konsulat*
crossroad	*sim*-pahng em-*paht*	*simpang empat*
embassy	ke-*doo*-tah-ahn be-*sahr*	*kedutaan besar*
hairdresser; hair salon	sa-*lon*; ke-*dai goon*-ting *rahm*-boot	*salon; kedai gunting rambut*
hospital	*hos*-pee-tahl	*hospital*
hotel	ho-*tehl*	*hotel*
money changer	tem-*paht* pe-*noo*-kahr-ahn wahng	*tempat penukaran wang*
museum	moo-*zee*-um	*muzium*
police station	*bah*-lai *po*-lis	*balai polis*
post office	pe-*jah*-baht pos	*pejabat pos*
public telephone	teh-*leh*-fon *ah*-wahm	*telefon awam*
public toilet	*tahn*-duhs *ah*-wahm	*tandas awam*
restaurant	*res*-to-rahn	*restoran*
school	se-*ko*-lah(h)	*sekolah*
temple	*chan*-dee/*poo*-rah	*candi/pura*
town square	dah-*tah*-rahn	*dataran*
traditional market	*pah*-sahr	*pasar*
village	*kahm*-pong	*kampong*
zoo	zoo	*zoo*

What time does it open/close?
poo-kool be-*rah*-puh
boo-kuh/too-*tup*
Pukul berapa buka/tutup?

Is it still open?
boo-kuh *lah*-gee tah(k)?
Buka lagi tak?

AT THE BANK **DI BANK**

All tourist areas and large towns have money changers as well as banks. Money changers, *tempat penukaran wang*, tem-*paht* pe-*noo*-kahr-ahn wahng, usually have longer opening hours and exchange rates are generally better than banks. Hotels and some department stores will also change money for you, but the rates aren't as good.

Can I exchange money here?
    bo-*leh(h) too*-kahr wahng
    dee *see*-nee?

Boleh tukar wang di sini?

Can I use my credit card to withdraw money?
    bo-*leh(h) sai*-yuh
    meng-*goo*-nah-kahn kahd
    kreh-dit *oon*-tu(k)
    me-nge-*loo*-ahr-kahn *doo*-it?

Boleh saya menggunakan kad kredit untuk mengeluarkan duit?

Please write it down.
    to-long *too*-lis-kahn

Tolong tuliskan.

Can I have smaller notes?
    ah-duh *doo*-it ke-*chil* tah(k)?

Ada duit kecil tak?

The ATM swallowed my card.
    kahd *sai*-yuh dee-*teh*-lahn
    ay tee em

Kad saya ditelan ATM.

Where can I cash a travellers cheque?
    dee *mah*-nuh *sai*-yuh bo-*leh(h)*
    me-*noo*-kahr-kahn chehk
    kem-*bah*-ruh *ee*-nee ke-*pah*-duh
    wahng *too*-nai?

Di mana saya boleh menukarkan cek kembara ini kepada wang tunai?

I want to change ...	*sai*-yuh nah(k) me-*noo*-kahr-kahn ...	*Saya nak menukarkan ...*
Australian dollars	*do*-lahr os-*trah*-lee-ah	*dolar Australia*
cash	wahng *too*-nai	*wang tunai*
Pounds Sterling	paun stuh-*ling*	*Pounds Stirling*
travellers cheques	chehk kem-*bah*-ruh	*cek kembara*
US dollars	*do*-lahr ah-*mehr*-ree-kah	*dolar Amerika*

AROUND TOWN

What's the exchange rate?
   ah-puh-kah(h) *kah*-dahr   *Apakah kadar*
   pe-*noo*-kahr-ahn?   *penukaran?*

Has any money arrived for me?
   ah-duh-kah(h) *hahn*-tahr-ahn   *Adakah hantaran wang*
   wahng *oon*-tu(k) *sai*-yuh?   *untuk saya?*

Can I transfer money
from my bank to here?
   bo-*leh(h)*-kah(h) bank   *Bolehkah bank*
   sai-yuh meng-*hahn*-tahr   *saya menghantar*
   doo-it ke bank *ee*-nee?   *duit ke bank ini?*

How long will it take?
   be-*rah*-puh *lah*-muh?   *Berapa lama?*

Do I have to pay commission?
   ah-duh-kah(h) ko-*mi*-shen   *Adakah komisyen perlu*
   per-*loo* dee-*bai*-yahr?   *dibayar?*

branch	chah-*wah*-gahn	*cawangan*
cash	wahng *too*-nai	*wang tunai*
cashier	*joo*-roo-wahng	*juruwang*
cashier's window	*ting*-kahp	*tingkap*
	joo-roo-wahng	*juruwang*
cheque	chehk	*cek*
coins	*doo*-it *shi*-ling	*duit syiling*
commission	ko-*mi*-shen	*komisyen*
credit card	kahd *kreh*-dit	*kad kredit*
ID card	kahd pe-nge-*nah*-lahn	*kad pengenalan*
main office	*ee*-boo pe-*jah*-baht	*ibu pejabat*
letter of credit	soo-*raht kreh*-dit	*surat kredit*
manager	pe-*ngoo*-rus	*pengurus*
money	wahng/*doo*-it	*wang/duit*
money order	wahng *ki*-ree-mahn	*wang kiriman*
note (bill)	*doo*-it *ker*-tahs	*duit kertas*
signature	*tahn*-duh *tah*-ngahn	*tanda tangan*
teller	*teh*-ler	*teler*

AT THE POST OFFICE

DI PEJABAT POS

Post offices, *pejabat pos*, pe-*jah*-baht pos, with their bright red facades, can be found in all towns.

I want to buy ...	*sai*-yuh nah(k) mem-be-*lee* ...	*Saya nak membeli ...*
envelopes	*sahm*-pul soo-*raht*	*sampul surat*
postcards	*pos*-kahd	*poskad*
stamps	se-*tehm*	*setem*
I want to send a/an ...	*sai*-yuh nah(k) meng-*hahn*-tahr ...	*Saya nak menghantar ...*
aerogram	*ehr*-o-gram	*aerogram*
letter	soo-*raht*	*surat*
parcel	*boong*-koo-sahn	*bungkusan*
telegram	*teh*-le-gram	*telegram*
Please send it (by) ... mail.	*to*-long *hahn*-tahr de-*ngahm* ...	*Tolong hantar dengan ...*
air	mehl oo-*dah*-ruh	*mel udara*
express	pos *lah*-joo	*pos laju*
registered	soo-*raht* ber-*dahf*-tahr	*surat berdaftar*
surface	pos bee-*ah*-suh	*pos biasa*

How much does it cost
to send this to ...?
be-*rah*-puh *hahr*-guh
peng-hahn-*tah*-rahn *ee*-nee ke ...?

*Berapa harga
penghantaran ini ke ...?*

How much is an airmail letter
to (the US)?
be-*rah*-puh ki-*ree*-mahn
soo-*raht* pos oo-*dah*-ruh ke
(ah-*mehr*-ee-kah)?

*Berapa kiriman
surat pos udara ke
(Amerika)?*

Please send this parcel to ...
by surface mail.

> *to*-long *ki*-reem-kahn
> *boong*-koo-sahn *ee*-nee ke ...
> de-*ngah* pos bee-*ah*-suh

*Tolong kirimkan
bungkusan ini ke ...
dengan pos biasa.*

Please weigh this letter.

> *to*-long *tim*-bahng
> soo-*raht* *ee*-nee

*Tolong timbang
surat ini.*

glue	gahm	*gam*
mailbox	pe-*tee* soo-*raht*	*peti surat*
pen	pen	*pen*
postcode	*pos*-kod	*poskod*
receiver	pe-ner-*ree*-muh	*penerima*
sender	pen-*gee*-rim	*pengirim*
string	*tah*-lee	*tali*

SIGNS

AWAS	CAUTION
BAHAYA	DANGER
BERHENTI	STOP
BUKA	OPEN
DILARANG ...	NO ...
MASUK	ENTRY
MEROKOK	SMOKING
DINGIN	COLD
HALAL	ALLOWED FOR MUSLIM CONSUMPTION
KELUAR	EXIT
LELAKI	MEN
MASUK	ENTRANCE
PANAS	HOT
TANDAS	TOILETS
TARIK	PULL
TOLAK	PUSH
TUTUP	CLOSED

TELECOMMUNICATIONS   TELEKOMUNIKASI

Making domestic telephone calls in Malaysia is easy. You can direct-dial local and long-distance calls using coins and there are card telephones operated by Telecom Malaysia and Uniphone. The cards are widely available at small shops, 7-Eleven stores, post offices and newsagents. Calling Singapore is not considered an international call. All operators speak English, although you may need to speak slowly.

Could I please use the telephone?
bo-*leh*(h) *pah*-kai teh-*leh*-fon? *Boleh pakai telefon?*

What's the area code for ...?
kod kah-*wah*-sahn teh-*leh*-fon *Kod kawasan telefon*
... be-*rah*-puh? *... berapa?*

I want to call ...
sai-yuh nah(k) me-neh-*leh*-fon ... *Saya nak menelefon ...*

The number is ...
nom-bor-nyuh ee-*ah*-lah(h) ... *Nombornya ialah ...*

I want to speak for (three) minutes.
sai-yuh nah(k) ber-*chah*-kahp *Saya nak bercakap selama*
se-*lah*-muh *(tee*-guh) *mi*-nit *(tiga) minit.*

How much is a
(three)-minute call to ...?
be-*rah*-puh *ring*-git *Berapa ringgit panggilan*
pang-*gil*-ahn *(tee*-guh) *(tiga) minit ke ...?*
mi-nit ke ...?

I want to make a
reverse-charge phone call.
sai-yuh nah(k) me-neh-*leh*-fon *Saya nak menelefon*
poong-*oo*-tahn *pungutan.*

When's a cheap time to call?
poo-kool be-*rah*-puh *mah*-suh *Pukul berapa masa*
moo-rah(h) *oon*-tu(k) *murah untuk*
meng-*goo*-nuh-kahn *menggunakan telefon?*
teh-*leh*-fon?

AROUND TOWN

Operator, I've been cut off.
    o-pe-*ray*-tor pang-*gil*-ahn *Operator, panggilan saya*
    sai-yuh ter-*poo*-toos   *terputus.*

The line is busy.
    tah-lee-ahn *ee*-too *see*-bu(k)/ *Talian itu sibuk/engage.*
    ehn-*gehj*

Sorry, you've got the wrong number.
    mah-*ahf* sah-lah(h) *nom*-bor   *Maaf, salah nombor.*

Hello, do you speak English?
    heh-lo bo-*leh(h) chah*-kahp   *Helo, boleh cakap bahasa*
    bah-*hah*-suh *ing*-ge-ris?   *Inggeris?*

Making a Call

Membuat Panggilan

Hello.
    heh-lo   *Helo.*

May I speak to ...?
    bo-*leh(h) sai*-yuh   *Boleh saya*
    ber-*chah*-kahp de-*ngahn* ...?   *bercakap dengan ...?*

Who's calling?
    see-*ah*-puh nee?   *Siapa ni?*

This is ... speaking.
    ee-nee ...   *Ini ...*

Yes, she's/he's here.
    yah *dee*-uh *ah*-duh dee *see*-nee   *Ya, dia ada di sini.*

One moment, please.
    toong-goo se-ke-*jahp*   *Tunggu sekejap.*

I'm sorry, they're not here.
    mah-*ahf* me-*reh*-kah tah(k)   *Maaf, mereka tak*
    ah-duh dee *see*-nee   *ada di sini.*

What time will she/he be back?
  poo-kool be-*rah*-puh dee-uh
  poo-*lahng*?   *Pukul berapa dia pulang?*

Can I leave a message?
  bo-*leh(h) ting*-gahl-kahn
  pe-*sah*-nahn?   *Boleh tinggalkan*
                       pesanan?

Please tell him/her I called.
  to-long be-ree-*ta*-hoo *dee*-uh
  sai-yuh teh-*leh*-fon   *Tolong beritahu dia saya*
                       telefon.

I'll call back later.
  sai-yuh teh-*leh*-fon
  ke-*moo*-dee-ahn   *Saya telefon kemudian.*

operator	o-pe-*ray*-tor	*operator*
phone book	*boo*-koo teh-*leh*-fon	*buku telefon*
phone box	teh-*leh*-fon *ah*-wahm	*telefon awam*
phone call	pahng-*gil*-ahn teh-*leh*-fon	*panggilan telefon*
phonecard	kad teh-*leh*-fon	*kad telefon*
reverse charges	*poong*-oo-tahn	*pungutan*
telephone	teh-*leh*-fon	*telefon*
to telephone	me-neh-*leh*-fon	*menelefon*
urgent call	pahng-*gil*-ahn *pen*-ting	*panggilan penting*

AROUND TOWN

Internet   **Internet**

Internet cafes have sprung up all over Malaysia in the past few years, offering cheap – yet sometimes slow – email access.

Is there a local Internet cafe?
  ah-duh *sai*-ber ka-*fay* tah(k)
  dee kah-*wah*-sahn *ee*-nee?   *Ada cyber cafe tak di*
                       kawasan ini?

Where can I get access
to the Internet?
  dee *mah*-nuh *sai*-yuh bo-*leh(h)*
  pah-kai *in*-ter-neht?   *Di mana saya boleh*
                       pakai internet?

What's the rate per hour?
  kah-dahr se-*jahm* be-*rah*-puh?   *Kadar sejam berapa?*

SIGHTSEEING

BERSIAR-SIAR

Malaysians love to go sightseeing, *makan angin*, *mah-kahn ah-ngin* (lit: to-eat air). You don't have to visit the big sights to enjoy Malaysia – the local markets and shopping areas are just as interesting. Notice the differences in multilingual signs, smells and sounds of the predominantly Chinese, Indian or Malay neighbourhoods.

Where's the tourist office?
    pe-*jah*-baht pe-*lahn*-chong-ahn   *Pejabat pelancongan*
    dee *mah*-nuh?   *di mana?*

What's that building?
    bahn-*goo*-nahn *ah*-puh *ee*-too?   *Bangunan apa itu?*

What's this monument?
    too-goo *ah*-puh *ee*-too?   *Tugu apa itu?*

Who lived there?
    see-*ah*-puh *per*-nah(h)   *Siapa pernah*
    ting-gahl dee *sah*-nuh?   *tinggal di sana?*

Do you have a local map?
    ah-duh pe-*tuh*   *Ada peta*
    tem-*pah*-tahn tah(k)?   *tempatan tak?*

Can I take (your) photo(s)?
    bo-*leh(h)* sai-yuh *ahm*-bil   *Boleh saya ambil*
    fo-to/*gahm*-bahr (*ahm*-dah)?   *foto/gambar (anda)?*

I'll send you the photograph.
    nahm-tee sai-yuh *hahn*-tahr   *Nanti saya hantar*
    fo-to/*gahm*-bahr *ee*-nee   *foto/gambar ini kepada*
    ke-*pah*-duh *ahm*-dah   *anda.*

Could you take a photo of (me)?
    to-long *ahm*-bil *fo*-to/   *Tolong ambil foto/*
    gahm-bahr (*sai*-yuh)?   *gambar (saya)?*

I want to see a/the ...	*sai*-yuh nah(k) me-*lee*-haht ...	*Saya nak melihat ...*
I'd like to go to a/the ...	*sai*-yuh nah(k) *per*-gee ke ...	*Saya nak pergi ke ...*
church	ge-*reh*-juh	*gereja*
garden	*tah*-mahn	*taman*
(botanical)	bo-*tahn*-i-kahl	*botanikal*
mosque	*mahs*-jid	*masjid*
museum	moo-*zee*-um	*muzium*
nightclub	ke-*lahb mah*-lahm	*kelab malam*
palace	ees-*tah*-nuh	*istana*
park	*tah*-mahn	*taman*
performance	per-*toon*-joo(k)-kahn	*pertunjukan*
public square	dah-*tah*-rahn	*dataran*
royal palace	ees-*tah*-nuh dee-*rah*-juh	*istana diraja*
statue	*pah*-tung	*patung*
university	yoo-ni-*ver*-si-tee	*universiti*

PAPERWORK   MENGISI BORANG

If you need to deal with the Malaysian government for any reason, you'll get further if you dress neatly and do your best to be polite and soft-spoken. Most government officials are Malays, who can be easily offended by obvious displays of impatience or anger, or what they define as loud voices or any form of arrogance. Many printed forms in Malaysia are in Malay and English, so you shouldn't have a lot of trouble.

Forms   Borang

name	*nah*-muh	*nama*
address	*ah*-lah-maht	*alamat*
date/place of birth	*tah*-rikh/tem-*paht* *lah*-*hir*	*tarikh/tempat lahir*
age	*oo*-moor	*umur*
sex	jahn-*tee*-nuh	*jantina*
nationality	*bahng*-suh	*bangsa*
religion	ah-*gah*-muh	*agama*
profession	pe-*ker*-jah-ahn	*pekerjaan*

marital status	*tah*-rahf	*taraf*
	per-*kah(h)*-wi-nahn	*perkahwinan*
single	be-*lum kah(h)*-win	*belum kahwin*
married	ber-*kah(h)*-win	*berkahwin*
divorced	ber-*che*-rai	*bercerai*
widow	*jahm*-duh	*janda*
widower	*doo*-duh	*duda*
identification	pe-*nge*-nahl-ahn	*pengenalan*
passport number	*nom*-bor *pahs*-port	*nombor pasport*
visa	*vee*-suh	*visa*
birth certificate	soo-*raht* ber-*ah*-nah(k)	*surat beranak*
drivers licence	*leh*-sehn me-*mahn*-doo	*lesen memandu*
purpose of visit	se-*bahb* lah-*wah*-tahn	*sebab lawatan*
business	pe-*ker*-jah-ahn	*pekerjaan*
holiday	per-*choo*-tee-ahn	*percutian*
visiting	me-*lah*-waht	*melawat*
relatives	ke-loo-*ahr*-guh	*keluarga*

BERJALAN-JALAN GOING OUT

When the hot sun goes down over Malaysia, the air cools and activity picks up! Bustling night markets open just before sunset, offering a myriad of food, goods and people-watching opportunities. Shopping malls are packed and the big cities have plenty of coffee shops, clubs, pubs and bars. Sampling the variety of Malaysian cuisine at some of the outdoor food stalls is a must.

Where's a ...?	... dee *mah*-nuh?	... *di mana?*
I'd like to go	*sai*-yuh nah(k)	*Saya nak*
to a ...	*per*-gee ke ...	*pergi ke ...*
bar	bahr	*bar*
cafe	ka-*fay*	*cafe*
food stalls	ge-*rai*	*gerai*
nightclub	ke-*lahb mah*-lahm	*kelab malam*
night market	*pah*-sahr *mah*-lahm	*pasar malam*
I feel like ...	*sai*-yuh nah(k) ...	*Saya nak ...*
dancing	me-*nah*-ree	*menari*
eating	*mah*-kahn	*makan*
watching a film	me-*non*-ton *fee*-lem	*menonton filem*

I feel like going	*sai*-yuh nah(k) ke ...	*Saya nak ke ...*
to a/the ...		
cinema	*pahng*-gung	*panggung*
	wai-yahng	*wayang*
concert	*kon*-sert	*konsert*
shadow	per-*toon*-joo(k)-ahn	*pertunjukan*
puppet show	*wai*-yahng *koo*-lit	*wayang kulit*
theatre	*tee*-ah-ter; *chan*-dee	*teater; candi*
	wah-rah	*wara*

INVITATIONS

JEMPUTAN

Would you like to go to a
cinema with me?
  nah(k) *per-gee* te-*ngo(k)*
  wai-yahng ber-*sah*-muh *sai*-yuh?

*Nak pergi tengok wayang
bersama saya?*

Do you know a good club?
  ahn-duh *tah*-hoo tah(k)
  ke-*lahb* yahng bah-*gus*?

*Anda tahu tak
kelab yang bagus?*

I'll pay.
  sai-yuh nah(k) *bai*-yahr-lah(h)

Saya nak bayarlah.

Come along.
  joom/*mah*-ree!

Jum/Mari!

The night's young!
  mah-lahm *mah*-si(h) *moo*-duh!

Malam masih muda!

Responding to Invitations

Jemputan Membalas

I'd like to.   yah/bo-*leh(h)*   *Ya/Boleh.*
I can't.   tah(k) bo-*leh(h)*   *Tak boleh.*

STAND BY ME

Apart from shaking hands, physical contact in public
between the sexes is very minimal in Malaysian society,
except perhaps in discos. Malaysians take a dim view
of canoodling couples, even if they're married.

Nightclubs & Bars

Kelab Malam & Bar

How should we get there?
  nai(k) *ah*-puh ke *sah*-nuh?

Naik apa ke sana?

Are these clothes OK?
  pah-*kai*-yahn *ee*-nee
  se-*swai* tah(k)?

Pakaian ini sesuai tak?

Is there an admission charge?
  ah-duh bai-*yahr*-ahn *mah*-su(k)
  tah(k)?

Ada bayaran masuk tak?

What sort of music do you like?
  ahn-*duh* soo-kuh *moo*-zik *ah*-puh?

Anda suka muzik apa?

I like techno.
  sai-yuh *soo*-kuh tek-no   *Saya suka tekno.*
Let's dance.
  joom *kee*-tuh me-*nah*-ree   *Jum kita menari.*

This place is ...	tem-*paht* ee-*nee* ...	*Tempat ini ...*
That person's ...	*dee*-uh ...	*Dia ...*
cool	behst	*best*
sleazy	*ko*-tor	*kotor*
strange	pe-*li(k)*	*pelik*

Let's go somewhere else.
  joom *per*-gee tem-*paht* lain   *Jum pergi tempat lain.*

DATING & ROMANCE
Looking for a Date

KELUAR BERDUA & PERCINTAAN
Mencari Pasangan

Remember the different pronouns in Malay. Usually the more casual, intimate and egalitarian pronouns (*aku* or *ku* for 'I' and *engkau* or *kau*, *kamu* or *mu* for 'you') are used in dating situations, especially after the first date or two (see the box on page 18).

Would you like to get together ...?	nah(k) ber-*joom*-puh ... tah(k)?	*Nak berjumpa ... tak?*
again	*lah*-gee	*lagi*
later tonight	*mah*-lahm *nahn*-tee	*malam nanti*
tomorrow	*eh*-so(k)	*esok*

I'd like to.	yah/bo-*leh(h)*	*Ya/Boleh.*
No thanks.	tah(k) nah(k)-*lah(h)*	*Tak naklah.*
Go away!	*per*-gee/be-*lah(h)*!	*Pergi/Belah!*
Don't hassle me.	*jah*-ngahn *kah*-chow ah-koo	*Jangan kacau aku.*

I have a ...	*sai*-yuh ah-duh ...	*Saya ada ...*
boyfriend	*pah(k)*-we	*pakwe*
girlfriend	*mah(k)*-we	*makwe*
husband	*swah*-mee	*suami*
wife	*ees*-te-ree	*isteri*

Love   Cinta

You're beautiful.	*kah*-moo *chahn*-ti(k)	*Kamu cantik.*
Let's kiss.	joom ber-*chee*-oom	*Jum bercium.*
(Don't) Stop!	(*jah*-ngahn) ber-*hen*-tee!	*(Jangan) Berhenti!*
Delicious!	se-*dahp*-nyuh!	*Sedapnya!*
Great!	heh-*baht*!	*Hebat!*

Do you have a condom?
  ah-duh *kon*-dom?   *Ada kondom?*

No condom, no sex.
  tah(k) bo-*leh(h)* *tahn*-puh   *Tak boleh tanpa*
  kon-dom   *kondom.*

Do you want to smoke?
  kah-moo nah(k) *ro*-ko(k)?   *Kamu nak rokok?*

Can I stay?
  bo-*leh(h)* *sai*-yuh   *Boleh saya*
  ber-*mah*-lahm dee *see*-nee?   *bermalam di sini?*

Can I see you again?
  bo-*leh(h)* *kee*-tuh ber-*te*-moo   *Boleh kita bertemu lagi?*
  lah-gee?

FORBIDDEN LOVE

Muslims can be arrested by Department of Religion officials for drinking alcohol and for eating or smoking in public during the fasting month, *Ramadhan*, rah-mah-dhahn. But there's another activity that's really not on. *Khalwat*, khahl-waht, is translated as 'close proximity' – when two people of the opposite sex are alone in a situation where sex might be a possibility. *Khalwat* is *haram*, hah-rahm, 'forbidden' in Islam.

Be aware that going alone to a secluded place, or entering a hotel room alone with a Muslim, might result in an embarrassing intrusion by the Department of Religion officials – and a fine (although usually the non-Muslim partner does not have to pay). Hope this box hasn't killed the mood!

I'll call you.
   nahm-tee *sai*-yuh teh-*leh*-fon   *Nanti saya telefon.*

Do you want to be my
girlfriend/boyfriend?
   kah-moo nah(k) *jah*-dee   *Kamu nak jadi pakwe/*
   pah(k)-we/*mah(k)*-we *sai*-yuh   *makwe saya tak?*
   tah(k)?

I like you.	*ah*-koo *soo*-kuh kow	*Aku suka kau.*
I love you.	*ah*-koo *chin*-tuh	*Aku cinta*
	pah-duh moo	*pada mu.*

HOT IN THE CITY

Malaysians are a fascinating combination of traditional
and modern, Asian and Western. You'll see Muslim
women and some Indian women completely covered
up, and others (of all backgrounds) in mini-skirts.
   Although Islam prohibits drinking alcohol and the
'close proximity' of people of the opposite sex, a lot of
both still goes on, particularly in the big cities. Chinese
Malaysians are probably the most accepting of dating,
the various Indian-Malaysian groups are not as happy
about it and the Malays are the most conservative.

Leaving & Breaking Up

Memutuskan Hubungan Percintaan

I leave tomorrow.
   eh-so(k) *sai*-yuh ber-*ahng*-kaht   *Esok saya berangkat.*

I'll miss you.
   ah-koo ah-*kahn* me-*rin*-doo-ee   *Aku akan merindui*
   kah-moo   *kamu.*

Let's keep in touch.
   ah-koo *hah*-rahp *kee*-tuh   *Aku harap kita akan*
   ah-*kahn* te-*tahp*   *tetap berkomunikasi.*
   ber-ko-*moon*-i-*kah*-see

This relationship isn't appropriate.
   hoo-*boong*-ahn *ee*-nee tah(k)   *Hubungan ini tak*
   se-*swai bah*-gee *kee*-tuh ber-*doo*-uh   *sesuai bagi kita berdua.*

'GOING TO THE CHAPEL'

- You will see mosques, large and small, everywhere in Malaysia, distinguished by their minarets and beautiful domes of different shapes. You'll certainly hear the call to prayer, *azan*, which blasts out five times a day and will notice the arrow on almost every hotel room ceiling, pointing to Mecca. Most Malays are not comfortable seeing travellers who appear to be non-Muslim entering their places of worship. Women should dress in loose-fitting clothes covering everything but their faces and hands; men should cover up too, in a long-sleeved shirt and pants. Ensure you don't walk in front of anyone who's praying.

- Hindu temples are usually ornate and colourful. The roofs are often a riot of vividly painted Hindu gods. Again, conservative dress is a good idea.

- Chinese temples have elaborate roofs, some with a multi-storey pagoda design. Inside the temples, incense spices the air and the hall is filled with carved and gilded wood and ornaments.

- Sikh temples, often modest buildings, can be recognised by the triangular flag flying outside. Any one is welcome within the temple, and as with all the other religions, you must take off your shoes before entering.

GOING OUT

KELUARGA   FAMILY

QUESTIONS   PERTANYAAAN

Family is all-important to Malaysians. Family ties are expressed
in everyday conversations through the use of words like *abang*,
ah-*bahng*, 'big brother' and *makcik*, *mah(k)*-chi(k), 'auntie'.
Whether at the market or in someone's home, you'll almost
certainly be asked questions about yourself and the members of
your family.

Are you married?   *soo*-dah(h) *kah(h)*-win?   *Sudah kahwin?*

Unless you have tied the knot, in which case you reply *soo*-dah(h)
'already', the best answer is:

Not yet.   be-*lum lah*-gee   *Belum lagi.*

Saying *tidak*, *tee*-dah(k), 'no', would be grammatically fine, but
many Malaysians might think it's weird if you're not married, or
at least thinking about it. Also, the word for 'friend', *kawan*,
kah-wahn, often implies a romantic relationship. *Ada kawan?*,
ah-duh *kah*-wahn?, may actually mean:

Do you have a boyfriend/girlfriend?
   ah-duh *pah(k)*-we/*mah(k)*-we?   *Ada pakwe/makwe?*
Is your husband/wife here?
   swah-mee/*ees*-te-ree *ahn*-duh   *Suami/Isteri anda di sini?*
   dee *see*-nee?
Do you have any brothers and sisters?
   ah-duh ah-*di(k)*-be-rah-di(k)?   *Ada adik-beradik?*
Do you have any children?
   soo-dah(h) *ah*-duh *ah*-nah(k)?   *Sudah ada anak?*
How many children do you have?
   be-*rah*-puh *o*-rahng *ah*-nah(k)?   *Berapa orang anak?*

FAMILY

REPLIES

JAWAPAN

I'm not married yet.
  sai-yuh be-*lum*
  kah(h)-win/*nee*-kah(h)

*Saya belum
kahwin/nikah.*

I'm still single.
  sai-yuh *mah*-si(h) *boo*-jahng

Saya masih bujang.

I'm married.
  sai-yuh *soo*-dah(h) *kah*(h)-win

Saya sudah kahwin.

I don't have any children (yet).
  sai-yuh *tee*-dah(k) (be-*lum*)
  ah-duh *ah*-nah(k)

*Saya tidak (belum)
ada anak.*

This is my ...	*ee*-nee ... *sai*-yuh	*Ini ... saya.*

I have ...	*sai*-yuh *ah*-duh ...	*Saya ada ...*
one son	se-*o*-rahng *ah*-nah(k) le-*lah*-kee	*seorang anak lelaki*
three sons	*tee*-guh *o*-rahng *ah*-nah(k) le-*lah*-kee	*tiga orang anak lelaki*
one daughter	se-*o*-rahng *ah*-nah(k) pe-*rem*-pwahn	*seorang anak perempuan*
three daughters	*tee*-guh *o*-rahng pe-*rem*-pwahn	*tiga orang perempuan*

I have two younger brothers.
  sai-yuh *ah*-duh *doo*-uh *o*-rahng
  ah-*di*(k) le-*lah*-kee

*Saya ada dua orang
adik lelaki.*

DID YOU KNOW ... One word for a second wife for Muslims is *madu*, *mah*-doo, which literally means honey, as in honey to the bee.

FAMILY MEMBERS   ANGGOTA KELUARGA

Brothers and sisters are always referred to as older or younger.

aunt	*mah(k)*-chi(k)	*makcik*
boyfriend	*pah(k)*-we/te-*mahn*	*pakwe/teman*
	le-*lah*-kee	*lelaki*
child(ren)	ah-nah(k)(-ah-nah(k))	*anak(-anak)*
cousin	se-*poo*-poo	*sepupu*
daughter	ah-nah(k)	*anak*
(unmarried)	pe-*rem*-pwahn	*perempuan*
	ah-nah(k) *dah*-ruh	*anak dara*
eldest	*soo*-long	*sulong*
family	ke-loo-*ahr*-guh	*keluarga*
father	*bah*-pah(k)/*ai*-yah(h)	*bapak/ayah*
friend	*kah*-wahn	*kawan*
girlfriend	*mah(k)*-we/te-*mahn*	*makwe/teman*
	wah-*nee*-tuh	*wanita*
grandchild	*choo*-choo	*cucu*
grandfather	*dah*-tu(k)	*datuk*
grandmother	neh-*neh(k)*	*nenek*
husband	*swah*-mee	*suami*
mother	mah(k)/*ee*-boo	*mak/ibu*
older brother	ah-*bahng* le-*lah*-kee	*abang lelaki*
older sister	*kah*-kah(k)	*kakak*
	pe-*rem*-pwahn	*perempuan*
partner	*pah*-sahng-ahn	*pasangan*
son	*ah*-nah(k) le-*lah*-kee	*anak lelaki*
uncle	*pah(k)*-chi(k)	*pakcik*
wife	*ees*-te-ree	*isteri*
younger brother	ah-*di(k)* le-*lah*-kee	*adik lelaki*
younger sister	ah-*di(k)* pe-*rem*-pwahn	*adik perempuan*
youngest	*bong*-soo	*bongsu*

FAMILY

IT'S A FAMILY AFFAIR

Malaysians of all backgrounds are very specific in relating to others in terms of how old people are and their placement in the family hierarchy. With larger families this can become a bit complicated. Introductions are often made simply by identifying relationships. If you meet the extended family, including the many aunts and uncles, you may be introduced to 'youngest uncle' *paksu*, *pah(k)-soo*. The wife of *paksu* will probably be called *maksu*, *mah(k)-soo*, except in her own family, where, if she were the middle auntie, she might be called *makngah*, *mah(k)-ngah(h)*. Of course there's always the eldest of the uncles in the family, *paklong*, *pah(k)-long*. Got it?

Malay women keep their own names when they marry, so it's not possible to keep track of family relations through surnames. Instead, each person has their own first name, followed by the words *bin*, bin, 'son of' or *binti*, bin-tee, 'daughter of', followed by their father's first name. So a family may actually have three different 'last' names.

When addressing male and female adults in a family respectively, you'd call them *Encik*, en-chi(k), (plus his first name) and *Puan*, poo-ahn, (plus her first name). People may also use this custom on you, and address you as 'Mr Mick' instead of 'Mr Jagger'.

COMMON INTERESTS   MINAT BERSAMA

Malaysians undertake leisure time with gusto. The worst feeling for many is *boringlah*, *boh*-reeng-lah(h), an adaption of the English word boring. The opposite feeling is *shiok*, shee-oh(k), 'delicious and wonderful'.

Do you like ...?	*ahn*-duh *soo*-kuh ...?	*Anda suka ...?*
I (don't) like ...	*sai*-yuh (tah(k)) *soo*-kuh ...	*Saya (tak) suka ...*
art	ke-se-*nee*-ahn	*kesenian*
cooking	me-*mah*-sah(k)	*memasak*
dancing	me-*nah*-ree	*menari*
(traditional)	trah-di-see-*o*-nahl	*tradisional*
discos	*dis*-ko	*disko*
film	*fee*-lem;	*filem;*
	wai-yahng	*wayang*
	gahm-bahr	*gambar*
going out	ber-*jah*-lahn-*jah*-lahn	*berjalan-jalan*
going shopping	mem-be-*lee*-be-*lah*(h)	*membeli-belah*
music	*moo*-zi(k)	*muzik*
photography	fo-to-*grah*-fee	*fotografi*
playing sport	ber-*soo*-kahn	*bersukan*
reading books	mem-*bah*-chuh	*membaca*
	boo-koo	*buku*
the theatre	*tee*-ah-ter;	*teater;*
	sahn-dee-*wah*-rah	*sandiwara*
travelling	men-gem-*bah*-ruh	*mengembara*
travel	kem-*bah*-ruh	*kembara*
watching TV	me-*non*-ton tee vee	*menonton TV*
writing	me-*noo*-lis	*menulis*

What do you do in your
spare time?
    ahm-duh *soo*-kuh *boo*-aht
    ah-puh *dah*-lahm *mah*-suh
    lah-pahng?
What hobby do you have?
    ah-puh *ho*-bee *ahn*-duh?

*Anda suka buat
apa dalam masa
lapang?*

Apa hobi anda?

HOW TO WINTER YOUR SHEEP

Malaysia's TV and radio improved drastically in the '90s. Long gone are the days of only two government TV channels, with incredibly boring and sometimes inappropriate programming – such as a documentary imported from England on 'How to Winter Your Sheep'.

The government sponsors two channels, TV1 and TV2, and there are three commercial stations. TV1 is almost all in Malay; TV2 has much more English as well as the other languages of Malaysia in its programming. Various satellite and cable companies bring an even wider array of foreign programming.

The modern Malaysian film industry has a lot of competition overseas, as Chinese, Indian, American and European films all crowd out local production. Modern Malay movies tend to be melodramatic and have simplistic story lines, maybe due to censorship or the view that morals are powerfully conveyed through film. Try to catch some of the older black and white films, especially those starring the famous and hilarious P Ramlee. They all have English subtitles.

INTERESTS

SPORT   SUKAN

Malaysians are into sport, especially *badminton*, *bahd*-min-ton, 'badminton' and *bola sepak*, *bo*-luh *seh*-pah(k), 'soccer'. Malaysian badminton players rank among the best in the world, and are in hot competition with the nearby Indonesians. The national soccer league *Liga Malaysia* also has a passionate following throughout the country. *Sepak takraw*, *seh*-pah(k) *tah*-kraw, is an impressive game, common in Malaysia, Indonesia and Thailand. Balls made of *rotan*, *ro*-tahn, 'rattan' are used like volleyballs. Players can only use their heads and feet to get the ball back and forth over the net, without letting it touch the ground.

Do you like sport?
ahm-duh *soo*-kuh
ber-*soo*-kahn?

*Anda suka
bersukan?*

I like playing sport.
sai-yuh *soo*-kuh
ber-*soo*-kahn

*Saya suka
bersukan.*

I prefer to watch rather
than play sport.
sai-yuh le-*bi(h) soo*-kuh
me-*non*-ton dah-ree-*pah*-duh
ber-*main soo*-kahn

*Saya lebih suka
menonton daripada
bermain sukan.*

Do you play ...?	*ahm*-duh main ... tah(k)?	*Anda main ... tak?*
Would you like to play/go/do ...?	*ahm*-duh nah(k) main ...?	*Anda nak main ...?*
badminton	*bahd*-min-ton	*badminton*
basketball	*bo*-luh ke-*rahm*-jahng	*bola keranjang*
boxing	*teen*-joo	*tinju*
diving	me-nye-*lahm*	*menyelam*
soccer	*bo*-luh *seh*-pah(k)	*bola sepak*
gymnastics	jim-*nahs*-tik	*gimnastik*
hockey	*ho*-kee	*hoki*
martial arts	se-*nee* mem-per-tah-*hahn*-kahn *di*-ree	*seni memperta-hankan diri*
rugby	*rahg*-bee	*ragbi*
water skiing	main skee air	*main ski air*
soccer	*bo*-luh *seh*-pah(k)	*bola sepak*
surfing	ber-se-*lahn*-chahr	*berselancar*
swimming	be-re-*nahng*	*berenang*
table tennis	*ping*-pong	*ping-pong*
tennis	*teh*-nis	*tenis*
takraw	*seh*-pah(k) *tah*-kraw	*sepak takraw*
top (spinning)	*gah*-sing	*gasing*

INTERESTS

WRITING LETTERS

MENULIS SURAT

Once you get back home, you may want to drop a line to people. Letter writing in Malay tends to be formal, so the sentences and phrases below are a little more serious than conversational Malay.

Dear ...,
ke-*pah*-duh ...
yahng dee-kah-*si(h)*-ee

Kepada ...
yang dikasihi,

I'm sorry it's taken me so long to write.
min-tuh mah-*ahf* se-*bahb*
dah(h) *lah*-muh *sai*-yuh
tee-dah(k) men-*gi*-reem soo-raht

Minta maaf sebab
dah lama saya
tidak mengirim surat.

It was great to meet you.
sai-yuh gem-*bee*-ruh kee-tuh
dah-paht ber-*te*-moo dah-*hoo*-loo

Saya gembira kita dapat
bertemu dahulu.

Thanks so much for your hospitality.
te-*ree*-muh *kah*-si(h) ah-*tahs*
ke-re-moo-tah-*mah*-hahn
ahm-duh

Terima kasih atas
keremutamahan
anda.

I miss you.
sai-yuh me-*rin*-doo-ee
ahm-duh/*kah*-lee-ahn (sg/pl)

Saya merindui
anda/kalian.

I had a fantastic time in ...
pe-ngah-*lah*-mahn *sai*-yuh
dee ... be-*gee*-too
me-nye-ro-*no(k)*-kahn

Pengalaman saya
di ... begitu
menyeronokkan.

My favourite place was ...
... ee-*ah*-la(h) tem-*paht*
yahng *pah*-ling *sai*-yuh
soo-kai

... ialah tempat
yang paling saya
sukai.

I hope to visit ... again.
se-*mo*-guh *sai*-yuh dah-paht
me-ngoon-joo-ngee ... *lah*-gee

Semoga saya dapat
mengunjungi ... lagi.

Send my regards to ...
to-long sahm-*pai*-kahn
sah-lahm *sai*-yuh ke-*pah*-duh ...

Tolong sampaikan
salam saya kepada ...

I'd love to see you again.
sai-yuh *ee*-ngin se-*kah*-lee
ber-*te*-moo de-*ngahn*
ahm-duh *lah*-gee

*Saya ingin sekali
bertemu dengan
anda lagi.*

Write soon!
to-long *bah*-lahs

Tolong balas!

With love/regards,
de-*ngahn kah*-si(h)

Dengan kasih,

SOCIAL ISSUES   ISU SOSIAL

Malaysians often enjoy talking about social issues, perhaps because so much that comes out in local papers and TV broadcasts is censored. Coffee shops are a great place to catch up on national gossip. Malaysians, however, do not appreciate criticism from foreigners, so be sensitive to 'what side' they are on. Politics in recent years have been very sensitive and fractured.

I (don't) agree.	*sai*-yuh (tah(k)) se-*too*-joo	*Saya (tak) setuju.*
Do you like ...?	*ahm*-duh *soo*-kuh ...?	*Anda suka ...?*
I (don't) like ...	*sai*-yuh (tah(k)) *soo*-kuh ...	*Saya (tak) suka ...*
Really?; Is that so?	be-*tul*-kah(h)?	*Betullkah?*
Really!	be-*tul!*	*Betul!*

What do people/you think about ...?
ah-puh pen-*dah*-paht
rah(k)-yaht/*ahm*-duh
ten-tahng ... ?

*Apa pendapat
rakyat/anda
tentang ...?*

I support the ... party.
sai-yuh me-*nyo*-kong *pahr*-tee ...

Saya menyokong parti ...

What party do you support?
pahr-tee yahng *mah*-nuh
ahm-duh me-*nyo*-kong?

*Parti yang mana
anda menyokong?*

In my country, we have a
conservative/liberal government.
ke-*rah*-jah-ahn dee ne-*gah*-ruh
sai-yuh kon-*ser*-vah-tif/
li-be-rahl

*Kerajaan di negara
saya konservatif/
liberal.*

INTERESTS

POLITICS

POLITIK

cronyism	kro-*nis*-me	*kronisme*
demonstration	*toon*-ju(k) pe-*rah*-sah-ahn	*tunjuk perasaan*
democracy	deh-*mo*-krah-see	*demokrasi*
general election	pi-lee-hahn-*rai*-yuh	*pilihanraya*
government	ke-*rah*-jah-ahn	*kerajaan*
monetary crisis	*kri*-sis ke-*wahng*-ahn	*krisis kewangan*
Malaysian	*ahng*-kah-tahn	*Angkatan*
Armed Forces	*ten*-te-ruh	*Tentera*
	mah-*lay*-see-ah	*Malaysia (ATM)*
Parliament	*pahr*-li-mehn	*Parlimen*
policy	*po*-li-see	*polisi*
politician	*ah*-lee *po*-li-tik	*ahli politik*
President	*preh*-si-dehn	*Presiden*
Prime Minister	per-*dah*-nuh *men*-te-ree	*Perdana Menteri*
reformation	reh-for-*mah*-see	*reformasi*
peaceful	*dah*-mai	*damai*
revolution	reh-vo-*loo*-see	*revolusi*
socialism	so-see-ahl-*is*-me	*sosialisme*
economy	eh-*ko*-no-mee	*ekonomi*
exploitation	ehks-ploy-*tah*-see	*eksploitasi*
history	se-*jah*-rah(h)	*sejarah*
justice	ke-*ah*-di-lahn	*keadilan*
the people	*rah*-kyaht	*rakyat*
poverty	ke-mis-*ki*-nahn	*kemiskinan*
riot	roo-*su*-hahn	*rusuhan*
unemployment	pe-*ngahng*-goo-rahn	*pengangguran*
welfare	ke-*bah*-jee-kahn	*kebajikan*
worker	pe-*ker*-juh	*pekerja*

INTERESTS

PRAISE YOU

Malaysians love to hear praise of their own country, but may perceive too many positive comments about the traveller's home country as 'boasting' or 'arrogance'. So, be humble about your own country's advantages.

INTERESTS

MUSIC   MUZIK

A variety of music abounds in Malaysia. You'll find well-known musicians and pop singers from many countries performing in the big cities or on TV. Around sunset, you might tune in to troops of *nasyid*, *nah*-sheed, singers, all-male or female groups who sing religious songs in Malay or Arabic, with a Middle-Eastern flavour. Featuring plenty of percussion instruments, traditional types of music include:

Dikir barat, *dee*-kir *bah*-raht
From Kelantan, men wearing traditional dress sit in a group and chant a story, accompanied by drums.

Dondang sayang, *don*-dahng *sai*-yahng
Mainly from Melaka, these are Chinese-influenced romantic songs with orchestral instrumentation .

Ghazal, *ghah*-zahl
Mainly found in Johor, these female singers are accompanied by an orchestra of Middle-Eastern instruments.

Zikir, *zee*-kir
A type of religious singing.

CRAFTS   KRAFTANGAN

The traditional arts and crafts of Malaysia are now mainly found on the east coast, and to a certain extent in East Malaysia. If you are looking for modern art, there are galleries and roadside artists in the bigger cities.

Batik, *bah*-teek, is the beautifully patterned material, usually cotton or silk, which is coloured with a wax and dye system that creates intricate and beautifully designed fabrics.

Kain songket, kain *song*-keht, is also a specialty of Kelantan and Terengganu. It is a hand-woven fabric with gold and silver threads through the material. This is the material traditionally worn in wedding ceremonies, coronations and other official functions.

Perak, *peh*-rah(k), is the fine silver filigree jewellery of the east coast.

FIGHTING KITES & BIG TOPS

These two traditional games are not child's play. The tops, *gasing*, *gah*-sing, made of polished hardwood and metal can weigh up to 7kg. The cords used to spin them are about 5m long, and it takes real strength to hurl the tops onto a polished mud slab. The player must then scoop up the spinning top with a thin wooden paddle and place it on a small, metal-tipped wooden post. Players compete to see whose top will spin the longest. Teams of players have traditionally played this game when the rice is ripening and there is less work to do.

Kite flying contests include events for the highest flyer and competitions between fighting kites. Both top spinning and kite, *wau*, wow, flying contests are held in the north-eastern states of Kelantan and Terrengannu. There are bird kites, cat kites and the ever-popular moon kite *wau bulan*, wow bu-lahn. They are superb works of art as well as flying instruments, and can be up to 2.5m wide. Kites and tops are popular souvenirs, and a traditional kite is the symbol of Malaysia Airlines.

INTERESTS

PERFORMING & MARTIAL ARTS
SENI PERSEMBAHAN DAN PERTAHANAN DIRI

Many of the traditional performing arts are finally dying out. Kelantan banned *wayang kulit*, wai-yahng koo-lit, and *mak yong*, mah(k) yong, for having 'unislamic influences'. They are only performed for tourists in that state. Tourism has saved these troops of performers from total extinction.

Wayang kulit, wai-yahng koo-lit
These shadow play puppets are found in many countries in South-East Asia. Performances, generally at night, can last for hours and are based on characters from the Hindu epic, the *Ramayana*.

Mak yong, mah(k) yong
A dance drama of Thai origin, with an all-female cast, associated with magical forces.

Menora, me-no-ruh
Similar to *mak yong*, with an all-male cast, wearing grotesque masks.

INTERESTS

MEMBELI BELAH   SHOPPING

LOOKING FOR ...   MENCARI ...

Malaysians are big on shopping, and you can join the frenzy in a
variety of shops, malls, traditional markets and stalls throughout
the country. Whether you're shopping for electronic goods,
handicrafts, antiques, brand name clothes or something that's
excitingly near the real thing, everything's a bargain, so get going!

Where's a/the ...?	... dee *mah*-nuh?	... *di mana*?
bakery	ke-*dai ro*-tee	*Kedai roti*
barber	ke-*dai goon*-ting *rahm*-but	*Kedai gunting rambut*
bookshop	ke-*dai boo*-koo	*Kedai buku*
camera shop	ke-*dai ka*-me-ruh	*Kedai kamera*
chemist	*fahr*-mah-see; ke-*dai oo*-baht	*Farmasi; Kedai ubat*
clothing store	ke-*dai* pah-*kai*-ahn	*Kedai pakaian*
general store	ke-*dai roon*-chit	*Kedai runcit*
market	*pah*-sahr	*Pasar*
music store	ke-*dai moo*-zi(k)	*Kedia muzik*
night market	*pah*-sahr *mah*-lahm	*Pasar malam*
shopping centre	*poo*-saht mem-be-*lee*-be-*lah(h)*	*Pusat membeli-belah*
souvenir shop	ke-*dai* chehn-de-rah-*mah*-tuh	*Kedai cenderamata*
supermarket	pah-sah-*rai*-yuh	*Pasaraya*
tailor	*too*-kahng *jah*-hit	*Tukang jahit*

MAKING A PURCHASE MEMBELI SESUATU

Shopkeepers might assume that you'll want a foreign product –
set them straight if you're looking for locally made things *barang
tempatan,* *bah*-rahng tem-*pah*-tahn

Where can I buy ...?
    ... dee-*joo*-ahl dee *mah*-nuh?   *... dijual di mana?*

Do you have any ...?
    ... *ah*-duh tah(k)?   *... ada tak?*

I'm looking for (a) ...
    sai-yuh nah(k) *chah*-ree ...   *Saya nak cari ...*

I'm just looking.
    sai-yuh nah(k) te-*ngo(k) sah*-juh   *Saya nak tengok saja.*

How much is it?
    be-*rah*-puh *hahr*-guh-nyuh?   *Berapa harganya?*

Can you write down the price?
    to-long *too*-lis-kahn   *Tolong tuliskan*
    hahr-guh-nyuh   *harganya.*

Can I try this on?
    bo-*leh(h) sai*-yuh *choo*-buh?   *Boleh saya cuba?*

Can I pay by credit card?
    bo-*leh(h)* bai-yahr   *Boleh bayar*
    de-*ngahn* kahd *kreh*-dit?   *dengan kad kredit?*

Do you have others?
    ah-duh yahng laiin?   *Ada yang lain?*

Where are these made?
    bah-rahng-*bah*-rahng *ee*-nee   *Barang-barang ini*
    dee-*boo*-aht dee *mah*-nuh?   *dibuat di mana?*

Can I see it?
    bo-*leh(h) sai*-yuh te-*ngo(k)*?   *Boleh saya tengok?*

I don't like it.
    sai-yuh tah(k) *soo*-kuh *ee*-nee   *Saya tak suka ini.*

It's beautiful!
    in-*dah(h)/chahn*-ti(k) se-*kah*-lee!   *Indah/Cantik sekali!*

I'll take it.
    sai-yuh nah(k) be-*lee ee*-nee   *Saya nak beli ini.*

BARGAINING   TAWAR-MENAWAR

Bargaining is something of a game to Malaysians. Be good-humoured in your bargaining: steady, but not aggressive pressure is the best. If you don't like the price, or think you can do better, there are usually other places to try.

It's too expensive.
    mah-*hahl*-nyuh!   *Mahalnya!*
Can you lower the price?
    bo-*leh(h)* koo-rahng-kahn   *Boleh kurangkan*
    hahr-guh tah(k)?   *harga tak?*

THEY MAY SAY ...

bo-*leh(h)* sai-yuh to-long *ahn*-duh?	Can I help you?
chah-ree ah-puh?	What are you looking for?
ah-duh, se-*ke*-jahp	We've got that, just a moment.
wahr-nuh ah-puh?	What colour?
ee-nee-kah(h) bah-rahng yahng ah-wah(k) chah-ree?	Is this what you're looking for?
hahr-guh-nyuh lee-muh poo-lu(h) ring-git	The price is RM50.
tee-dah(k)/tah(k) ah-duh	We don't have any.

SHOPPING

How much discount?
be-*rah*-puh-kah *dis*-kown?   *Berapakah diskaun?*
I'll give you ...
sai-yuh *bah*-gee *ahn*-duh ...   *Saya bagi anda ...*
No more/less than ...
tah(k) le-*bi(h)*/   *Tak lebih/*
koo-rahng dah-ree-*pah*-duh ...   *kurang daripada ...*
This is my final offer.
ee-nee *tah*-wahr-ahn   *Ini tawaran*
te-*rah*-khi(r) *sai*-yuh   *terakhir saya.*

cheap	*moo*-rah(h)	*murah*
discount	*dis*-kown	*diskaun*
expensive	mah-*hahl*	*mahal*

ESSENTIAL ITEMS BARANGAN YANG PERLU

I'm looking for (a) ...	*sai*-yuh *chah*-ree ...	*Saya cari ...*
batteries	*bah*-te-ree	*bateri*
bread	*ro*-tee	*roti*
butter	men-*teh*-guh	*mentega*
cheese	*keh*-joo	*keju*
chocolate	*chok*-laht	*coklat*
eggs	te-*lur*	*telur*
flour	te-*pung*	*tepung*
ham	*dah*-ging *bah*-bee	*daging babi*
honey	*mah*-doo	*madu*
margarine	men-*teh*-guh	*mentega*
matches	*mahm*-chis	*mancis*
milk	*soo*-soo	*susu*
toilet paper	*tee*-soo	*tisu*
toothpaste	*oo*-baht gee-gee	*ubat gigi*
torch (flashlight)	*lahm*-poo *soo*-lu(h)	*lampu suluh*
towel	*twah*-luh	*tuala*
washing powder	*ser*-bu(k) *choo*-chee	*serbuk cuci*
yogurt	*yo*-gurt	*yogurt*

SHOPPING

SOUVENIRS   CENDERA HATI

Traditional handicraft production has declined due to changes in national lifestyle, so arty items you see may often be from Indonesia. The east coast, Sabah and Sarawak still have some excellent crafts; Melaka is a centre for antiques, as is Penang.

basket	*bah*-kool	bakul
... batik	*bah*-ti(k) ...	batik ...
hand painted	*loo*-kis *tah*-ngahn	lukis tangan
printed	chahp	cap
bracelet	ge-*lahng*	gelang
cane ware	*bah*-rahng-ahn *ro*-tahn	barangan rotan
... carving	*oo*-ki-rahn	ukiran ...
stone	*bah*-too	batu
wood	*kai*-yoo	kayu
earrings	*soo*-bahng	subang
handcrafts	krahf-*tah*-ngahn	kraftangan
jewellery	*bah*-rahng ke-*mahs*	barang kemas
machete	*pah*-rahng	parang
carved masks	*to*-peng yahng	topeng
	dee-*oo*-kir	yang diukir
material (fabric)	kain	kain
necklace	*rahm*-tai *leh*-hehr	rantai leher
Malay knives	ke-*ris*	keris
paintings	loo-*kee*-sahn	lukisan
pottery	tem-*bee*-kahr	tembikar
shadow puppets	*wai*-yahng *koo*-lit	wayang kulit
ring	*chin*-chin	cincin
sarong	*sah*-rung	sarung
statue	*pah*-tung	patung

SHOPPING

CLOTHING   PAKAIAN

bra	*cho*-lee	*coli*
cardigan	*bah*-joo se-*joo(k)* yahng	*baju sejuk yang*
	ber-*boo*-tahng de-*pahm*	*berbutang depan*
dress	*bah*-joo gown	*baju gaun*
gloves	*sah*-rung tah-*ngahm*	*sarung tangan*
hat	*to*-pee	*topi*
jacket	jah-*keht*	*jaket*
jeans	jeens	*jeans*
jumper	*bah*-joo se-*ju(k)*	*baju sejuk*
pants	se-*loo*-ahr *pahm*-jahng	*seluar panjang*
raincoat	*bah*-joo hoo-jahn	*baju hujan*
sandals	se-*lee*-pahr	*selipar*
shirt	*bah*-joo/ke-*meh*-juh	*bajul kemeja*
shoelaces	*tah*-lee *kah*-sut	*tali kasut*
shoes	*kah*-sut	*kasut*
shorts	se-*loo*-ahr *pehm*-deh(k)	*seluar pendek*
skirt	sket	*skirt*
socks	*sto*-king	*stoking*
swimsuit	pah-*kai*-ahn/	*pakaian/*
	bah-joo *reh*-nahng	*baju renang*
tie	*tah*-lee *leh*-hehr	*tali leher*
trousers	se-*loo*-ahr *pahm*-jahng	*seluar panjang*
Tshirt	*bah*-joo tee	*baju T*
underwear	se-*loo*-ahr *dah*-lahm	*seluar dalam*

HOT AND COLD

Think hot, hot, hot. It simply never cools down, except
during the rainy season on the east coast. You'll need
cotton clothes that breathe, and protect you from the
sun (and any eager eyes checking you out). If you head
into the highlands you may need to rug up, so take
waterproof gear or a light jumper.

MATERIALS

BAHAN

The *Jalan Masjid India* and *Jalan Tuanku Abdul Rahman* areas of Kuala Lumpur have a huge variety of shops selling material.

bone	*too*-lahng	tulang
cotton	*kah*-pahs	kapas
gold	e-*mahs*	emas
jackfruit wood	kai-yoo *nahng*-kuh	kayu nangka
leather	*koo*-lit	kulit
rattan/cane	*ro*-tahn	rotan
sandalwood	chehn-*dah*-nuh	cendana
shell	*koo*-lit *see*-put	kulit siput
silk	*soo*-te-ruh	sutera
silver	*peh*-rah(k)	perak
wood	*kai*-yoo	kayu
wool	*boo*-loo *bi*-ree-*bi*-ree	bulu biri-biri

THE REAL McCOY

When looking for souvenirs or items made in Malaysia, ask:
'Is this made in Malaysia?'

ee-nee *bah*-rahng   Ini barang
boo-ah-tahn mah-*lay*-see-ah?   buatan Malaysia?

SHOPPING

COLOURS

		WARNA
black	*hee*-tahm	hitam
blonde/tan	*peh*-rahng	perang
blue	*bee*-roo	biru
brown	*chok*-laht	coklat
dark ...	... *too*-uh	... tua
green	*hee*-jow	hijau
grey	ke-*lah*-boo/*ah*-sahp	kelabu/asap
light ...	... *moo*-duh	... muda
multicoloured	ber-*wahr*-nah-*wahr*-nee	berwarna-warni
orange	o-rehn/*jing*-guh	oren/jingga
pink	*meh*-rah(h) *jahm*-boo	merah jambu
purple	*oon*-goo	ungu
red	*meh*-rah(h)	merah
white	*poo*-ti(h)	putih
yellow	*koo*-ning	kuning

TOILETRIES

BARANGAN BILIK AIR

In smaller towns you may find some of these items in traditional Chinese medicine shops.

comb	*see*-kaht	sikat
condoms	*kon*-dom	kondom
contraceptive ...	*oo*-baht/	ubat/
device/	*ah*-laht pe-*rahm*-chang	alat perancang
medicine	ke-loo-*ahr*-guh	keluarga
deodorant	dee-*o*-do-rahn	deodoran
laxative	*joo*-lahp	julap
lip balm	bahm *bee*-bir	bam bibir
lipstick	*gin*-choo/chaht *bee*-bir	gincu/cat bibir
moisturising	kreem	krim
cream	pe-*lehm*-bahb *koo*-lit	pelembab kulit
mosquito repellent	*oo*-baht *nyah*-mu(k)	ubat nyamuk
razor	pen-*choo*-kur	pencukur
razor blade	*pee*-sow *choo*-kur	pisau cukur
sanitary napkins	*twah*-luh wah-*nee*-tuh	tuala wanita
shampoo	*shahm*-poo	syampu
shaver	pen-*choo*-kur	pencukur
shaving cream	kreem *choo*-kur	krim cukur
soap	*sah*-bun	sabun
sunblock cream	kreem pe-*lin*-dung	krim pelindung
	chah-*hai* yuh	cahaya
	mah-tuh-*hah*-ree	matahari
tampons	*tahm*-pohn	tampon
tissues	*ti*-soo	tisu
toothbrush	be-*roos gee*-gee	berus gigi

FRESH IS BEST

Malaysians have at least two showers a day to combat the extreme heat and humidity. Take the hint. As well as ensuring you're sweet-smelling, more frequent showers and using talcum powder will help to avoid fungal infections.

SHOPPING

FOR THE BABY

UNTUK BAYI

baby's bottle	*bo*-tol *bah*-yee	*botol bayi*
baby clothes	pah-*kai*-ahn *bah*-yee	*pakaian bayi*
(children's)	*(kah*-nah(k)-*kah*-nah(k))	*(kanak-kanak)*
baby food	*mah*-kah-nahn *bah*-yee	*makanan bayi*
baby powder	be-*dahk bah*-yee	*bedak bayi*
bib	bib	*bib*
boiled water	air *mah*-sah(k)	*air masak*
lukewarm	swahm	*suam*
disposable nappies	kain *lahm*-pin yahng	*kain lampin yang*
(diapers)	bo-*leh(h)* dee-*boo*-ahng	*boleh dibuang*
dummy (pacifier)	*poo*-ting	*puting*
nappy rash cream	kreem *roo*-ahm *bah*-yee	*krim ruam bayi*
powdered milk	*soo*-soo *ser*-bu(k)	*susu serbuk*

MUSIC

MUZIK

I'm looking for a ... CD.
   sai-yuh nah(k)
   men-*chah*-ree CD ...   *Saya nak*
                                mencari CD ...
Do you have ...?
   ah-duh ...?   *Ada ...?*
I heard a band/singer called ...
   sai-yuh *per*-nah(h)
   men-*deh*-ngahr *koom*-poo-lahn/   *Saya pernah*
   pe-*nyah*-nyee ber-*nah*-muh ...   *mendengar kumpulan/*
                                  penyanyi bernama ...
Can I listen to this CD here?
   bo-*leh(h)* tah(k) *sai*-yuh
   men-*deh*-ngahr CD *ee*-nee   *Boleh tak saya*
   dee *see*-nee?   *mendengar CD ini*
                                  di sini?
I want a blank tape.
   sai-yuh nah(k) *ka*-seht *ko*-song   *Saya nak kaset kosong.*

STATIONERY & PUBLICATIONS
ALAT TULIS-MENULIS & PENERBITAN

There are many bookstores and newsagents in the larger cities that carry English titles. Stock up before you head out.

Is there an English-language bookshop here?

ah-duh ke-*dai boo*-koo	*Ada kedai buku*
bah-*hah*-suh *ing*-ge-ris tah(k)	*bahasa Inggeris*
dee *see*-nee?	*tak di sini?*

Is there an English-language section?

ah-duh bah-*hah*-gee-ahn	*Ada bahagian*
bah-*hah*-suh *ing*-ge-ris tah(k)?	*bahasa Inggeris tak?*

Do you sell ...?	*ah*-duh-kah(h) ... dee-*joo*-ahl?	*Adakah ... dijual?*
envelopes	*sahm*-pool *soo*-raht	*sampul surat*
magazines	mah-*jah*-luh(h)	*majalah*
newspapers (English-language)	soo-*raht khah*-bahr (bah-*hah*-suh *ing*-ge-ris)	*surat khabar (bahasa Inggeris)*
novels	no-vel/*boo*-koo che-*ree*-tuh	*novell buku cerita*
pens	pehn	*pen*
postcards	*pos*-kahd	*poskad*
stamps	se-*tehm*	*setem*
writing paper	ker-tahs *too*-lis	*kertas tulis*
... dictionaries	*kah*-moos ...	*kamus ...*
bilingual	*dwee*-bah-hah-suh	*dwibahasa*
pocket	*po*-keht	*poket*
... maps	*peh*-tuh ...	*peta ...*
city	bahn-duh-*rai*-yuh	*bandaraya*
regional	dah-*eh*-rah(h)/ *rahn*-tow	*daerah/ rantau*
road	*jah*-lahn	*jalan*

SHOPPING

PHOTOGRAPHY FOTOGRAFI

There are film and processing shops all over Malaysia, which also take passport photos. Photo processing is good quality and it's much cheaper than many places overseas. You can bargain for cameras and other equipment, unless you're buying them in a department store.

I'd like a film for this camera.
sai-yuh nah(k) *fee*-lem   *Saya nak filem*
oon-tu(k) ka-me-ruh *ee*-nee?   *untuk kamera ini.*

How much is it for
processing and developing?
be-*rah*-puh *hahr*-guh   *Berapa harga*
pen-*choo*-chee-ahn   *pencucian filem ini?*
fee-lem *ee*-nee?

When will it be ready?
bee-luh see-*ahp*?   *Bila siap?*

Do you repair cameras here?
bo-*leh(h)* *bai*-kee   *Boleh baiki*
ka-me-ruh tah(k) dee *see*-nee?   *kamera tak di sini?*

battery	*ba*-te-ree	*bateri*
B&W (film)	(*fee*-lem) *hee*-tahm	(*filem*) *hitam*
	poo-ti(h)	*putih*
camera	ka-me-ruh	*kamera*
colour (film)	(*fee*-lem) ber-*wahr*-nuh	(*filem*) *berwarna*
to develop	men-*choo*-cee	*cuci*
film	(*fee*-lem)	*filem*
flash(bulb)	pahn-*chah*-rahn	*pancaran*
	(*mehm*-tul)	(*mentul*)
lens	*lehm*-suh	*lensa*
light meter	*mee*-ter chah-*hai*-yuh	*meter cahaya*
photograph	*fo*-to/*gahm*-bahr	*foto/gambar*
to print	men-*choo*-chee	*mencuci*
(make) reprints	(*boo*-aht) *sah*-lee-nahn	(*buat*) *salinan*
slides	slaid	*slaid*
videotape	*pee*-tuh *vi*-dee-o	*pita video*

SMOKING   MEROKOK

Some cigarettes in Malaysia have a higher tar/nicotine content than they do in other countries. If you're smoking 'lights' they may not be as 'light' as you think! The intense spicy aroma of the imported Indonesian 'clove cigarettes', *kretek*, *kreh-teh(k)*, will be the smell of your Malaysian memories. Smuggling *kretek* into Malaysia is a big but illegal business.

A packet of cigarettes, please.
  to-long *bah*-gee
  se-*ko*-tah(k) *ro*-ko(k)

*Tolong bagi
sekotak rokok.*

Do you have a light?
  ah-duh *mahm*-chis?

Ada mancis?

Are these cigarettes strong or mild?
  ah-duh-kah(h) *ro*-ko(k)
  ee-nee ke-*rahs* ah-*tow* ri-*ngahm*?

*Adakah rokok
ini keras atau ringan?*

Can I smoke here?
  bo-*leh(h)* tah(k)
  me-*ro*-ko(k) dee *see*-nee?

*Boleh tak
merokok di sini?*

Do you have an ashtray?
  ah-duh-kah(h) be-*kahs*
  ah-boo *ro*-ko(k)?

*Adakah bekas
abu rokok?*

Please don't smoke.
  to-long jah-*ngahn* me-*ro*-ko(k)

Tolong jangan merokok.

I'm trying to give up smoking.
  sai-yuh se-*dahng* men-*choo*-buh
  ber-*hen*-tee me-*ro*-ko(k)

*Saya sedang mencuba
berhenti merokok.*

cigarette papers	*ker*-tahs *ro*-ko(k)	*kertas rokok*
cigarettes	*ro*-ko(k)	*rokok*
clove cigarette	*kreh*-teh(k)	*kretek*
filter	*fil*-ter	*filter*
lighter	*mahn*-chis *ah*-pee	*mancis api*
matches	*mahn*-chis	*mancis*
menthol	*mehm*-tol	*mentol*
pipe	paip	*paip*
smoke	*ah*-sahp	*asap*
to smoke	me-*ro*-ko(k)	*merokok*
tobacco	tehm-*bah*-kow	*tembakau*

SIZES & COMPARISONS

UKURAN & PERBANDINAGAN

a little bit	se-*dee*-kit	*sedikit*
big	be-*sahr*	*besar*
bigger	le-*bi(h)* be-*sahr*	*lebih besar*
biggest	*pah*-ling be-*sahr*	*paling besar*
enough	*choo*-kup	*cukup*
heavy	be-*raht*	*berat*
too much/many	ter-*lah*-loo *bah*-nyah(k)	*terlalu banyak*
less	koo-*rahng*	*kurang*
light	ri-*ngahn*	*ringan*
long	pahn-*jahng*	*panjang*
many	*bah*-nyah(k)	*banyak*
more	le-*bi(h)* *bah*-nyah(k)	*lebih banyak*
narrow	sem-*pit*	*sempit*
short	*pehm*-deh(k)	*pendek*
small	ke-*chil*	*kecil*
smaller	le-*bi(h)* ke-*chil*	*lebih kecil*
smallest	*pah*-ling ke-*chil*	*paling kecil*
spacious	loo-*ahs*	*luas*
tall	*ting*-gee	*tinggi*
too big	ter-*lah*-loo be-*sahr*	*terlalu besar*
very big	*sah*-ngaht be-*sahr*	*sangat besar*
wide	le-*bahr*	*lebar*

WEIGHTS & MEASURES

millimetre	*mi*-li-*mee*-ter	*milimeter*
centimetre	*sen*-ti-*mee*-ter	*sentimeter*
metre	*mee*-ter	*meter*
kilometre	*ki*-lo-*mee*-ter	*kilometer*
litre	*lee*-ter	*liter*
gram	gram	*gram*
kilogram	*ki*-lo-gram	*kilogram*

BERAT & UKURAN

STREET LIFE

You are unlikely to be harassed by people on the streets, even in the rougher parts of town.

Come here!
see-nee-lah(h)/*mah*-ree
see-nee-lah(h)
Sinilah/Mari sinilah.

Go away!
per-gee!/be-*lah*(h)!
Pergi!/Belah!

I don't have any money.
tah(k) *ah*-duh *doo*-it
Tak ada duit.

alley	lo-*rong*	*lorong*
footpath	*ping*-gir *jah*-lahn	*pinggir jalan*
hawker	pen-*joo*-ahl	*penjual*
homeless person	*o*-rahng *gee*-luh	*orang gila*
thief	pen-*choo*-ree	*pencuri*
street	*jah*-lahn	*jalan*
street stall (food)	ge-*rai*/*wah*-rung	*gerai/warung*
traffic lights	*lahm*-poo	*lampu*
	ee-*shah*-raht	*isyarat*

SHOPPING

USEFUL WORDS

PERKATAAN YANG BERGUNA

to buy	mem-be-*lee*	*membeli*
cheap	*moo*-rah(h)	*murah*
to export	meng-*ehk*-sport	*mengeksport*
to import	meng-*im*-port	*mengimport*
made in	dee-per-*boo*-aht dee	*diperbuat di*
old	*too*-uh/*lah*-muh	*tua/lama*
to order	me-*nehm*-pah(h)	*menempah*
quality	*moo*-too/*kwah*-li-tee	*mutu/kualiti*
to sell	men-*joo*-ahl	*menjual*
type (of product)	je-*nis*/*mah*-chahm	*jenis/macam*

SHOPPING

The fabulous array of Malaysian food will impress you from the moment you arrive. You'll probably eat a lot of your meals in *kedai kopi*, *ke-dai ko-*pee, coffee shops or *gerai*, *ge-rai*, hawker stalls that serve tasty dishes, snacks and cooling drinks. Cooked up on the spot or served buffet-style, these are clean and delicious. Of course there are also restaurants in bigger cities, and fast food outlets are spreading around the country like fat on a hot grill. But for authentic tastes, try the hawkers' stalls and smaller restaurants, teeming with people from early in the morning till late at night.

During fasting month in the Malay areas, only Chinese or non-Muslim Indian shops will be open during daylight hours. Fast food chains usually remain open for non-Muslim clientele. However, in northern states and some rural areas, you should keep a low profile while eating and drinking in public out of respect for those who are fasting.

breakfast	*mah*-kahn *pah*-gee;	*makan pagi;*
	sah-rah-pahn	*sarapan*
lunch	*mah*-kahn	*makan*
	te-ngah-*hah*-ree	*tengahari*
dinner	*mah*-kahn *mah*-lahm	*makan malam*

BREAKFAST   MAKAN PAGI

Having breakfast out is a national pastime. Some roadside stalls and *mamak*, *mah*-mah(k), (Muslim Indian) restaurants open before sunrise. A mid-morning snack or meal is also called breakfast, and many of these foods are available all day. Sweet *teh tarik*, *teh tah*-rik, is a must for a true Malaysian-style breakfast. Of course, for the unadventurous, hotels and fast food chains serve Western style breakfasts, and the big cities have patisseries and bakeries.

COMMON MALAYSIAN BREAKFASTS:

nasi lemak   nah-see le-mah(k)
rice cooked with coconut milk and pandan leaves, served with a very spicy anchovy sauce, peanuts, a hardboiled egg, tomato and cucumber, and sometimes chicken. Utterly, utterly delicious. Don't leave Malaysia without trying it.

roti canai   ro-tee chah-nai
flat bread fried in ghee and served with curried lentils or some other spicy sauce. A little milder than nasi lemak.

tosai   to-sai
similar to *roti canai*, but lighter and roasted rather than fried

kueh   koo-eh(h)
include the savoury curry puff, as well as small sweet cakes. Bite-sized, to add to your breakfast.

nasi dagang   nah-see dah-gahng
an east coast specialty, this super-rich coconut rice – served with some form of curry or meat dish – will fill you up immediately

VEGETARIAN & SPECIAL MEALS
MAKANAN SAYURAN & MAKANAN KHAS

If you're a vegetarian, you can specify *tanpa daging*, *tahn-pah dah-ging*, 'without meat', or *sayur saja*, *sai-yur sah-juh*, 'vegetables only'. To some Malays *daging*, 'meat', means beef only, so you may need to elaborate: *tanpa daging, ayam dan lain-lain*, *tahn-pah dah-ging, ai-yahm dahn lain-lain*, 'without meat/beef, chicken and other things.'

I'm vegetarian.
sai-yuh mah-kahn sai-yur   Saya makan sayur
sah-juh/sai-yuh tah(k)   saja/saya tak
mah-kahn dah-ging   makan daging.

I don't/	sai-yuh tah(k) soo-kuh/	Saya tak suka/
can't eat ...	bo-leh(h) mah-kahn ...	boleh makan ...
chicken	ai-yahm	ayam
beef	dah-ging lehm-boo	daging lembu
eggs	te-lur	telur
fish	ee-kahn	ikan
ham	dah-ging bah-bee;	daging babi;
	hahm	ham
meat	dah-ging	daging
milk and cheese	soo-soo dahn keh-joo	susu dan keju
prawns	oo-dahng	udang

I'm allergic to ...	sai-yuh ah-ler-jik	Saya alergik
	kah-low mah-kahn ...	kalau makan ...
dairy products	soo-soo	susu
peanuts	kah-chahng	kacang

Do you have any vegetarian dishes?
ah-duh mah-kah-nahn
sai-yu-rahn sah-juh?

Ada makanan
sayuran saja?

Does this dish have meat/chicken?
ah-duh dah-ging/
ai-yahm tah(k) dah-lahm
mah-sah-kahn ee-nee?

Ada daging/
ayam tak dalam
masakan ini?

Can I get this without meat/chicken?
bo-leh(h) tah(k) mah-sah(k)
tahn-puh dah-ging/ai-yahm?

Boleh tak masak
tanpa daging/ayam?

Does it contain eggs?
mah-kah-nahn ee-nee
ah-duh te-lur tah(k)?

Makanan ini
ada telur tak?

Kosher restaurants are unknown in Malaysia, however *halal*, *hah-lahl*, restaurants do not use pork products.

Is there a halal restaurant here?
ah-duh reh-sto-rahn
hah-lahl dee see-nee?

Ada restoran
halal di sini?

Is this halal?
ee-nee hah-lahl-kah(h)?

Ini halalkah?

FOOD

EATING OUT

Where can I find a ... ?	... dee *mah*-nuh?	**MAKAN DI LUAR** ... *di mana?*
food stall	ge-*rai*	*Gerai*
night market	*pah*-sahr *mah*-lahm	*Pasar malam*
restaurant	*reh*-sto-rahn	*Restoran*

Where's a ... restaurant?	*reh*-sto-rahn ... dee *mah*-nuh?	*Restoran ...* *di mana?*
cheap	moo-*rah(h)*	*murah*
fish head curry	*kah*-ree ke-*pah*-luh *ee*-kahn	*kari kepala* *ikan*

We'd like a table for (five), please.
   to-long *bah*-gee *meh*-juh   *Tolong bagi meja*
   oon-tu(k) (*lee*-muh) o-rahng   *untuk (lima) orang.*

I want to eat ...
   sai-yuh nah(k) *mah*-kahn ...   *Saya nak makan ...*

What dish is that?
   mah-sah-kahn *ah*-puh *ee*-too?   *Masakan apa itu?*

What's in that dish?
   ah-duh *ah*-puh dah-*lahm*   *Ada apa dalam*
   mah-sah-kahn *ee*-too?   *masakan itu?*

Is it spicy?
   pe-*dahs* tah(k)?   *Pedas tak?*

How much does one portion cost?
   ber-*rah*-puh *hahr*-guh *oon*-tu(k)   *Berapa harga untuk*
   sah-too bah-*hah*-gee-ahn?   *satu bahagian?*

FOOD

THEY MAY SAY ...

mah-kahn *ah*-puh?	What would you like to eat?
mee-num *ah*-puh?	What would you like to drink?

We're in a hurry. Please
bring our food quickly.
   kah-mee nah(k) che-*paht* nee.   *Kami nak cepat ni.*
   to-long *bah*-wuh *mah*-kah-nahn   *Tolong bawa makanan*
   che-*paht* see-*kit*   *cepat sikit.*
Do I get it myself or
do they bring it to us?
   lai-yahn *di*-ree ah-*tow*   *Layan diri atau*
   me-*reh*-kuh yahng *bah*-wuh?   *mereka yang bawa?*

UP TO YOUR ELBOWS

There's a certain finesse that needs to be developed when eating food with your hands. Always use your right hand only. Hold a piece of *roti canai*, ro-tee chah-nai, or meat between your thumb and two smallest fingers and then use your pointer and index fingers to separate a bite-sized chunk. If you're eating rice, use your fingers like a scoop and shovel the food into your mouth with your thumb. Tastes even better!

Please bring a/an/the ...	*to*-long *bah*-wuh ...	*Tolong bawa ...*
ashtray	be-*kahs ah*-boo ro-ko(k)	*bekas abu rokok*
bill	bil	*bil*
cup	*chah*-wahn	*cawan*
fork	*gahr*-foo	*garfu*
glass	ge-*lahs*	*gelas*
glass of water (with/ without ice)	se-ge-*lahs* air ko-song (de-*ngahn*/ *tahn*-puh ais)	*segelas air kosong (dengan/ tanpa ais)*
knife	*pee*-sow	*pisau*
menu	*meh*-noo	*menu*
plate	*ping*-gahn	*pinggan*
spoon	*soo*-doo	*sudu*
toothpick	pen-*choo*-li(k) *gee*-gee	*penculik gigi*

This isn't cooked properly.
    tah(k) *choo*-kup *mah*-sah(k) nee   *Tak cukup masak ni.*
Not too spicy please.
    jah-*ngahn* ter-*lah*-loo pe-*dahs*   *Jangan terlalu pedas.*
No MSG please.
    to-long jah-*ngahn*   *Tolong jangan*
    pah-kai *ah*-jee-no-*mo*-to   *pakai ajinomoto.*
No ice, please.
    tahm-puh ais   *Tanpa ais.*
Less oily please.
    koo-*rahng* min-yah(k)   *Kurang minyak.*

FOOD FOR THOUGHT

Bear hugs or a peck on the cheek as a way of greeting are totally foreign to the vast majority of Malaysians, and are best avoided. Keep in mind that there are simply some things you shouldn't do with your left hand, because Malays use their left hand for cleaning themselves. It's a good idea to get into the habit of using your right hand for passing items – and definitely for eating. It's shocking and filthy to touch food with your left hand. So don't do it. Ever!

This is (too) ...	*mah*-kah-nahn	*Makanan*
	ee-nee (ter-*lah*-loo) ...	*ini (terlalu)* ...
bitter	pah-*hit*	*pahit*
cold	se-*joo(k)*	*sejuk*
delicious	se-*dahp*/ eh-nah(k)	*sedap/enak*
fresh	se-*gahr*	*segar*
hot	*pah*-nahs	*panas*
salty	*mah*-sin	*masin*
sour	*mah*-sahm	*masam*
spicy	pe-*dahs*	*pedas*
spoiled	*bah*-see	*basi*
stale	*mah*-su(k) *ah*-ngin	*masuk angin*
sweet	*mah*-nis	*manis*
unripe	be-*lum mah*-sah(k)	*belum masak*
uncooked	men-*tah*(h)	*mentah*

TYPICAL DISHES

MAKANAN BIASA

Many small restaurants, stalls and coffee shops don't have menus –
what's available is usually advertised on the wall, the stall tarpaulin
or the side of the *kaki-lima*, kah-*kee lee*-muh, 'footpath'.

The names of many dishes specify how they're prepared, such
as *ayam bakar*, ai-yahm *bah*-kahr, 'grilled chicken'.

MENU DECODER		
Main Course		**Makanan Utama**
arnab	*ahr*-nahb	rabbit
ayam ...	*ai*-yahm ...	... chicken
bakar	*bah*-kahr	grilled
goreng	*go*-rehng	fried
babi	*bah*-bee	pig
bakso/ba'so	*bah(k)*-so/*bah*-so	meatball soup
bubur nasi	*boo*-bur *nah*-see	rice porridge with anchovies, vegetables, and chicken
bubur kacang hijau	*boo*-bur kah-chahng *hee*-jow	mung bean porridge (sweet)
capati	chah-*pah*-tee	Indian flat flour pancake
daging lembu	*dah*-ging *lehm*-boo	beef
daging biri-biri	*dah*-ging *bi*-ree-*bi*-ree	lamb/mutton
gado-gado	*gah*-do-*gah*-do	boiled vegetables and peanut sauce
hati	*hah*-tee	(chicken) liver
ikan	*ee*-kahn	fish
air tawar	air *tah*-wahr	freshwater
air masin	air *mah*-sin	saltwater
ikan bilis	*ee*-kahn *bi*-lis	dried anchovies, usually made into a spicy sauce
ikan keli	*ee*-kahn ke-*lee*	catfish
itik	*ee*-tik	duck
jagung bakar	*jah*-gung *bah*-kahr	roasted corn
kambing	*kahm*-bing	goat
kangkung	*kahng*-kung	water spinach

FOOD

kari	kah-ree	curry
kentang	ken-tahng	potatoes
kepah	ke-pah(h)	mussels
ketam	ke-tahm	crab
ketupat	ke-too-paht	boiled pressed rice
kicap	kee-chahp	soy sauce
kuay teow	koo-ay tee-ow	flat, wide rice noodles
laksa Kelantan	lah(k)-suh ke-lahn-tahn	spicy rice noodle soup with coconut milk
laksa Penang	lah(k)-suh pe-nahng	rice noodle soup in fish sauce
mee	mee	wheat noodles
mee ...	mee ...	
goreng	go-rehng	fried noodles with meat and vegetables
kuah/sup	koo-ah(h)/ soop	noodle soup with meat and vegetables
rebus	ree-bus	noodle soup with starchy, spicy sauce, fried tofu and vegetables
murtabak	moor-tah-bah(k)	pancakes stuffed with beef or chicken filling with onions and spices

THAT'S NOT A KNIFE!

When you eat in stalls or small restaurants, you'll usually receive a large spoon and a fork (in Chinese restaurants, of course, you'll get chopsticks). No knife is provided. Malaysians, if they're eating with their hands, have a technique of pinning down the meat with their thumb and tearing it with the other fingers (the left hand is not involved at all, since it is considered dirty). If you want a knife, you'll have to ask for one!

FOOD

nan	nahn	Indian grilled bread
nasi	nah-see	cooked rice
nasi ...	nah-see ...	
campur	chahm-pur	cooked rice with a selection of meat and vegetable dishes on one plate
goreng	go-rehng	fried rice
goreng istimewa	go-rehng is-tee-meh-wuh	special fried rice
ayam	ai-yahm	chicken rice
beriyani	be-ree-yah-nee	Indian rice with spicy chicken, beef, or lamb curry
dagang	dah-gahng	special rice cooked with coconut milk eaten with fish shrimp, or eggs (Peninsular East Coast specialty)
impit	im-pit	cubes of pressed rice, often served with peanut sauce
kerabu	ke-rah-boo	rice with cut up vegetables and a roasted grated coconut (Peninsular East Coast specialty)
lemak	le-mah(k)	rice cooked in coconut milk with spicy sauce and anchovies, with or without meat
minyak	min-yah(k)	ghee rice with curries
patprik	paht-pri(k)	rice with beef in a special Thai sauce
otak	o-tah(k)	brains

FOOD

perut	pe-*rut*	tripe
petai	pe-*tai*	large, tasty bean
pulut	pu-lut	glutinous rice
rendang	rehn-dahng	meat cooked slowly in spices and coconut
rojak	ro-jah(k)	fruit and vegetables cut up with a sweet and spicy peanut sauce
roti	ro-tee	bread
roti ...	ro-tee ...	
bakar	bah-kahr	toast with jam
canai	chah-nai	Indian breakfast bread, shaped like a pancake, served with curry or lentils
jala	jah-luh	thin, yellow netted bread eaten with curry
sambal	sahm-bahl	spicy sauce to eat with rice
sate ...	sah-teh ...	... satay
ayam	ai-yahm	chicken
daging	dah-ging	beef
kambing	kahm-bing	goat
soto	so-to	chicken soup with rice cubes
sotong	so-tong	squid
tahu	tah-hoo	tofu
telur ...	te-lur ...	... egg
goreng	go-rehng	fried
rebus	ree-bus	boiled
masak	mah-sah(k)	soft-boiled
separuh	se-pahr-u(h)	
telur dadar	te-lur dah-dahr	omelette

FOOD

tempeh	*tehm*-peh(h)	tempeh (fermented soybean cakes)
tempeh goreng	*tehm*-peh(h) *go*-rehng	fried tempeh
tiram	*ti*-rahm	oysters
ubi	*oo*-bee	potatoes
udang	*oo*-dahng	shrimp
udang karang	*oo*-dahng *kah*-rahng	lobster

Snacks & Sweets

Makanan Ringan & Makanan Manis

agar-agar	ah-*gahr*-ah-*gahr*	gelatine (made with seaweed)
ais krim	ais krim	ice cream
dodol	*do*-dol	chewy, toffee-like sweet pudding, also in durian flavour
karipap	*kah*-ree-pahp	curry puff
keropok	ke-*ro*-po(k)	prawn or rice crackers
kueh	*koo*-eh(h)	sweet or savoury snacks (various kinds)
kueh (lapis)	*koo*-eh(h) *lah*-pis	(layer) cake
manisan	*mah*-nee-sahn	sweets
onde-onde; buah melaka	on-*deh*-on-*deh*; *boo*-uh(h) me-*lah*-kuh	glutinous rice ball stuffed with palm sugar
pau	pow	steamed rice flour buns with a variety of fillings
pisang goreng	*pee*-sahng *go*-rehng	fried banana
rojak	*ro*-jah(k)	fruit salad in a sweet, spicy peanut sauce
tahu	*tah*-hoo	tofu

FOOD

SELF-CATERING

Can I please have ...?	to-long bah-gee ... ?
an orange	o-rehn se-bee-jee
a kilo of oranges	o-rehn se-kee-lo
two kilos of oranges	doo-uh kee-lo o-rehn
half a kilo of oranges	se-te-ngah(h) kee-lo o-rehn
seven mangoes	too-juh bee-jee mahng-guh

MASAKAN SENDIRI

Tolong bagi ...?
oren sebiji
oren sekilo
dua kilo oren
setengah kilo oren
tujuh biji mangga

AT THE MARKET   DI PASAR

Delicious fresh fruit, exotic vegetables and spices, fresh fish and meats abound in the Malaysian *pasar*, *pah-sahr*. Whether you want to cook a meal yourself or try to find a taste of home, this should be your first stop – the nucleus of any Malaysian town. A multitude of other goods are on offer: rice and grains, packaged goods, kitchenware, tobacco and so on. Your nose will tell you when you've hit the meat section.

FOOD

How much is this?
   be-*rah*-puh
   hahr-guh-nyuh ee-nee?   *Berapa*
                             harganya ini?

How much is a kilogram of ...?
   be-*rah*-puh
   hahr-guh se-*kee*-lo ... ?   *Berapa*
                             harga sekilo ...?

Can I taste it?
   bo-*leh(h) choo*-buh?   *Boleh cuba?*

I don't want that one.
   tah(k) nah(k) yahng ee-too   *Tak nak yang itu.*

Please give me another one.
   to-long *bah*-gee yahng lain   *Tolong bagi yang lain.*

bread	*ro*-tee	*roti*
noodles	mee	*mee*
rice (cooked)	*nah*-see	*nasi*
rice (uncooked)	be-*rahs*	*beras*

WORLD FOOD

In Malaysia you'll find a variety of Chinese cuisines, including Cantonese, Hokkien, Szechuan, Teochew, Hakka, Shanghai, and Beijing styles of cooking.

Among the Indian restaurants, stalls and *kedai kopi*, ke-*dai ko*-pee, you'll get to try South Indian, Muslim Indian, *mamat*, *mah*-maht, and North Indian and Pakistani dishes. Of course Malay food is widely available, as is Indonesian – the two are very similar. *Nyonya* is a unique blend of Chinese and Malay styles of cooking, and *Baba-Nyonya* or *Peranakan* is the style of early Chinese immigrants who adopted some of the cooking of the Malays. Thai cuisine is also widely available in Malaysia.

FOOD

Meat | Daging

beef	*dah*-ging *lehm*-boo	*daging lembu*
brains	*o*-tahk	*otak*
chicken	*ai*-yahm	*ayam*
duck	*ee*-tik	*itik*
goat	*kahm*-bing	*kambing*
lamb	*ah*-nah(k) *bi*-ree-*bi*-ree	*anak biri-biri*
liver	*hah*-tee	*hati*
mutton	*bi*-ree-*bi*-ree	*biri-biri*
pig	*bah*-bee	*babi*
rabbit	*ahr*-nahb	*arnab*

Seafood | Makanan Laut

catfish	*ee*-kahn ke-*lee*	*ikan keli*
cockles	ke-*rahng*	*kerang*
crab	ke-*tahm*	*ketam*
freshwater fish	*ee*-kahn air *tah*-wahr	*ikan air tawar*
lobster	*oo*-dahng *kah*-rahng	*udang karang*
mussels	ke-*pah(h)*	*kepah*
oysters	*ti*-rahm	*tiram*
saltwater fish	*ee*-kahn air *mah*-sin	*ikan air masin*
salted dried fish	*ee*-kahn ke-*ring*	*ikan kering*
shrimp	*oo*-dahng	*udang*
squid	*so*-tong	*sotong*

Vegetables | Sayur-Sayuran

beans	*kah*-chahng	*kacang*
cabbage	*ku*-bis	*kubis*
carrot	*lo*-ba(k)	*lobak*
cauliflower	*ku*-bis *boo*-nguh	*kubis bunga*
corn	*jah*-gung	*jagung*
cucumber	*tee*-mun	*timun*
eggplant	te-*rung*	*terung*
mushrooms	*chen*-dah-wahn/*koo*-laht	*cendawan/kulat*
onion	*bah*-wahng	*bawang*
potato	*ken*-tahng	*kentang*
pumpkin	*lah*-boo	*labu*
tomato	to-*mah*-to	*tomato*

FOOD

Fruit   **Buah-Buahan**

Malaysia is the land of heavenly fruit. Whether you shop at road-side stalls, in the markets or in supermarkets, you'll find a devastatingly delicious variety of tropical and temperate fruits. Some fruits are only found here, like the *ciku*, *chee*-koo, which resembles a fuzzy potato with a hint of vanilla flavour.

FEAST ON FRUIT

guava   *jahm*-boo   *jambu*
  a hard, pear-shaped fruit. The small black seeds should not be eaten. *Jambu air*, *jahm*-boo air, is a small, pink, smooth, strawberry shaped variety with a fragrant taste.

jackfruit   *nahng*-kah   *nangka*
  sellers often break the fruit up into segments, which are then packed, ready to eat. The flesh is rubbery, sweet and strongly flavoured. Jackfruit trees are everywhere and can be recognised by their huge pendulous fruit, often wrapped in plastic bags for protection while they ripen on the tree.

mangosteen   *mang*-gis   *manggis*
  easily recognised by its thick, purple-brown, fibrous skin, which protects mouth-watering, sweet-sour, white flesh

rambutan   *rahm*-boo-tahn   *rambutan*
  bright red fruit covered in soft, hairy spines, and containing a delicious, lychee-like, sweet white flesh

salak   *sah*-lah(k)   *salak*
  brown snake-skin fruit of the Zalacca palm, the flesh of which is crunchy and nutty. An Indonesian fruit, occasionally sold in Malaysian markets.

starfruit   be-*lim*-bing   *belimbing*
  A watery, thirst-quenching fruit shaped like a star, end on. It's one of the few fruits eaten without being peeled.

FOOD

apple	*eh*-pahl	*epal*
avocado	ah-vo-*kah*-do	*avokado*
banana	*pee*-sahng	*pisang*
cempedak	*chem*-pe-dah(k)	*cempedak*
coconut	ke-*lah*-puh	*kelapa*

Look for *kelapa muda*, (ke-*lah*-puh *moo*-duh), 'young coconut', which makes a refreshing drink.

lemon	*leh*-mon	*lemon*
lime	*lee*-mow	*limau*
mango	*mang*-guh	*mangga*
orange	*o*-rehn	*oren*
papaya	*beh*-ti(k)	*betik*
peanuts	*kah*-chang	*kacang*
pineapple	*neh*-nahs	*nenas*
strawberry	*strah*-beh-ree	*strawberi*
soursop	doo-*ree*-ahn be-*lahm*-duh	*durian belanda*
watermelon	tem-*bee*-kai	*tembikai*

ROYAL STINK

An encounter with *durian*, *doo-ree-ahn*, the 'king of fruits', is a memorable experience for the fruit lover. *Durians* announce themselves in any market by exuding an incredibly pungent stench. If you can hold your breath long enough to approach, and swallow the rich, creamy flesh, you may get to crave the unique flavour.

Spices & Condiments
Rempah-Rempahan

English	Pronunciation	Malay
chilli	*chi*-lee	*cili*
chilli shrimp paste	*sam*-bahl be-*lah*-chahn	*sambal belacan*
chilli sauce	*sam*-bahl; sos *chi*-lee	*sambal; sos cili*
cinnamon	*kai*-yoo *mah*-nis	*kayu manis*
cloves	*cheng*-ki(h)	*cengkih*
curry	*kah*-ree	*kari*
garlic	*bah*-wahng *poo*-ti(h)	*bawang putih*
ginger	*hah*-lee-uh	*halia*
mortar and pestle	*bah*-too *toom*-bu(k)	*batu tumbuk*
MSG	*ah*-jee-no-mo-to	*ajinomoto*
oil	*min*-yah(k)	*minyak*
black pepper	*lah*-duh *hee*-tahm	*lada hitam*
salt	*gah*-rahm	*garam*
soy sauce (salty)	*kee*-chahp *(mah*-sin)	*kicap (masin)*
sugar	*goo*-luh	*gula*
sweet soy sauce	*kee*-chahp *mah*-nis	*kicap manis*
tomato sauce	sos to-*mah*-to	*sos tomato*
turmeric	*koon*-yit	*kunyit*
vinegar	*choo*-kuh	*cuka*

FEELING HOT HOT HOT

cili (the smaller, the hotter)	*chi*-lee	chilli
pedas	pe-*dahs*	spicy
sambal	*sahm*-bahl	chilli sauce/paste

Cooking Methods
Cara Masakan

English	Pronunciation	Malay
baked	bah-*kahr dah*-lahm o-vehn/ke-*too*-hahr	*bakar dalam oven/ketuhar*
boiled	*ree*-bus	*rebus*
cooked in coconut milk	*mah*-sah(k) le-*mah*(k); *goo*-lai	*masak lemak; gulai*
fried	go-*rehng*	*goreng*
grilled	*bah*-kahr	*bakar*
smoked	*ah*-sahp	*asap*
spit-roasted	*pahng*-gang	*panggang*
steamed	*koo*-koos	*kukus*

FOOD

DRINKS   **MINUMAN**

I want to drink ...
sai-yuh nah(k) *mee*-num ...   *Saya nak minum ...*
Do you have ...?
ah-duh ...?   *Ada ...?*

Hot/Warm Drinks   **Minuman Panas/Suam**

Except in upmarket restaurants and hotels, tea and coffee are nearly always served sweet and milky. If you want black coffee or plain tea, ask for *teh/kopi kosong*, 'empty tea/coffee'.

coffee ...	*ko*-pee ...	*kopi ...*
without sugar	*tahm*-puh *goo*-luh	*tanpa gula*
without milk	o	*o*
without milk and sugar	o *ko*-song	*o kosong*
coffee with milk	*ko*-pee *soo*-soo	*kopi susu*
tea without sugar	teh *tahm*-puh *goo*-luh	*teh tanpa gula*
tea without milk	teh o	*teh o*
tea with milk	teh *soo*-soo	*teh susu*
frothed tea	teh *tah*-rik	*teh tarik*
boiled water	air *mah*-sah(k)	*air masak*
warm water	air swahm	*air suam*
ginger tea	teh *hah*-lee-uh	*teh halia*

TOO MUCH IS BARELY ENOUGH

Most Malaysians can't imagine drinking tea or coffee or any other drink without a lot of sweeteners in it. Coffee and tea, as well as iced tea, will be served with sweetened condensed milk unless you specify *kopi o* or *teh o* which will then be sweetened with sugar before it is brought to you! In traditional restaurants and stalls, the milk used in drinks is usually sweetened condensed milk. Drinks like 'ABC', *air batu campur*, 'mixed ice', are more of a dessert than a drink, and are often served in a bowl. Drinks served in Malaysian homes are almost always sweetened, too.

FOOD

Cold Drinks		Minuman Sejuk
cincau		*chin*-chow
black *agar*, 'seaweed' jelly with fruit syrup and ice		
air limau		air *lee*-mow
citrus juice		
air kelapa muda		air ke-*lah*-puh *moo*-duh
coconut milk		
cendol		*chehn*-dol
coconut milk with rice jelly and ice		
air batu campur		air *bah*-too *chahm*-pur
ABC or coconut milk with fruit, jelly, nuts, sweet milk and shaved ice		
pekatan		pe-*kah*-tahn
cordial		
kopi ais		*ko*-pee ais
iced coffee with milk		
kopi o ais		*ko*-pee o ais
iced coffee without milk		
teh ais		teh ais
iced tea with milk		
teh o ais		teh o ais
iced tea without milk		
the o ais kosong		teh o ais *ko*-song
iced tea without milk or sugar		
teh o ais limau		teh o ais *lee*-mow
iced tea with lime		
Horlicks ais		*hor*-liks ais
iced milky malt drink		
Milo ais		*mi*-lo ais
iced chocolate milk		
milk	*susu*	*soo*-soo
water	*air*	air
bottled ...	... *botol*	... *bo*-tol

FOOD

Alcohol

		Minuman Keras
beer	bir	*bir*
grape wine	wain	*wain*
palm tree spirits	*to*-dee	*todi*
rice wine	*too*-ah(k)	*tuak*

FOOD

DI LUAR BANDAR

IN THE COUNTRY

CAMPING

BERKHEMAH

Malaysia offers cheap camping options: many of the national parks have camping grounds, and you can set up anywhere in the country. Sites near waterfalls and other jungle areas easily accessible by road are popular, so they can be crowded and a bit messy. Men and women can camp together, but again, it's best to say you're married to avoid any hassles.

The weather is wet, warm and humid and there are plenty of bugs. Make sure your tent has mosquito netting.

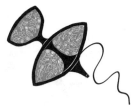

Can we camp here?
  bo-*leh(h)* ber-*kheh*-mah(h)
  dee *see*-nee?

Boleh berkhemah di sini?

How much is it per person/tent?
  be-*rah*-puh *hahr*-guh-nyuh
  oon-tu(k) *sah*-too *o*-rahng/
  kheh-mah(h)?

*Berapa harganya
untuk satu orang/
khemah?*

Where can I hire a tent?
  kheh-mah(h) dee-*seh*-wuh
  dee *mah*-nuh?

Khemah disewa di mana?

Are there shower facilities?
  ah-duh tem-*paht*
  mahn-dee tah(k)?

*Ada tempat
mandi tak?*

backpack	behg *sahn*-dahr	*beg sandar*
campground	kah-*wah*-sahn	*kawasan*
	per-*kheh*-mah(h)-ahn	*perkhemahan*
camping	ber-*kheh*-mah(h)	*berkhemah*
campsite	*tah*-pah(k)	*tapak*
	per-*kheh*-mah(h)-ahn	*perkhemahan*
firewood	*kai*-yoo *ah*-pee	*kayu api*
mat	*tee*-kahr	*tikar*
mosquito net	ke-*lahm*-boo	*kelambu*
national park	*tah*-mahn ne-*gah*-ruh	*taman negara*
penknife	*pee*-sow *lee*-paht	*pisau lipat*
sleeping bag	*kahm*-tung *tee*-dur	*kantung tidur*
stove (burner)	*dah*-pur	*dapur*
tent	*kheh*-mah(h)	*khemah*
torch (flashlight)	*lahm*-poo *soo*-luh	*lampu suluh*

HIKING

MERENTAS HUTAN

Are there any tourist attractions near here?
ah-duh tem-*paht* tah-ree-kahn
pe-*lahn*-cong de-*kaht* see-nee?

*Ada tempat tarikan
pelancong dekat sini?*

Where's the nearest village?
dee *mah*-nuh *kahm*-pung
yahng *pah*-ling de-*kaht*?

*Di mana kampung
yang paling dekat?*

Is it safe to climb this mountain?
se-*lah*-maht-kah(h) *oon*-tu(k)
men-*dah*-kee *goo*-nung ee-nee?

*Selamatkah untuk
mendaki gunung ini?*

Is there a hut up there?
ah-duh *pon*-do(k)-kah(h) dee *ah*-tahs?

Ada pondokkah di atas?

Do I need a guide?
ah-duh-kah(h) *sai*-yuh per-*loo*
pe-*mahn*-doo pe-*lahn*-chong?

*Adakah saya perlu
pemandu pelancong?*

Where can I find out about hiking
trails in the region?
dee *mah*-nuh *ah*-duh
mah(k)-loo-maht *tehm*-tahng
je-*jah*-kahn me-*rehn*-tahs
hoo-tahn dee dah-*eh*-rah(h) ee-nee?

*Di mana ada
maklumat tentang
jejakan merentas
hutan di daerah ini?*

I'd like to talk to someone who
knows this area.
sai-yuh nah(k) ber-*chah*-kahp
de-ngahn se-se-*o*-rahng
yahng *tah*-hoo *tehm*-tahng
dah-*eh*-rah(h) ee-nee

*Saya nak bercakap
dengan seseorang
yang tahu tentang
daerah ini.*

How long is the trail?
be-*rah*-puh *pahm*-jahng
lo-rong me-*rehn*-tahs
hoo-tahn ee-nee?

*Berapa panjang
lorong merentas
hutan ini?*

Is the track well marked?
ah-duh-kah(h) *trehk*-nyuh
dee-*tahn*-duh *de*-ngahn bai(k)?

*Adakah treknya
ditanda dengan baik?*

How high is the climb?
be-*rah*-puh *ting*-gee
pen-dah-*kee*-ahn ee-nee?

*Berapa tinggi
pendakian ini?*

IN THE COUNTRY

Which is the shortest/easiest route?
yahng *mah*-nuh
lah-loo-ahn yahng
pah-ling che-*paht*/moo-dah(h)?

*Yang mana
laluan yang
paling cepat/mudah?*

When does it get dark?
bee-luh-kah(h)
hah-ree moo-luh ge-*lahp*?

*Bilakah
hari mula gelap?*

Is it very scenic?
pe-*mahm*-dahng-ahn-nyuh
in-dah(h) se-*kah*-lee tah(k)?

*Pemandangannya
indah sekali tak?*

Where can I hire mountain gear?
ah-laht men-*dah*-kee
goo-nung dee-*seh*-wuh
dee *mah*-nuh?

*Alat mendaki
gunung disewa
di mana?*

Where can we buy supplies?
be-*kah*-lahn dee-*joo*-ahl
dee *mah*-nuh?

*Bekalan dijual
di mana?*

On the Path

Dalam Perjalanan

Where have you come from?
ahn-duh *dah*-tahng
dah-ree *mah*-nuh?

*Anda datang
dari mana?*

How long did it take you?
be-*rah*-puh *lah*-muh
per-*jah*-lah-nahn *ah*-wah(k)?

*Berapa lama
perjalanan awak?*

Does this path go to ...?
ah-duh-kah(h) *jah*-lahn
ee-nee me-*noo*-joo ke ...?

*Adakah jalan
ini menuju ke ...?*

Where can we spend the night?
dee *mah*-nuh *kah*-mee
bo-*leh*(h) ber-*mah*-lahm?

*Di mana kami
boleh bermalam?*

Can I leave some things
here for a while?
bo-*leh*(h) *sim*-pahn bah-*rahng*
dee *see*-nee se-ke-*jahp*?

*Boleh simpan barang
di sini sekejap?*

There's a cave here.
ah-duh *goo*-ah dee *see*-nee

Ada gua di sini.

IN THE COUNTRY

I'm lost.	*sai*-yuh ter-*seh*-saht	*Saya tersesat.*
altitude	ke-*ting*-gee-ahn	*ketinggian*
binoculars	te-*ro*-pong	*teropong*
candles	*lee*-lin	*lilin*
to climb	men-*dah*-kee/ me-*nai*-kee	*mendaki/ menaiki*
compass	*kom*-pahs	*kompas*
downhill	*too*-roon *boo*-kit	*turun bukit*
first-aid kit	*ko*-tah(k) ke-che-*mah*-sahn	*kotak kecemasan*
gloves	*sah*-rung tah-*ngahn*	*sarung tangan*
guide	pe-*mahn*-doo	*pemandu*
guided trek	trehk yahng ber-*pahn*-doo	*trek yang berpandu*
hiking	me-*rehn*-tahs *hoo*-tahn	*merentas hutan*
hiking boots	*kah*-sut me-*rehn*-tahs *hoo*-tahn	*kasut merentas hutan*
hunting	ber-*boo*-roo	*berburu*
ledge	*bi*-rai	*birai*
lookout	tem-*paht* me-*mahn*-dahng	*tempat memandang*
map	*peh*-tuh	*peta*
mountain climbing	men-*dah*-kee *goo*-nung	*mendaki gunung*
pick	be-*lee*-ung	*beliung*
provisions	be-*kah*-lahn	*bekalan*
rock climbing	me-*mahn*-jaht *bah*-too	*memanjat batu*
rope	*tah*-lee	*tali*
short cut	*jah*-lahn *pin*-tahs	*jalan pintas*
signpost	*tahn*-duh *jah*-lahn	*tanda jalan*
steep	*choo*-rahm	*curam*
track	trehk; *jah*-lahn ke-*chil; lo*-rong	*trek; jalan kecil; lorong*
trek	trehk	*trek*
uphill	nai(k) *boo*-kit	*naik bukit*
to walk	ber-*jah*-lahn *kah*-kee	*berjalan kaki*

IN THE COUNTRY

AT THE BEACH

DI PANTAI

Can we swim here?
  bo-*leh(h)* be-re-*nahng*
  dee *see*-nee?

*Boleh berenang
di sini?*

Is it safe to swim here?
  se-lah-*maht*-kah(h)
  be-re-*nahng* dee *see*-nee?

*Selamatkah
berenang di sini?*

What time is high/low tide?
  poo-kool be-*rah*-puh air
  pah-sahng *ting*-gee/*rehm*-dah(h)?

*Pukul berapa air
pasang tinggi/rendah?*

coast	*pahn*-tai	*pantai*
diving	me-nye-*lahm*	*menyelam*
fishing	me-*mahn*-ching	*memancing*
marine reserve	*tah*-mahn	*taman*
	sim-pah-nahn lowt	*simpanan laut*
reef	*bah*-too *kah*-rahng	*batu karang*
sand	*pah*-sir	*pasir*
sea	lowt	*laut*
snorkelling	*snor*-kel	*snorkel*
sunblock	pe-*lin*-dung	*pelindung*
	chah-*hai*-yuh	*cahaya*
	mah-tuh-*hah*-ree	*matahari*
sunglasses	cher-*min mah*-tuh	*cermin*
	hee-tahm	*mata hitam*
surf	*om*-bah(k)	*ombak*
surfboard	*pah*-pahn se-*lahm*-chahr	*papan selancar*
surfing	ber-se-*lahn*-chahr	*berselancar*
swimming	be-re-*nahng*	*berenang*
tide	air *pah*-sahng	*air pasang*
towel	*twah*-luh	*tuala*
waterski	skee air	*ski air*
waves	*om*-bah(k)	*ombak*
windsurfing	ber-se-*lahn*-chahr	*berselancar*
	ah-ngin	*angin*

Diving

Are there good diving sites here?
  ah-duh tem-*paht*
  pe-nye-*lah*-mahn
  yahng bah-*gus* dee *see*-nee?

Can we hire a diving boat/guide?
  bo-*leh(h)*-kah(h) *kah*-mee
  me-*nyeh*-wuh bot/
  pe-*mahn*-doo *oon*-tu(k)
  me-nye-*lahm*?

We'd like to hire diving equipment.
  kah-mee nah(k) me-*nyeh*-wuh
  ke-leng-*kah*-pahn
  pe-nye-*lah*-mahn

I'm interested in exploring wrecks.
  sai-yuh ber-*mee*-naht
  oon-tuk men-*chah*-ree
  kah-pahl *kah*-rahm

Penyelaman

*Ada tempat
penyelaman
yang bagus di sini?*

*Bolehkah kami
menyewa bot/
pemandu untuk
menyelam?*

*Kami nak menyewa
kelengkapan
penyelaman.*

*Saya berminat
untuk mencari
kapal karam.*

WEATHER

CUACA

Weather reports in Malaysia are always the same. Rain in some places, dry in others. Hot during the day, slightly cooler at night. Humidity: high. In the Klang Valley (Kuala Lumpur and surrounding area) afternoon thunderstorms are common.

What's the weather like?
  bah-gai-*mah*-nuh
  choo-*ah*-chuh-nyuh?

*Bagaimana
cuacanya?*

Today it's ...	choo-*ah*-chuh	*Cuaca hari ini ...*
	hah-ree *ee*-nee ...	
cloudy	*men*-dung/	*mendung/*
	be-*rah*-wahn	*berawan*
cold	se-*joo(k)*	*sejuk*
flooding	*bahn*-jir	*banjir*
hot	*pah*-nahs	*panas*
humid/wet	lem-*bahb*	*lembab*
raining heavily	*hoo*-jahn leh-*baht*	*hujan lebat*
raining lightly	ge-*ree*-mis	*gerimis*
warm	koo-*rahng pah*-nahs	*kurang panas*
windy	be-*rah*-ngin	*berangin*

What time is ...?	*poo*-kool be-*rah*-puh ...?	*Pukul berapa ...?*
sunrise	mah-tuh-*hah*-ree ter-*bit*	*matahari terbit*
sunset	mah-tuh-*hah*-ree	*matahari*
	ter-be-nahm	*terbenam*

cloud	*ah*-wahn	*awan*
fog	*kah*-boos	*kabus*
moon	*bu*-lahn	*bulan*
mud	*loom*-pur	*lumpur*
rain	hoo-*jahn*	*hujan*
sky	lah-*ngit*	*langit*
smoke	*ah*-sahp	*asap*
storm	*ree*-but	*ribut*
sun	mah-tuh-*hah*-ree	*matahari*
typhoon	*tow*-fahn	*taufan*

BLAME IT ON THE RAIN

Malaysia is monsoonal, but only the east coast has a clear season of rain, when it buckets down for days and days. The driest part of the Peninsula is Kuala Pilah, Negeri Sembilan.

| *musim hujan* | the rainy (monsoon) season, October to March |
| *musim kemarau* | the dry season, April to September |

GEOGRAPHICAL TERMS ISTILAH GEOGRAFI

atoll	*poo*-low *chin*-chin	*pulau cincin*
beach	*pahn*-tai	*pantai*
bridge	*jahm*-bah-tahn	*jambatan*
cave	*goo*-uh	*gua*
city	*bahn*-dahr	*bandar*
cliff	te-*bing ting*-gee	*tebing tinggi*
earth	*boo*-mee	*bumi*
earthquake	*gehm*-puh *boo*-mee	*gempa bumi*
estuary	moo-*ah*-ruh	*muara*
farm	*lah*-dahng/ ke-*bun*	*ladang/ kebun*
footpath	*lo*-rong ber-*jah*-lahn *kah*-kee	*lorong berjalan kaki*
forest	*hoo*-tahn/*rim*-buh	*hutan/rimba*
gap (narrow pass)	*lah*-loo-ahn sem-*pit*	*laluan sempit*
harbour	pe-*lah*-boo-hahn	*pelabuhan*
hill	*boo*-kit	*bukit*
hot spring	*mah*-tuh air *pah*-nahs	*mata air panas*
jungle	*hoo*-tahn/*rim*-buh	*hutan/rimba*
island	*poo*-low	*pulau*
lake	*tah*-si(k)	*tasik*
mountain (path)	(*lah*-loo-ahn) *goo*-nung	*(laluan) gunung*
pass	*lah*-loo-ahn	*laluan*
peak	*poon*-chah(k)	*puncak*
plain	dah-*tah*-rahn	*dataran*
river	*soo*-ngai	*sungai*
rock	*bah*-too	*batu*
town	*ko*-tuh	*kota*
valley	*lehm*-bah(h)	*lembah*
village	*kahm*-pung/*deh*-suh	*kampung/desa*
volcano	*goo*-nung ber-*ah*-pee	*gunung berapi*
waterfall	air ter-*joon*	*air terjun*

FAUNA | | ## DUNIA BINATANG

English	Pronunciation	Malay
bird	*boo*-rung	*burung*
buffalo	ker-*bow*	*kerbau*
cat	*koo*-ching	*kucing*
chicken	*ai*-yahm	*ayam*
civet cat	*moo*-sahng	*musang*
cow	*lehm*-boo	*lembu*
crocodile	boo-*ai*-yuh	*buaya*
dog	*ahm*-jing	*anjing*
fish	*ee*-kahn	*ikan*
frog	*kah*-tah(k)/*ko*-do(k)	*katak/kodok*
gecko	*chi*(k)-chah(k)	*cikcak*
goat	*kahm*-bing	*kambing*
horse	*koo*-duh	*kuda*
monitor lizard	bee-*ah*-wah(k)	*biawak*
monkey	*mo*-nyeht	*monyet*
mouse deer	*kahm*-chil	*kancil*
pig	*bah*-bee	*babi*
python	*sah*-wah(h)	*sawah*
rooster	*ai*-yahm *jah*-tahn	*ayam jantan*
sheep	*bi*-ree-*bi*-ree	*biri-biri*
(poisonous) snake	*oo*-lahr (ber-*bee*-suh)	*ular (berbisa)*
tiger	*hah*-ree-mow	*harimau*

TINY BUT CLEVER

The tales of *Sang Kancil,* sahng *kahn*-chil, the tiny but clever mouse deer, are favourites among Malay children. The mouse deer (which you can see at the National Zoo) weighs only a few pounds, but manages to outwit many other bigger predators in these traditional tales. The smallest of Malaysian-made cars is appropriately called the *Kancil.*

Insects / Serangga

Insects		Serangga
... ant	se-*mut* ...	*semut* ...
fire	*ah*-pee	*api*
biting	*gee*-git	*gigit*
butterfly	*koo*-poo-*koo*-pool/ *rah*-muh-*rah*-muh	*kupu-kupu*/ *rama-rama*
centipede	*lee*-pahn	*lipan*
cockroach	*lee*-pahs	*lipas*
fly	*lah*-laht	*lalat*
leech (large, in rivers)	*lin*-tah(h)	*lintah*
(small, in grass)	*pah*-chaht	*pacat*
mosquito	*nyah*-mu(k)	*nyamuk*
spider	*lah*-bah(h)-*lah*-bah(h)	*labah-labah*
termite	*ah*-nai-*ah*-nai	*anai-anai*

FLORA & AGRICULTURE / DUNIA TUMBUHTUMBUHAN & PERTANIAN

agriculture	per-*tah*-nee-ahn	*pertanian*
coconut palm	*po*-ko(k) ke-*lah*-puh	*pokok kelapa*
coconut	ke-*lah*-puh	*kelapa*
corn	*jah*-gung	*jagung*
flower	*boo*-nguh	*bunga*
fruit tree	*po*-ko(k) *boo*-ah(h)	*pokok buah*
to harvest	me-me-*ti(k)*	*memetik*
irrigation	*sah*-li-rahn	*saliran*
leaf	down	*daun*
oil palm	ke-*lah*-puh *sah*-wit	*kelapa sawit*
orchard	*doo*-sun	*dusun*
plantation	eh-*steht*/lah-*dahng*	*estet/ladang*
to plant	me-*nah*-nahm	*menanam*
rice field	*sah*-wah(h)	*sawah*
rice terrace	*peh*-tah(k) *sah*-wah(h)	*petak sawah*
rubber	*geh*-tah(h)	*getah*
sugar cane	*teh*-boo	*tebu*
tobacco	tem-*bah*-kow	*tembakau*

PULL YOUR SOCKS UP!

When camping, be aware that South-East Asia has a tremendous number of venomous snakes and some enormous pythons. One was caught during the '90s with a grisly mouthful: the head and shoulders of a man. It had presumably dropped on him in an overgrown area near his house, and squeezed him into submission.

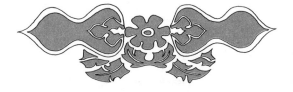

KESIHATAN   HEALTH

Public health is generally excellent and you're unlikely to get seriously ill during your travels in Malaysia. If you do need to talk about illness, the all-purpose word is *sakit*, *sah*-kit, which means 'to feel sick' or 'to hurt'. Government clinics and hospitals can accommodate foreigners, although there is usually a long wait. Private clinics and hospitals are fast, do not generally require appointments and are reasonably priced.

AT THE DOCTOR   DI KLINIK

Almost all doctors and most nurses speak English, even in rural areas. Most doctors dispense medicine and prescriptions as you need them, so there is seldom the need make an extra trip to a pharmacy. Malaysia enjoys a good standard of health, so as long as you observe the general guidelines for health in the tropics, you should be fine.

HEALTH

Where's a ...	... dee *mah*-nuh?	... *di mana?*
chemist	*fahr*-mah-see	*farmasi*
dentist	*dok*-tor *gee*-gee	*doktor gigi*
doctor	*dok*-tor	*doktor*
hospital	hos-*pi*-tahl	*hospital*
clinic	*kli*-nik	*klinik*

I'm sick.
   sai-yuh *sah*-kit   *Saya sakit.*
My friend is sick.
   kah-wahn *sai*-yuh *sah*-kit   *Kawan saya sakit.*
Is there a doctor here
who speaks English?
   ah-duh *dok*-tor yahng   *Ada doktor yang*
   ber-*bah*-hah-suh *ing*-ge-ris?   *berbahasa Inggeris?*
Could the doctor come to the hotel?
   bo-*leh(h)*-kah(h)   *Bolehkah*
   dok-tor *dah*-tahng ke *ho*-tehl? *doktor datang ke hotel?*

HEALTH

I've had a blood test.
dah-rah(h) *sai*-yuh *soo*-dah(h)
dee-per-*eek*-suh

Darah saya sudah diperiksa.

I need a blood test.
sai-yuh me-mer-*loo*-kahn
pe-mer-*eek*-sah-ahn *dah*-rah(h)

Saya memerlukan pemeriksaan darah.

Is that a new syringe?
jah-*rum* soon-*ti(k)*
ee-too bah-*roo*-kah(h)?

Jarum suntik itu barukah?

Please use this syringe.
to-long *pah*-kai jah-*rum*
soon-*ti(k)* ee-nee

Tolong pakai jarum suntik ini.

What are you doing?
ahm-duh *boo*-aht *ah*-puh?

Anda buat apa?

What do you want to do?
ahm-duh *boo*-aht nah(k) *ah*-puh?

Anda buat nak apa?

I feel better/worse.
sai-yuh be-*rah*-suh le-*bi(h)*
bai(k)/te-*ru(k)*

Saya berasa lebih baik/teruk.

This is my usual medicine.
ee-nee *oo*-baht
bee-*ah*-suh *sai*-yuh

Ini ubat biasa saya.

I've been vaccinated.
sai-yuh *soo*-dah(h)
dee-i-moo-ni-*sah*-see

Saya sudah diimunisasi.

I don't want a
blood transfusion.
sai-yuh tah(k) nah(k)
pe-nahm-*bah*-hahn *dah*-rah(h)

Saya tak nak penambahan darah.

I need a receipt for
my insurance.
sai-yuh per-*loo*-kahn *reh*-sit
oon-tu(k) in-*soo*-rans *sai*-yuh

Saya perlukan resit untuk insurans saya.

THEY MAY SAY ...

sah-kit *ah*-puh?   *Sakit apa?*
  What's the matter?

ahn-duh ber-*rah*-suh   *Anda berasa*
sah-kit dee *mah*-nuh?   *sakit di mana?*
  Where does it hurt?

ahn-duh *ah*-duh *ah*-lah-hahn? *Anda ada alahan?*
  Are you allergic to anything?

ahn-duh ... ?   Do you ...?   *Anda ...?*
  me-*ro*-ko(k)   smoke   *merokok*
  mee-num   drink   *minum*
    mee-nu-mahn   *minuman*
    ke-*rahs*   *keras*
  men-*goo*-nah-kahn take drugs *mengunakan*
  dah-dah(h)   *dadah*

ahn-duh de-*mahm pah*-nahs? *Anda demam panas?*
  Do you have a temperature?

ah-duh-kah(h) *ahn*-duh   *Adakah anda*
se-*dahng dah*-tahng haid? *sedang datang haid?*
  Are you menstruating?

ahn-duh me-*ngahn*-dung/ *Anda mengandung/*
hah-mil?   *hamil?*
  Are you pregnant?

ahn-duh te-*rah*-suh *sah*-kit? *Anda terasa sakit?*
  Do you feel any pain?

per-nah(h) ke-*nuh*   *Pernah kena*
pe-*nyah*-kit *ee*-nee tah(k)? *penyakit ini tak?*
  Have you had this before?

ahn-duh se-*dahng*   *Anda sedang*
mah-kahn oo-baht? *makan ubat?*
  Are you on medication?

soo-dah(h) be-*rah*-puh *Sudah berapa*
lah-muh *ahn*-duh   *lama anda*
be-*rah*-suh be-*gee*-nee? *berasa begini?*
  How long have you been like this?

HEALTH

AILMENTS   **PENYAKIT**

I feel under the weather.
sai-yuh *koo*-rahng   *Saya kurang*
se-*dahp bah*-dahn   *sedap badan.*

I feel nauseous.
sai-yuh *moo*-ahl   *Saya mual.*

I've been vomiting.
sai-yuh *soo*-dah(h) *moon*-tah(h)   *Saya sudah muntah.*

I'm having a hard time sleeping.
sai-yuh *soo*-sah(h) *tee*-dur   *Saya susah tidur.*

I feel ...	*sai*-yuh ber-*rah*-suh ...	*Saya berasa ...*
dizzy	pe-*ning*	*pening*
shivery	meng-*gee*-gil	*menggigil*
weak	le-*mah(h)*	*lemah*

My leg is broken.
too-lahng *kah*-kee   *Tulang kaki saya patah.*
sai-yuh *pah*-tah(h)

My foot is sprained.
kah-kee *sai*-yuh   *Kaki saya tersiliuh.*
ter-see-*lee*-u(h)

I have low/high blood pressure.
sai-yuh *ah*-duh te-*kah*-nahn   *Saya ada tekanan*
dah-rah(h) *rehm*-dah(h)/*ting*-gee   *darah rendah/tinggi.*

My ... hurts
... *sai*-yuh *sah*-kit   *... saya sakit.*

I'm suffering from (a/an) ...	*sai*-yuh *sah*-kit ...	*Saya sakit ...*
addiction	ke-*tah*-gee-hahn	*ketagihan*
allergy	*ah*-ler-gee/*ah*-lah-hahn	*alergi/alahan*
anaemia	ah-*nee*-mee-uh	*anemia*
asthma	*leh*-lah(h)	*lelah*
bite	gee-gee-tahn	*gigitan*
burns	ke-*nuh ah*-pee	*kena api*
cancer	kan-ser	*kanser*
cholera	*tah*-oon	*taun*
cold	sel-*seh*-muh	*selsema*
constipation	sem-be-*lit*	*sembelit*
cough	*bah*-tu(k)	*batuk*
cystitis	*sah*-kit *ken*-ching	*sakit kencing*
diarrhoea	*chir*-rit-*bir*-it	*cirit-birit*
dog bite	gee-gee-tahn *ahn*-jing	*gigitan anjing*
dysentery	*di*-sen-tree	*disentri*
fever	de-*mahm pah*-nahs	*demam panas*
food poisoning	ke-*rah*-choo-nahn *mah*-kah-nahn; *sah*-lah(h) *mah*-kahn	*keracunan makanan; salah makan*
gastroenteritis	*sah*-kit gas-trik	*sakit gastrik*
headache	*sah*-kit ke-*pah*-luh	*sakit kepala*
heart condition	mah-*sah*-ah-lah(h) *jahm*-tung	*masalah jantung*
hepatitis	heh-*pah*-tai-tis	*hepatitis*
high blood pressure	te-*kah*-nahn *dah*-rah(h) *ting*-gee	*tekanan darah tinggi*
indigestion	tah(k) *hah*-zahm *mah*-kah-nahn	*tak hazam makanan*
infection	in-*fehk*-see	*infeksi*
influenza	sel-*seh*-muh/floo	*selsema/flu*
itch	*gah*-tahl	*gatal*
lice	*koo*-too	*kutu*
malaria	mah-*lah*-ree-uh	*malaria*
migraine	*sah*-kit ke-*pah*-luh be-*raht*; *mai*-grehn	*sakit kepala berat; migraine*

HEALTH

pain	*sah*-kit	*sakit*
rabies	*ray*-bees; pe-*nyah*-kit *ahn*-jing *gee*-luh	*rabies; penyakit anjing gila*
rheumatism	*sah*-kit *sen*-dee	*sakit sendi*
sore throat	*sah*-kit te-*kah*(k)	*sakit tekak*
sprain	ter-se-*lee*-oo(h)	*terseliuh*
stomachache	*sah*-kit pe-*root*	*sakit perut*
sunburn	ter-*bah*-kar mah-tuh-*hah*-ree	*terbakar matahari*
travel sickness	*mah*-buk per-*jah*-lah-nahn	*mabuk perjalanan*
typhoid	de-*mahm* ke-pee-*ah*-loo	*demam kepialu*
urinary tract infection	*sah*-kit *ken*-ching	*sakit kencing*
venereal disease	pe-*nyah*-kit ke-*lah*-meen	*penyakit kelamin*
worms	*chah*-ching	*cacing*

WOMEN'S HEALTH   KESIHATAN WANITA

Private maternity clinics would have information on specific matters to do with women's health. Testing for STDs is available at most clinics and larger hospitals.

Is there a female doctor here?
  ah-duh *dok*-tor
  wah-*nee*-tuh dee *see*-nee?

Ada doktor wanita di sini?

Is there a doctor especially for women?
  ah-duh *dok*-tor *khoo*-soos
  oon-tu(k) wah-*nee*-tuh?

Ada doktor khusus untuk wanita?

I'd like to use contraception.
  sai-yuh nah(k) *goo*-nuh *ah*-laht/
  oo-baht pen-*ceh*-gah(h) *hah*-mil

Saya nak guna alat/ ubat pencegah hamil.

I haven't menstruated for ... weeks.
  sai-yuh be-*lum dah*-tahng
  haid se-*lah*-muh ... *ming*-goo

Saya belum datang haid selama ... minggu.

I'm on the Pill.
    sai-yuh *mah*-kahn pil   *Saya makan pil*
    men-*cheh*-gah(h) *hah*-mil   *mencegah hamil.*

(Maybe) I'm pregnant.
    (moong-kin) *sai*-yuh   *(Mungkin) Saya*
    me-*ngahn*-dung/*hah*-mil   *mengandung/hamil.*

abortion	peng-*goo*-goo-rahn *ah*-nah(k)	*pengguguran anak*
cystitis	*sah*-kit *ken*-ching	*sakit kencing*
diaphragm	*dai*-ah-frahm	*diaphram*
IUD	ai oo deh	*IUD*
mammogram	*mah*-mo-gram	*mamogram*
menstruation	*dah*-tahng haid	*datang haid*
miscarriage	ke-*goo*-goo-rahn	*keguguran*
pap smear	smir	*smear*
period pain	se-*goo*-gup	*segugup*
the Pill	pil pen-*cheh*-gah(h) *hah*-mil	*pil pencegah hamil*
premenstrual tension	ke-*teh*-gah-ngahn se-be-*lum* *dah*-tahng haid	*ketegangan sebelum datang haid*
thrush	*goo*-ahm	*guam*
ultrasound	*ul*-trah-sownd	*ultrasound*

HEALTH

THEY MAY SAY ...

pil *ee*-nee *mes*-tee   *Pil ini mesti*
dee *ahm*-bil *tee*-guh   *di ambil tiga*
kah-lee se-*hah*-ree   *kali sehari*

    These pills must be
    taken three times a day.

gon-chahng-kahn   *Goncangkan*
bo-tol doo-loo   *botol dulu*
se-be-*lum* mee-num   *sebelum minum.*

    Shake the bottle
    before taking.

HEALTH

SPECIAL HEALTH NEEDS		KEPERLUAN KHUSUS KESIHATAN
anaemia	ah-*nee*-mee-uh	*anaemia*
asthma	*leh*-lah(h)	*lelah*
diabetes	*ken*-ching *mah*-nis	*kencing manis*
I'm allergic to ...	*sai*-yuh ah-*ler*-jik ke-pah-duh ...	*Saya alergik kepada ...*
antibiotics	an-tai-bai-*o*-tik	*antibiotik*
aspirin	*as*-pi-rin	*aspirin*
bees	*leh*-bah(h)	*lebah*
codeine	ko-deen	*kodein*
dairy products	*pro*-duk ber-*soo*-soo	*produk bersusu*
penicillin	pe-ni-*si*-lin	*penisilin*
pollen	de-*boo*-nguh	*debunga*

I have a skin allergy.
sai-yuh *ah*-duh
ah-lah-hahn *koo*-lit
    Saya ada alahan kulit.

I have my own syringe.
sai-yuh *ah*-duh *jah*-rum
soon-*ti(k)* sen-*di*-ree
    Saya ada jarum suntik sendiri.

I need a new pair of glasses.
sai-yuh per-*loo*-kahn
cher-*min mah*-tuh *bah*-roo
    Saya perlukan cermin mata baru.

I'm on medication for ...
sai-yuh se-*dahng pah*-kai
oo-baht *oon*-tu(k) ...
    Saya sedang pakai ubat untuk ...

ALTERNATIVE TREATMENTS

PENGUBATAN ALTERNATIF

Although Western-style medical treatment is the norm, alternative treatments, including some that are unique to Malaysia, are widely practised.

aromatherapy	ah-ro-mah-*teh*-rah-pee	*aromaterapi*
acupuncture	ah-koo-*punk*-toor	*akupunktur*
faith healer	*bo*-mo(h)/*doo*-koon/	*bomoh/dukun/*
	pah-wahng	*pawang*
herbalist	*ah*-lee *jah*-moo	*ahli jamu*
massage	*oo*-root	*urut*
masseur/masseuse	*too*-kahng *oo*-root	*tukang urut*
meditation	per-*tah*-pah-ahn	*pertapaan*
physiotherapy	fi-see-o-*tehr*-ah-pee	*fisioterapi*
reflexology	ree-flek-*so*-lo-gee	*refleksologi*
yoga	*yo*-guh	*yoga*

HEALTH

PARTS OF THE BODY

BAHAGIAN TUBUH

ankle	ke-*ting*	*keting*
anus	*doo*-bur	*dubur*
appendix	ah-*pehm*-dik	*apendik*
arm	*leh*-ngahn	*lengan*
back	be-*lah*-kahng	*belakang*
bladder	kahn-*du*-ngahn	*kandungan*
	ken-ching	*kencing*
blood	*dah*-rah(h)	*darah*
bone	*too*-lahng	*tulang*
breast	*boo*-ah(h) *dah*-duh	*buah dada*
buttocks	*pong*-gong	*ponggong*
chest	*dah*-duh	*dada*
chin	*dah*-goo	*dagu*
ear	te-*li*-nguh	*telinga*
eye	*mah*-tuh	*mata*
face	*moo*-kuh	*muka*
finger	*jah*-ree *tah*-ngahn	*jari tangan*
foot	*kah*-kee	*kaki*

HEALTH

hands	*tah*-ngahn	*tangan*
head	ke-*pah*-luh	*kepala*
heart	*jahm*-tung	*jantung*
hip	*ping*-gahn	*pinggan*
kidney	*boo*-ah(h) *ping*-gahng	*buah pinggang*
knee	*loo*-tut	*lutut*
leg	*kah*-kee	*kaki*
liver	*hah*-tee	*hati*
lung	*pah*-roo-*pah*-roo	*paru-paru*
mouth	*moo*-lut	*mulut*
muscle	*o*-tot	*otot*
neck	*leh*-hehr	*leher*
nose	*hee*-dung	*hidung*
penis	*zah*-kahr	*zakar*
ribs	*too*-lahng *roo*-su(k)	*tulang rusuk*
shoulder	*bah*-hoo	*bahu*
skin	*koo*-lit	*kulit*
stomach	pe-*root*	*perut*
testicles	*boo*-ah(h) *peh*-lir	*buah pelir*
throat	te-*kah(k)*	*tekak*
toes	*jah*-ree *kah*-kee	*jari kaki*
tooth	*gee*-gee	*gigi*
vagina	*fah*-rahj	*faraj*
vein	*oo*-*raht dah*-rah(h)	*urat darah*
	hah-loos	*halus*

AT THE CHEMIST   DI FARMASI

Some internationally known painkillers are not sold off the shelf in
Malaysian pharmacies. Although you do not need a prescription,
you will have to ask the chemist to dispense them to you.

I need medicine for ...
    sai-yuh per-*loo*-kahn   *Saya perlukan*
    oo-baht *oon*-tu(k) ...   *ubat untuk ...*
How many times a day?
    be-*rah*-puh *kah*-lee se-*hah*-ree?   *Berapa kali sehari?*

antibiotics	an-tai-bai-*o*-tik	*antibiotik*
antiseptic	an-ti-*sehp*-tik	*antiseptik*
aspirin	*as*-pi-rin	*aspirin*
Band-aids	*plas*-ter	*plaster*
bandage	pem-bah-loot	*pembalut*
condoms	*kon*-dom	*kondom*
contraceptives	*ah*-laht/*oo*-baht	*alat/ubat*
	pen-*ceh*-gah(h) *hah*-mil	*pencegah hamil*
cotton wool	*kah*-pahs	*kapas*
cough medicine	*oo*-baht *bah*-tu(k)	*ubat batuk*
gauze	kain *kah*-suh	*kain kasa*
gastrolyte	ga-*stroh*-leet	*gastrolyte*
headache tablets	*oo*-baht *sah*-kit	*ubat sakit*
	ke-*pah*-luh	*kepala*
laxatives	*joo*-lahp	*julap*
painkillers	*oo*-baht *tah*-hahn	*ubat tahan sakit*
	sah-kit	
penicillin	pe-ne-*si*-lin	*penisilin*
quinine	*kwee*-nin	*kuinin*
rubbing alcohol	*al*-ko-hol *go*-so(k)	*alkohol gosok*
sleeping pills	*oo*-baht *tee*-dur	*ubat tidur*
tablet	*tab*-leht	*tablet*
vitamins	vee-*tah*-min	*vitamin*

Useful Words

accident	ke-*mahl*-ah-ngahn	*kemalangan*
breath	*nah*-fahs	*nafas*
disease	pe-*nyah*-kit	*penyakit*
faeces	*tah*-hee	*tahi*
fast (n)	*pwah*-suh	*puasa*
to fast	ber-*pwah*-suh	*berpuasa*
health	ke-see-*hah*-tahn	*kesihatan*
injection	*soon*-tee-kahn	*suntikan*
injury	ke-che-de-*rah*-ahn	*kecederaan*
medicine	*oo*-baht	*ubat*
poisonous	be-*rah*-choon	*beracun*
urine	air *ken*-ching	*air kencing*
wound	*loo*-kuh	*luka*

HEALTH

HEALTH

AT THE DENTIST

I have a toothache.
  sai-yuh *sah*-kit *gee*-gee
I have a cavity.
  ah-duh *gee*-gee ber-*loo*-bahng
My tooth is broken.
  gee-gee *sai*-yuh *pah*-tah(h)
I've lost a filling.
  tahm-pah-lahn
  gee-gee *sai*-yuh *hee*-lang
My gums hurt.
  goo-see *sai*-yuh *sah*-kit
Don't extract it.
  jah-*ngahn* *chah*-but
Please give me an anaesthetic.
  to-long *kah*-si(h)
  oo-baht bee-*oos*

DI DOKTOR GIGI

Saya sakit gigi.

Ada gigi berlubang.

Gigi saya patah.

Tampalan
gigi saya hilang.

Gusi saya sakit.

Jangan cabut.

Tolong kasih
ubat bius.

Ouch!   ah-*doo(h)!*   *Aduh!*

KEPERLUAN KHUSUS

SPECIFIC NEEDS

DISABLED TRAVELLERS   ORANG CACAT

Few facilities cater to the disabled in Malaysia. In most cities and towns there are seldom any sidewalks, and if there are, the curbs tend to be high and uneven. Toilets for the disabled are few and far between. Some of the newer mass transit and train systems in Kuala Lumpur have more accessibility. Malays in particular tend to stare at any one who looks different (this includes most non-Asian travellers) so be prepared to be gawked at.

I'm disabled.
   sai-yuh *chah*-chaht   *Saya cacat.*

I need assistance.
   sai-yuh per-*loo*-kahn   *Saya perlukan bantuan.*
   bahn-*too*-ahn

What services do you
have for disabled people?
   ah-duh per-*keed*-mah-tahn   *Ada perkhidmatan untuk*
   oon-tu(k) o-rahng *chah*-chaht?   *orang cacat?*

Is there wheelchair access?
   ah-duh *jah*-lahn *mah*-su(k)   *Ada jalan masuk untuk*
   oon-tu(k) ke-*roo*-see be-*ro*-duh?   *kerusi beroda?*

I'm deaf.
   sai-yuh pe-*kah(k)*   *Saya pekak.*

I can lipread.
   sai-yuh *dah*-paht mem-*bah*-chuh   *Saya dapat membaca*
   ge-*rah*-kahn *bee*-bir   *gerakan bibir.*

Does anyone here know
sign language?
   ah-duh *o*-rahng yahng *tah*-hoo   *Ada orang yang tahu*
   bah-*hah*-suh ee-*shah*-raht?   *bahasa isyarat?*

I have a hearing aid.
   sai-yuh *ah*-duh *ah*-laht   *Saya ada alat bantu*
   bahn-too de-*ngahr*   *dengar.*

Speak more loudly please.
   to-long *chah*-kahp
   kwaht see-*kit*

*Tolong cakap
kuat sikit.*

Are guide dogs permitted?
   bo-*leh(h)*-kah(h) *sai*-yuh
   mem-*bah*-wuh *mah*-su(k)
   ahn-jing pe-*mahn*-doo?

*Bolehkah saya membawa
masuk anjing pemandu?*

Braille library	per-poos-tah-*kah*-ahn	*perpustakaan*
	brehl	*Braille*
disabled person	*o*-rahng *chah*-chaht	*orang cacat*
guide dog	*ahn*-jing pe-*mahn*-doo	*anjing pemandu*
wheelchair	ke-*roo*-see be-*ro*-duh	*kerusi beroda*

GAY TRAVELLERS   ORANG HOMOSEKSUAL

Despite negative views of homosexuality and laws which allow
for the punishment of homosexual acts by imprisonment or
caning, Malaysia is amazingly tolerant of transvestites, *pondan*,
pon-dahn. Public displays of affection are not okay, however.

   There is a gay scene in Kuala Lumpur. The word 'gay',
pronounced geh, will be understood.

Where are the gay hangouts?
   dee *mah*-nuh tem-*paht*
   ber-*koom*-pool *o*-rahng geh/
   ho-mo-*sek*-soo-ahl?

*Di mana tempat
berkumpul orang
gay/homoseksual?*

Where are the gay clubs?
   ke-*lahb* mah-lahm *oon*-tu(k)
   o-rahng geh dee *mah*-nuh?

*Kelab malam untuk
orang gay di mana?*

[Are we; Am I] likely to be harassed?
   ah-duh-kah *o*-rahng geh
   se-*ring* de-*gahng*-goo dee
   see-nee?

*Adakah orang gay
sering diganggu di sini?*

Is there a gay organisation
in Kuala Lumpur?
   ah-duh or-gahn-i-*sah*-see geh
   dee *kwah*-luh *loom*-pur tah(k)?

*Ada organisasi gay di
Kuala Lumpur tak?*

TRAVELLING WITH THE FAMILY

PERJALANAN DENGAN KELUARGA

Malaysians love children, and if you have some it can be a real icebreaker. Discounts are available for children at most attractions and on public transport. You will see children eating out with adults, even in pricey restaurants, at almost any time of day.

Are there facilities for babies?
  ah-duh ke-moo-*dah(h)*-ahn
  oon-tu(k) *bah*-yee tah(k)?

Ada kemudahan untuk bayi tak?

Do you have a childminding service?
  ah-duh per-*kheed*-mah-tahn
  pen-*jah*-gah-ahn *ah*-nah(k) tah(k)?

Ada perkhidmatan penjagaan anak tak?

Where can I find a/an
(English-speaking) babysitter?
  dee *mah*-nuh *sai*-yuh bo-*leh(h)*
  men-*chah*-ree pen-*jah*-guh
  ah-nah(k) (yahng *tah*-hoo
  ber-*chah*-kahp *dah*-lahm
  bah-*hah*-suh *ing*-ge-ris)?

Di mana saya boleh mencari penjaga anak (yang tahu bercakap dalam Bahasa Inggeris)?

Can you put an (extra)
bed/cot in the room?
  bo-*leh(h)* *sai*-yuh *min*-tuh
  sah-too *(lah*-gee) *kah*-til *oon*-tu(k)
  bee-li(k) *kah*-mee?

Boleh saya minta satu (lagi) katil untuk bilik kami?

I need a car with a child seat.
  sai-yuh per-*loo*-kahn ke-*reh*-tuh
  de-*ngahn* ke-*roo*-see
  kah-nah(k)-*kah*-nah(k)

Saya perlukan kereta dengan kerusi kanak-kanak.

Is it suitable for children?
  ah-duh-kah(h) *ee*-nee se-*swai*
  oon-tu(k) *kah*-nah(k)-*kah*-nah(k)?

Adakah ini sesuai untuk kanak-kanak?

Are there any activities for children?
  ah-duh ke-gee-*ah*-tahn *oon*-tu(k)
  kah-nah(k)-*kah*-nah(k)?

Ada kegiatan untuk kanak-kanak?

Is there a family discount?
ah-duh *dis*-kown *oon*-tu(k)   *Ada diskaun untuk*
ke-loo-*ahr*-guh?   *keluarga?*

Are children allowed?
ah-duh-kah(h)   *Adakah kanak-kanak*
kah-nah(k)-*kah*-nah(k)   *dibenarkan masuk?*
dee-be-*nahr*-kahn *mah*-su(k)?

Do you have a children's menu?
ah-duh *meh*-nyoo *oon*-tu(k)   *Ada menu untuk*
kah-nah(k)-*kah*-nah(k) tah(k)?   *kanak-kanak tak?*

ON BUSINESS   PERJALANAN PERNIAGAAN

We're attending a ...	*kah*-mee	*Kami*
	meng-hah-*di*-ree ...	*menghadiri ...*
conference	per-*see*-dah-ngahn/	*persidangan/*
	kon-fer-*ehn*-see	*konferensi*
meeting	me-shoo-*ah*-raht	*mesyuarat*
trade fair	*pehs*-tuh	*pesta*
	per-*toon*-joo-kahn	*pertunjukan*
	per-*dah*-gah-ngahn	*perdagangan*

I'm on a course.
sai-yuh se-*dahng* ber-*koor*-sus   *Saya sedang berkursus.*

I have an appointment with ...
sai-yuh *ah*-duh te-moo-*jahn*-jee   *Saya ada temujanji*
de-*ngahn* ...   *dengan ...*

Here's my business card.
ee-nee kahd *nah*-muh *sai*-yuh   *Ini kad nama saya.*

I need an interpreter.
sai-yuh per-*loo*   *Saya perlu penterjemah.*
pen-ter-*jeh*-mah(h)

I'd like to use a computer.
sai-yuh per-*loo* meng-*goo*-nuh   *Saya perlu mengguna*
kom-*poo*-ter   *komputer.*

I'd like to send [a fax; an email].

   sai-yuh nah(k) meng-*hahn*-tahr   *Saya nak menghantar*
   fahks/*ee*-mehl   *faks/e-mel.*

client	pe-*lahng*-gahn/*klai*-ehn	*pelanggan/klien*
colleague	*rah*-kahn se-*ker*-juh	*rakan sekerja*
distributor	pe-*ngeh*-dahr	*pengedar*
email	*ee*-mehl	*e-mel*
exhibition	*pah*-meh-rahn	*pameran*
manager	pe-*ngoo*-roos	*pengurus*
mobile phone	teh-*leh*-fon *bim*-bit	*telefon bimbit*
profit	*oon*-tung	*untung*
proposal	*oo*-sool/*chah*-dah-ngahn	*usul/cadangan*

FILM & TV CREWS

KRU FILEM & TELEVISYEN

Can we film here?

   bo-*leh(h)* *kah*-mee
   me-rah-*kahm*-kahn   *Boleh kami*
   fee-lem dee *see*-nee?   *merakamkan*
                    filem di sini?

We're filming!

   kah-mee se-*dahng*
   mem-*boo*-aht *fee*-lem!   *Kami sedang*
                    membuat filem!

We're making a ...   *kah*-mee   *Kami membuat ...*
                 mem-*boo*-aht ...

film	*fee*-lem	*filem*
documentary	do-koo-*mehn*-tah-ree	*dokumentari*
TV series	si-ree *rahm*-chah-ngahn teh-le-vi-shen	*siri rancangan televisyen*

PILGRIMAGE & RELIGION

NAIK HAJI & KEAGAMAAN

Malaysian Muslims can be a little touchy about discussing religion. Approach Islam with great respect. If you're asking questions it's better to ask a Chinese or Indian Malaysian who is less likely to be a Muslim. Talking too much to a Malay about religions other than Islam might be perceived as trying to convert them, which is against the law. Remember that in order to enter a mosque, a man must wear a shirt, preferably with sleeves, and pants (or a *sarong*) falling below the knees. Women must wear clothing that covers their head and body with the exception of their hands and face – usually a skirt rather than pants. Don't walk in front of people who are performing their prayers.

Can I attend this service?
    bo-*leh(h)* meng-hah-*di*-ree
    oo-pah-*chah*-ruh *ee*-nee?

Boleh menghadiri upacara ini?

Can I pray here?
    bo-*leh(h)* sai-yuh
    ber-sehm-*bai*-yahng dee *see*-nee?

Boleh saya bersembayang di sini?

Where can I pray/worship?
    dee *mah*-nuh tem-*paht* yahng
    sai-yuh bo-*leh(h)*
    ber-sehm-*bai*-yahng?

Di mana tempat yang saya boleh bersembayang?

Where can I make confession
(in English)?
    pe-*ngah*-koo-ahn (*dah*-lahm
    bah-*hah*-suh *ing*-ge-ris)
    dee-lah-*koo*-kahn dee *mah*-nuh?

Pengakuan (dalam Bahasa Inggeris) dilakukan di mana?

May I enter this mosque?
    bo-*leh(h)* tah(k) *sai*-yuh
    mah-su(k) *mahs*-jid *ee*-nee?

Boleh tak saya masuk masjid ini?

Where may I stand/
walk in the mosque?
    dee *mah*-nuh *sai*-yuh bo-*leh(h)*
    ber-*di*-ree/*jah*-lahn *dah*-lahm
    mahs-jid?

Di mana saya boleh berdiri/jalan dalam masjid?

SPECIFIC NEEDS

baptism	*bahp*-tis	*baptis*
christening	*bahp*-tis	*baptis*
church	ge-*reh*-juh	*gereja*
communion	per-*jah*-moo-ahn soo-chee	*perjamuan suci*
confession	pe-*ngah*-koo-ahn	*pengakuan*
fasting month	*rah*-mah-dahn	*Ramadhan*
Friday prayers	sem-*bah(h)*-yahng joo-mah-aht	*sembahyang Jumaat*
funeral	pe-*mah*-kah-mahn	*pemakaman*
God (Muslim)	*too*-hahn/*ahl*-lah(h)	*Tuhan/Allah*
monk	*rah*-hib	*rahib*
mosque	*mahs*-jid	*masjid*
pilgrim (Muslim)	*hah*-jee/*haj*-jah(h)	*haji/hajjah* (m/f)
pilgrimage to Mecca	hahj	*hajj*
prayer	do-ah/*sem*-bah(h)-yahng	*doa/sembahyang*
priest (Catholic)	*pah*-dree	*padri*
pastor (Protestant)	*pah*-dree/*pahs*-tor	*padri/pastor*
relic	pe-*ning*-gah-lahn	*peninggalan*
religious	pe-*rah*-rah-kahn	*perarakan*
procession	*ah*-gah-muh	*agama*
religious tax	*zah*-kaht	*zakat*
saint	o-rahng soo-chee/*wah*-lee	*orang suci/wali*
shrine	tem-*paht* soo-chee	*tempat suci*
... temple	*to*-kong ...	*tokong ...*
Buddhist	*boo*-dah	*Buddha*
Chinese	*chee*-nah	*Cina*
Hindu	*koo*-il	*kuil*

SPECIFIC NEEDS

BAREFOOT & FANCY FREE

All Malaysians take off their shoes before entering accommodation of any kind, so remember to remove yours and put them next to the pile. Footwear must also be removed when visiting mosques and some temples, and beware – expensive shoes can walk off on their own.

TRACING ROOTS & HISTORY

MENCARI ASAL-USUL & SEJARAH

I think my ancestors came
from this area.

   sai-yuh *rah*-suh neh-*neh(k)*
   mo-yahng *sai*-yuh ber-*ah*-sahl
   dah-ree *kah*-wah-sahn *ee*-nee

*Saya rasa nenek
moyang saya berasal
dari kawasan ini.*

I'm looking for my relatives.

   sai-yuh men-*chah*-ree *ah(h)*-lee
   ke-loo-*ahr*-guh *sai*-yuh

*Saya mencari ahli
keluarga saya.*

I have/had a relative who
lives around here.

   doo-loo ke-loo-*ahr*-guh *sai*-yuh
   ting-gahl dee *kah*-wah-sahn *ee*-nee

*Dulu keluarga saya
tinggal di kawasan ini.*

Is there anyone here
by the name of ...?

   ah-duh *o*-rahng dee *see*-nee
   yahng ber-*nah*-muh ...?

*Ada orang di sini
yang bernama ...?*

I'd like to go to the cemetery/
burial ground.

   sai-yuh *i*-ngin me-*lah*-waht
   per-*koo*-bu-rahn

*Saya ingin melawat
perkuburan.*

My father used to work here.

   ai-yah(h) *sai*-yuh per-*nah(h)*
   ber-*ker*-juh dee *see*-nee

*Ayah saya pernah
berkerja di sini.*

SPECIFIC NEEDS

MASA, TARIKH & PERAYAAN

TIME, DATES & FESTIVALS

Malaysians, especially in the big cities, tend to be punctual for business (although heavy rain and traffic jams may wreak havoc with schedules from time to time). However, for social functions, it's okay to be fashionably late.

TELLING THE TIME   MENENTUKAN MASA

In Malay, 'am' and 'pm' are replaced by whole words.

8 am
poo-kool *lah*-pahn *pah*-gee

pukul lapan pagi
(lit: hour eight morning)

8 pm
poo-kool *lah*-pahn *mah*-lahm

pukul lapan malam
(lit: hour eight night)

morning (12 midnight – 12 noon)
pah-gee

pagi

afternoon (12 noon – 3 pm)
te-ngah-*hah*-ree

tengahari

evening (3 – 7 pm)
pe-*tahng*

petang

night (7 pm – 12 midnight)
mah-lahm

malam

o'clock	*poo*-kool	*pukul*
second	sa-*aht*/de-ti(k)	*saat/detik*
minute	*mi*-nit	*minit*
to	se-be-*lum*	*sebelum*
past	se-le-*pahs*	*selepas*
half	se-te-*ngah(h)*	*setengah*
quarter	*soo*-koo	*suku*
one hour	se-*jahm*	*sejam*
two hours	*doo*-uh jahm	*dua jam*

What time is it?
  poo-kool be-*rah*-puh
  (se-*kah*-rahng)?   *Pukul berapa*
                       (sekarang)?

It's three o'clock.
  poo-kool *tee*-guh   *Pukul tiga.*

It's a quarter to four.
  lah-gee *soo*-koo jahm   *Lagi suku jam*
  poo-kool em-*paht*   *pukul empat.*

It's ten past three.
  se-*poo*-lu(h) *mi*-nit se-le-*pahs*   *Sepuluh minit selepas*
  poo-kool *tee*-guh   *pukul tiga.*

It's five-thirty.
  poo-kool *lee*-muh   *Pukul lima*
  se-te-*ngah(h)*   *setengah.*

Half past one.
  poo-kool *sah*-too se-te-*ngah(h)*   *Pukul satu setengah.*

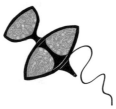

DAYS   HARI DALAM SEMINGGU

Monday	*hah*-ree *ees*-nin	*hari Isnin*
Tuesday	*hah*-ree se-*lah*-suh	*hari Selasa*
Wednesday	*hah*-ree *rah*-boo	*hari Rabu*
Thursday	*hah*-ree *khah*-mis	*hari Khamis*
Friday	*hah*-ree *joo*-mah-aht	*hari Jumaat*
Saturday	*hah*-ree *sahb*-too	*hari Sabtu*
Sunday	*hah*-ree *ah*-hahd	*hari Ahad*
on Monday	*pah*-duh *hah*-ree *ees*-nin	*pada hari Isnin*

MONTHS

		BULAN
January	*jahm*-oo-ah-ree	*Januari*
February	*feh*-broo-ah-ree	*Februari*
March	mahch	*Mac*
April	*ah*-pril	*April*
May	may	*Mei*
June	joon	*Jun*
July	*joo*-lai	*Julai*
August	o-gos	*Ogos*
September	sehp-*tehm*-ber	*September*
October	ok-*to*-ber	*Oktober*
November	no-*vehm*-ber	*November*
December	dee-*sehm*-ber	*Disember*
during June	se-*mah*-suh *bu*-lahn joon	*semasa bulan Jun*

THE NIGHT BEFORE

Nights refer to the following day – 'Saturday night' is expressed as 'the night before Sunday', rather like saying 'Christmas Eve'.

Thursday night
mah-lahm *joo*-mah-aht   *malam Jumaat*
(lit: at-night Friday)

DATES   TARIKH

Date order in Malaysia is expressed as day, month, year, eg:

17 August 1945
too-ju(h) be-*lahs* o-gos   *Tujuh belas Ogos*
sem-*bee*-lahn be-*lahs* em-*paht* *sembilan belas*
poo-lu(h) lee-muh   *empat puluh lima*

What date is it today?
ah-puh *tah*-rikh *hah*-ree ee-nee?   *Apa tarikh hari ini?*

It's 28 June.
hah-ree ee-nee *doo*-uh *poo*-lu(h)   *Hari ini dua puluh lapan*
lah-pahn hah-ree-*bu*-lahn joon   *haribulan Jun.*

TIME, DATES &
FESTIVALS

PRESENT | SEKARANG

immediately	ser-*tah*-mer-*tah*	*serta-merta*
now	se-*kah*-rahng/*kee*-nee	*sekarang/kini*
currently	se-*dahng*	*sedang*
today	*hah*-ree *ee*-nee	*hari ini*
this morning	*pah*-gee *ee*-nee	*pagi ini*
during the day	*pah*-duh *hah*-ree *ee*-nee	*pada hari ini*
tonight	*mah*-lahm *ee*-nee;	*malam ini*;
	mah-lahm *nahm*-tee	*malam nanti*
this week	*ming*-goo *ee*-nee	*minggu ini*
this month	*boo*-lahn *ee*-nee	*bulan ini*
this year	*tah*-hoon *ee*-nee	*tahun ini*

PAST | YANG LALU

just now	*bah*-roo *sah*-juh	*baru saja*
before	se-be-*lum*	*sebelum*
recently	*bah*-roo-*bah*-roo *ee*-nee	*baru-baru ini*
already	*soo*-dah(h)	*sudah*
yesterday	se-*mah*-lahm	*semalam*
yesterday morning	*pah*-gee se-*mah*-lahm	*pagi semalam*
yesterday afternoon	te-ngah-*hah*-ree se-*mah*-lahm	*tengahari semalam*
last night	*mah*-lahm se-*mah*-lahm	*malam semalam*
day before yesterday	kel-*mah*-rin	*kelmarin*
last week	*ming*-goo le-*pahs*	*minggu lepas*
two weeks ago	*doo*-uh *ming*-goo le-*pahs*	*dua minggu lepas*
last month	*boo*-lahn le-*pahs*	*bulan lepas*
last year	*tah*-hoon le-*pahs*	*tahun lepas*
ago	yahng *lah*-loo; le-*pahs*	*yang lalu; lepas*
a while ago	se-*dee*-kit *mah*-suh doo-*loo*	*sedikit masa dulu*
long ago	*lah*-muh doo-*loo*	*lama dulu*

FUTURE

as soon as possible	se-che-*paht* *moong*-kin	*secepat mungkin*
soon	se-*geh*-ruh	*segera*
not yet	be-*lum lah*-gee	*belum lagi*
later	ke-*moo*-dee-ahn/ *nahm*-tee	*kemudian/ nanti*
after	se-le-*pahs*/se-*soo*-dah(h)	*selepas/sesudah*
tomorrow	*eh*-so(k)	*esok*
morning	*eh*-so(k) *pah*-gee	*esok pagi*
afternoon	*eh*-so(k) te-ngah-*hah*-ree	*esok tengahari*
evening	*eh*-so(k) pe-*tahng*	*esok petang*
day after tomorrow	*loo*-suh	*lusa*
next week	*ming*-goo de-*pahn*	*minggu depan*
next month	*boo*-lahn de-*pahn*	*bulan depan*
next year	*tah*-hoon de-*pahn*	*tahun depan*
forever	se-*lah*-muh-*lah*-muh-nyuh	*selama-lamanya*

MASA DEPAN

moment	se-*behm*-tahr	*sebentar*
minute	*mi*-nit	*minit*
hour	jahm	*jam*
day	*hah*-ree	*hari*
week	*ming*-goo	*minngu*
month	*boo*-lahn	*bulan*
year	*tah*-hoon	*tahun*
decade	*deh*-kahd	*dekad*
century	*ah*-bahd	*abad*
millennium	mi-*leh*-nee-um	*milenium*

DURING THE DAY

		SEPANJANG HARI
dawn	*sen*-juh	*senja*
day	*hah*-ree	*hari*
early	*ah*-wahl	*awal*
early morning	*ah*-wahl *pah*-gee	*awal pagi*
midday	te-ngah-*hah*-ree	*tengahari*
midnight	te-*ngah(h)* mah-lahm	*tengah malam*
sunrise	mah-tuh-*hah*-ree ter-*bit*	*matahari terbit*
sunset	mah-tuh-*hah*-ree ter-*be*-nahm	*matahari terbenam*

SEASONS

		MUSIM
spring	*moo*-sim *boo*-nguh	*musim bunga*
summer	*moo*-sim *pah*-nahs	*musim panas*
autumn	*moo*-sim *loo*-ru(h); *goo*-gur	*musim luruh; gugur*
winter	*moo*-sim se-*joo(k)*	*musim sejuk*
dry season	*moo*-sim ke-*mah*-row/ ke-*ring*	*musim kemarau/ kering*
rainy season	*moo*-sim *hoo*-jahn	*musim hujan*

LIKE A PRAYER

Malays sometimes refer to prayer times, rather than the time of day. If you hear a Malay saying the following, they mean:

Selepas zohor
following the midday prayers, which usually occur around 12:30 – 1:00 pm

Selepas asar
after the mid-afternoon prayers, which usually start around 3:30 – 4:30 pm

Selepas mahgrib
following the sunset prayers; sunset on the Peninsula usually falls between 7:00 – 7:30 pm

Selepas isyak
after the commencement of night prayers, which is usually about one hour after sunset. 'After *isyak*' could actually mean any time before dawn the next morning!

HOLIDAYS & FESTIVALS

PERCUTIAN & PERAYAAN

Malaysia loves a festival! There are many religious dates observed and celebrated by various communities. The dates on which Muslim holidays fall change from year to year, because they follow the (lunar) Islamic calendar.

Some festivals will affect your stay. Almost everything shuts down during Chinese New Year. For *Hari Raya Aidl Fitri*, there's a big parade and lots of flag waving in Kuala Lumpur. Travel before and during *Hari Raya Puasa* can be difficult, as the whole country endeavours to *balik kampung*, *bah*-li(k) *kahm*-pung, (lit: go-back village) get home for celebrations. Flights will be full, trains will be packed and traffic will be jammed.

Chinese New Year

Chinese New Year is a major national event which falls in January or February. Dragon dances are held and Chinese families have a reunion dinner on the eve of Chinese New Year, opening their homes for family and friends during the first two days of the festival. Children and unmarried relatives receive *ang pow*, *ahng pow*, (money in small red envelopes) and everyone wishes you *Gong Si Fatt Choy* (a happy and prosperous New Year). In a true overlapping of cultures, the Malays have adopted the use of a green *ang pow* envelope for giving money (also a Muslim tradition during *Hari Raya*, *hah*-ree *rai*-yuh). These envelopes are widely available for free at banks throughout Malaysia, before the festive periods.

Deepavali

Deepavali, dee-pah-*vah*-lee, the Hindu 'Festival of Lights', celebrates *Rama's* victory over the demon *Ravana*. It's the most important of Hindu festivals in Malaysia. Oil lamps are lit to celebrate this victory and to invite *Lakshmi*, the goddess of wealth, into the home. The Malaysian Indians who celebrate *Deepavali* also hold open houses.

Hari Kebangsaan

Hari Kebahngsaan, *hah*-ree ke-bahng-*sah*-ahn, Malaysia's Independence Day, falls on 31 August and is marked with a national holiday.

TIME, DATES & FESTIVALS

Hari Raya Aidil Adha/Hari Raya Haji

Hari Raya, hah-**ree** rai-**yuh**, literally means 'day celebration'. This Muslim festival commemorates Ibrahim's devotion to God. On being ordered by God to kill his son, Isaac, Ibrahim was about to do the deed when God put a stop to it and told him to kill a sheep instead. It's the day upon which the Muslim pilgrims to Mecca complete their pilgrimage. Almost every Muslim in Malaysia has some member of the family in Mecca every year.

The sacrifice – of a goat or a sheep – is re-enacted throughout the Muslim areas of Malaysia on *Aidil Adha*, followed by great feasting. Muslims hold open houses, *rumah terbuka*, roo-**mah**(h) ter-**boo**-kuh, for friends and families, with a smorgasbord of delicious foods.

Hari Raya Aidil Fitri/Hari Raya Puasa

The first day of the tenth month marks the end of *Ramadan*, rah-mah-dahn, and the celebration of *Hari Raya Puasa*, hah-ree rai-yuh pwah-suh – also known as *Aidil Fitri*, ai-dil fee-tree. It begins with mass prayers at mosques and in city squares, followed by two days of open houses, family visits and culinary engorgement.

> **BODY & SOUL**
>
> During *Aidl Fitri*, children ask forgiveness from their parents for any wrongdoings, using the words *Maaf zahir batin*, mah-ahf zah-hir bah-tin, 'I apologise with my body and soul'.

Ramadan

The ninth month of the Muslim calendar is the month of *Ramadan*, rah-mah-dahn, also known as *bulan puasa*, bu-lahn pwah-suh, 'the fasting month'. During *Ramadan*, most adult Muslims don't drink, eat, smoke, have sex or indulge in other pleasures during daylight hours. The fast is symbolic of a person's faith, and is also a way for Muslims to feel an affinity with those who are too poor to afford food.

Children, pregnant or menstruating women, and people who are sick or elderly aren't expected to fast. However, some women 'make up' for missed fasting days later in the year. No one is forced to fast, but it's best to eat indoors, out of sight. Many restaurants and food stalls remain open, with a shade-cloth over the door.

Thaipusam

During *Thaipusam*, tai-poo-sahm, in January, Hindu devotees honor Lord *Subramaniam* with acts of physical endurance. The festival is celebrated primarily in Kuala Lumpur, at Batu Caves, and in Penang, at the Waterfall Hilltop Temple. The devotees march in a procession carrying *kavadi*, kah-vah-dee, heavy metal frames decorated with fruit, flowers and feathers. The *kavadi* are hung from their bodies with metal hooks and spikes driven through their flesh.

CROWDED HOUSE

Selamat Hari se-*lah*-maht *hah*-ree (lit: safe ... day)

If you arrive near a festival period, and express interest in the traditions and practices of any Malaysian, you might get a flag to an 'open house', a Malaysian tradition practised by all races and religions. Traditional foods are prepared, and every guest is treated to full hospitality. You're not expected to bring a gift — however it is appropriate to give small quantities of money to children and unmarried adults. Just feel free to go and enjoy the food and company.

This is one tradition during which racial tensions are often put aside. You'll see people of all origins at each other's homes. Chinese families who are expecting Muslim guests will often prepare food that is *halal* (allowed) for Muslims. If you don't get an invitation on *Hari Raya Puasa*, you can always go to the Prime Minister's house, where everyone in the nation is welcome!

Happy/Merry (festival name)!	se-*lah*-maht ...!	*Selamat ...!*
ang pow	ahng pow	*ang pow*
open house	*roo*-mah(h) ter-*boo*-kuh	*rumah terbuka*
Please come in.	*see*-luh *mah*-su(k)	*Sila masuk.*
Please help yourself.	*see*-luh *mah*-kahn/ *mee*-num	*Sila makan/ minum.* (lit: please eat/drink)
Thank you.	te-*ree*-muh *kah*-si(h)	*Terima kasih.*
What are these?	*mah*-kah-nahn *ah*-puh nee?	*Makanan apa ni?*

WEDDINGS   PERKAHWINAN

Weddings are big business in Malaysia, often with hundreds of guests. Whole streets can be blocked off, tents set up and tables and decorations set on the road. Depending on the faith and/or wealth of the family, weddings can last for days. Even if you've never met the couple, it's not uncommon to be invited to the reception and wedding feast, *kenduri*, ken-*doo*-ree, rather than the actual religious ceremony, *nikah*, *nee*-kah(h).

Although offering gifts is acceptable, it's customary to give money in an envelope to the parents who are hosting the reception.

Congratulations!	*tah(h)*-nee-ah(h)!	*Tahniah!*
wedding	per-*kah(h)*-wi-nahn/ per-*nee*-kah(h)-ahn	*perkahwinan/ pernikahan*
reception	ken-*doo*-ree	*kenduri*

THEY SAY IT'S YOUR BIRTHDAY

Birthdays aren't a big deal once people have finished school. Malaysians sing the same happy birthday song that Westerners do – usually in English.

Happy Birthday!	
se-*lah*-maht *hah*-ree *jah*-dee!	*Selamat Hari Jadi!*
When is your birthday?	
bee-luh *hah*-ree *jah*-dee ahn-duh?	*Bila hari jadi anda?*
My birthday's on ...	
hah-ree *jah*-dee *sai*-yuh *pah*-duh ...	*Hari jadi saya pada ...*
How old are you?	
oo-mur be-*rah*-puh-kah(h)?	*Umur berapakah?*

TIME, DATES & FESTIVALS

FUNERALS PEMAKAMAN/PERKEBUMIAN

Muslims believe that the corpse must be buried as soon as possible, and burial usually occurs within 24 hours of death. Chinese and Indian funerals, which sometimes feature processions with professional mourners, tend to be more public.

| My condolences. | *tahk*-zee-ah(h) | *Takziah.* |
| When did he/ she die? | *bee*-luh *dee*-uh me-*ning*-gahl? | *Bila dia meninggal?* |

BILANGAN & JUMLAH

NUMBERS & AMOUNTS

In Malay, numbers from 12 to 19 are comprised of the numbers one to nine plus *(-)belas*, (-)be-*lahs*. Numbers from 20 to 99 are counted with *(-)puluh*, *(-)poo*-lu(h), '10'. The number 10 is *sepuluh*, se-*poo*-lu(h), 20 is *dua puluh*, *doo*-uh *poo*-lu(h), and so on.

In the hundreds, *(-)ratus*, *(-)rah*-toos, is used. So, *seratus*, se-*rah*-toos, is 100, *duaratus*, *doo*-uh *rah*-toos, is 200, and so on. For thousands, use *(-)ribu*, *(-)ree*-boo, and for millions, use *(-)juta*, *(-)joo*-tuh.

CARDINAL NUMBERS

BILANGAN POKOK

0	*ko*-song/see-*fahr*	*kosong/sifar*
1	*sah*-too	*satu*
2	*doo*-uh	*dua*
3	*tee*-guh	*tiga*
4	em-*paht*	*empat*
5	*lee*-muh	*lima*
6	e-*nahm*	*enam*
7	*too*-ju(h)	*tujuh*
8	*lah*-pahn	*lapan*
9	sem-*bee*-lahn	*sembilan*
10	se-*poo*-lu(h)	*sepuluh*
11	se-be-*lahs*	*sebelas*
12	*doo*-uh be-*lahs*	*dua belas*
13	*tee*-guh be-*lahs*	*tiga belas*
14	em-*paht* be-*lahs*	*empat belas*
15	*lee*-muh be-*lahs*	*lima belas*
16	e-*nahm* be-*lahs*	*enam belas*
17	*too*-ju(h) be-*lahs*	*tujuh belas*
18	*lah*-pahn be-*lahs*	*lapan belas*
19	sem-*bee*-lahn be-*lahs*	*sembilan belas*
20	*doo*-uh *poo*-lu(h)	*dua puluh*
21	*doo*-uh *poo*-lu(h) *sah*-too	*dua puluh satu*
22	*doo*-uh *poo*-lu(h) *doo*-uh	*dua puluh dua*
30	*tee*-guh *poo*-lu(h)	*tiga puluh*
40	em-*paht* *poo*-lu(h)	*empat puluh*

50	*lee*-muh *poo*-lu(h)	lima puluh
100	se-*rah*-toos	seratus
200	*doo*-uh rah-toos	dua ratus
268	*doo*-uh rah-toos e-*nahm*	dua ratus enam
	poo-lu(h) *lah*-pahn	puluh lapan
300	*tee*-guh rah-toos	tiga ratus
1000	se-*ree*-boo	seribu
2000	*doo*-uh ree-boo	dua ribu
3000	*tee*-guh ree-boo	tiga ribu
51,783	*lee*-muh poo-lu(h)	lima puluh satu
	sah-too ree-boo, *too*-ju(h)	ribu, tujuh ratus
	rah-toos *lah*-pahn	lapan puluh tiga
	poo-lu(h) *tee*-guh	
1 million	se-*joo*-tuh	sejuta
2 million	*doo*-uh *joo*-tuh	dua juta

ORDINAL NUMBERS BILANGAN TINGKAT

1st	per-*tah*-muh	pertama
2nd	ke-*doo*-uh	kedua
3rd	ke-*tee*-guh	ketiga
4th	ke-em-*paht*	keempat
5th	ke-*lee*-muh	kelima
6th	ke-e-*nahm*	keenam
7th	ke-*too*-ju(h)	ketujuh
8th	ke-*lah*-pahn	kelapan
9th	ke-sem-*bee*-lahn	kesembilan
10th	ke-se-*poo*-lu(h)	kesepuluh

the first bus
   bahs (yahng) per-*tah*-muh   *bas (yang) pertama*
the third building
   bah-*ngoo*-nahn (yahng) ke-*tee*-guh   *bangunan (yang) ketiga*

FRACTIONS PECAHAN

1/3	se-per-*tee*-guh	sepertiga
1/4	*soo*-koo	suku
1/2	se-te-*ngah(h)*	setengah
3/4	*tee*-guh pe-rem-*paht*	tiga perempat

QUANTITY

JUMLAH

Quantity can either be indicated by a number, or by a quantity word placed before a noun.

all	se-*moo*-uh	semua
both	ke-*doo*-uh-nyuh/	keduanya/
	ke-*doo*-uh-*doo*-uh-nyuh	kedua-duanya
double	*doo*-uh kah-lee *gahn*-duh	dua kali ganda
each	se-*tee*-ahp/	setiap/tiap-tiap
	tee-ahp-*tee*-ahp	
enough	*choo*-kup	cukup
every	se-*tee*-ahp/	setiap/
	mah-sing-*mah*-sing	masing-masing
few	be-be-*rah*-puh	beberapa
a little	se-*dee*-kit	sedikit
many (for things)	*bah*-nyah(k)	banyak
(for people)	rah-*mai*	ramai
much	*bah*-nyah(k)	banyak
one more	sah-too *lah*-gee	satu lagi

There are many people.

    ah-duh rah-*mai* o-rahng   *Ada ramai orang.*
                                (lit: there-are many person)

about	le-*bi(h)* *koo*-rahng/	lebih kurang/
	ki-ruh-*ki*-ruh	kira-kira
amount	*jum*-lah(h)	jumlah
to count	me-*ngi*-ruh	mengira
minus	*to*-lah(k)/*koo*-rahng	tolak/kurang
more	le-*bi(h)*	lebih
number	*nom*-bor/*ahng*-kuh/	nombor/angka/
	bee-*lah*-ngahn	bilangan
a pair	se-*pah*-sahng	sepasang
percent	pe-*rah*-toos	peratus
plus	*tahm*-bah(h)	tambah
quantity	bee-*lah*-ngahn/	bilangan/
	koo-*ahn*-ti-tee	kuantiti
some	be-be-*rah*-puh	beberapa

COUNT DOWN

Malay uses 'counters' before most numbers (see page 36, under Classifiers), like in English when we say 'a *piece* of paper'. However, in Malay these counters are used nearly all the time for specific numbers of things or people.

Common counters include:

batang   *bah*-tahng
   long, roundish things such as pencils, rivers, trees, cigarettes
biji   *bee*-jee
   small round things such as fruit, sweets, beans
buah   *boo*-ah(h)
   large objects such as cars, houses, furniture, airplanes, buildings, mountains, planets
ekor   *eh*-kor
   animals
helai   *heh*-lai
   flat, thin, saggy things such as clothing and paper
keping   *ke*-ping
   flat, thin, hard things such as a sheet of metal or wood
kotak   *ko*-tah(k)
   box shaped things, like a cigarette carton or box
orang   *o*-rahng
   people
potong   *po*-tong
   a piece of something you can cut, eg, cake

I want to buy three shirts.
  sai-yuh nah(k) be-*lee tee*-guh   *Saya nak beli tiga helai*
  heh-lai *bah*-joo   *baju.*
                            (lit: I want buy three *helai* shirt)

KECEMASAN   EMERGENCIES

Ambulance and paramedic services in Malaysia are slow at best. It's often better to get yourself to the nearest hospital if you need medical services.

Help!	*to*-long!	*Tolong!*
Stop!	ber-*hehn*-tee!	*Berhenti!*
Go away!	*per*-gee/be-*lah(h)*!	*Pergi/Belah!*
Watch out!	*ah*-wahs/	*Awas/*
	ber-*hah*-ti-*hah*-ti!	*Berhati-hati!*
Thief!	pen-*choo*-ree!	*Pencuri!*
Pickpocket!	pe-nye-*luk sah*-koo!	*Penyeluk saku!*
Fire!	ke-*bah*-kah-rahn!	*Kebakaran!*
It's an emergency!	ke-che-*mah*-sahn!	*Kecemasan!*

There's been an accident.
    ah-duh ke-*mah*-lah-ngahn!   *Ada kemalangan!*

Help me please!
    min-tuh *to*-long!   *Minta tolong!*

Could I use the telephone?
    bo-*leh(h) goo*-nai teh-*leh*-fon?   *Boleh gunai telefon?*

I'm lost.
    sai-yuh ter-*seh*-saht   *Saya tersesat.*

Where are the toilets?
    tahn-duhs dee *mah*-nuh?   *Tandas di mana?*

Call the police!
    pahng-gil *po*-lis!   *Panggil polis!*

I'll get the police!
    sai-yuh ah-*kahm pahng*-gil *po*-lis!   *Saya akan panggil polis!*

Where's the police station?
    bah-lai *po*-lis dee *mah*-nuh?   *Balai polis di mana?*

I've been robbed!
    sai-yuh te-*lah(h)* dee-*rom*-pah(k)!   *Saya telah dirompak!*

I speak English.
    sai-yuh *tah*-hoo ber-*chah*-kahp   *Saya tahu bercakap*
    bah-*hah*-suh *ing*-ge-ris   *bahasa Inggeris.*

EMERGENCIES

I've lost my ...	... *sai*-yuh *hee*-lahng	... *saya hilang.*
My ... was/were stolen.	... *sai*-yuh dee-*choo*-ree	... *saya dicuri.*

backpack	behg *sahm*-dahr	*beg sandar*
bags	behg	*beg*
handbag	behg *tah*-ngahn	*beg tangan*
money	*doo*-it/wahng	*duit/wang*
papers	*do*-koo-mehn/ ker-*tahs*	*dokumen/ kertas*
passport	*pahs*-port	*pasport*
travellers cheques	chehk kem-*bah*-ruh	*cek kembara*
wallet	*dom*-peht	*dompet*

DEALING WITH THE POLICE
BERURUSAN DENGAN POLIS

Good manners go a long way in Malaysia. As a foreign visitor you are considered a guest, and guests are on best behaviour! At least be patient and try to keep your voice low.

My possessions are insured.
　　sai-yuh *ah*-duh in-*soo*-rahns
　　oon-tu(k) *bah*-rahng-
　　bah-rahng *sai*-yuh

Saya ada insurans untuk barang-barang saya.

What am I accused of?
　　sai-yuh dee-*too*-du(h) *ah*-puh?

Saya dituduh apa?

I (don't) understand.
　　sai-yuh (tah(k)) *fah*-hahm

Saya (tak) faham.

I didn't realise I was doing anything wrong.
　　sai-yuh tah(k) se-*dahr sai*-yuh
　　ber-sah-*lah(h)*

Saya tak sedar saya bersalah.

I didn't do it.
sai-yuh *tee*-dah(k)
me-lah-*koo*-kahn *ee*-too

Saya tidak melakukan
itu.

I'm sorry; I apologise.
sai-yuh me-nye-*sahl*;
sai-yuh *min*-tuh mah-*ahf*

Saya menyesal; Saya
minta maaf.

We're innocent.
kah-mee *tee*-dah(k)
ber-sah-*lah(h)*

Kami tidak bersalah.

We're foreigners.
kah-mee o-rahng *ah*-sing

Kami orang asing.

Can I call someone?
bo-*leh(h)*-kah(h) *sai*-yuh
me-neh-*leh*-fon se-se-o-rahng?

Bolehkah saya
menelefon seseorang?

Can I see a lawyer
who speaks English?
bo-*leh(h)*-kah(h) *sai*-yuh
ber-*jum*-puh de-*ngahn*
pe-*gwahm* yahng
ber-bah-*hah*-suh *ing*-ge-ris?

Bolehkah saya berjumpa
dengan peguam yang
berbahasa Inggeris?

Is there a fine we
can pay to clear this?
bo-*leh(h)*-kah(h) *kah*-mee
mem-*bai*-yahr *den*-duh
oon-tu(k) me-nye-le-*sai*-kahn
mah-*sah*-luh(h) *ee*-nee?

Bolehkah kami
membayar denda
untuk menyelesaikan
masalah ini?

Can we pay an on-the-spot fine?
bo-*leh(h)* *bai*-yahr *den*-duh
se-*kah*-rahng?

Boleh bayar denda
sekarang?

I know my rights.
sai-yuh *tah*-hoo hahk *sai*-yuh

Saya tahu hak saya.

I want to contact my
embassy/consulate.
sai-yuh nah(k)
meng-hoo-*boo*-ngee
ke-*doo*-tah-ahn/*kon*-soo-laht
sai-yuh

Saya nak
menghubungi
kedutaan/konsulat
saya.

EMERGENCIES

THE POLICE MAY SAY ...

ahn-duh dee-*too*-duh me-lah-*koo*-kahn ...	*Anda dituduh melakukan ...*	You'll be charged with ...
dee-uh dee-*too*-duh me-lah-*koo*-kahn ...	*Dia dituduh melakukan ...*	She'll/He'll be charged with ...
be-*ker*-juh tahn-puh ee-zin	*bekerja tanpa izin*	working without a permit
ke-*gee*-ah-tahn sub-*ver*-sif	*kegiatan subversif*	anti-government activity
mah-su(k) tahn-puh ee-zin *mah*-su(k) tahn-puh vee-suh	*masuk tanpa izin masuk tanpa visa*	illegal entry entry without a visa
meng-*gahng*-goo ke-*ah*-mah-nahn	*mengganggu keamanan*	disturbing the peace
me-*mee*-li-kee *bah*-rah-ngahn *hah*-rahm	*memiliki barangan haram*	possession of illegal substances
pe-*lahng*-gah-rahn pe-*rah*-tu-rahn lah-loo-*lin*-tahs	*pelanggaran peraturan lalulintas*	traffic violation
pem-*boo*-noo-hahn	*pembunuhan*	murder
pen-*choo*-ree-ahn	*pencurian*	theft
pen-*choo*-ree-ahn dee ke-*dai*	*pencurian di kedai*	shoplifting
pe-*rom*-pah-kahn	*perompakan*	robbery
pe-*ro*-go-lahn	*perogolan*	rape
se-*rahng*-ahn	*serangan*	assault
me-le-*bee*-hee *tehm*-po(h) sah(h) vee-suh	*melebihi tempoh sah visa*	overstaying your visa

arrested	dee-*tahng*-kahp	*ditangkap*
cell	sehl	*sel*
consulate	*kon*-soo-laht	*konsulat*
court	*mah(h)*-khah-mah(h)	*mahkamah*
embassy	ke-*doo*-tah-ahn	*kedutaan*
fine	*dehm*-duh	*denda*
(not) guilty	(*tee*-dah(k)) ber-sah-*lah(h)*	(*tidak*) *bersalah*
lawyer	pe-*gwahm*	*peguam*
police officer	pe-*gah*-wai *po*-lis	*pegawai polis*
police station	*bah*-lai *po*-lis	*balai polis*
prison	pen-*jah*-ruh	*penjara*
trial	pe-*ngah*-di-lahn	*pengadilan*

EMERGENCIES

THE BILL

It's best to address the police as 'sir' or 'ma'am'.

| Sir | twahn/en-*chi(k)* | *tuan/encik* |
| Ma'am | pwahn/*chi(k)* | *puan/cik* |

HEALTH   KESIHATAN

For common ailments head to a walk-in clinic; go to a private hospital if you're really ill.

I'm ill.
   sai-yuh *sah*-kit   *Saya sakit.*
My friend is ill.
   kah-wahn *sai*-yuh *sah*-kit   *Kawan saya sakit.*
Call an ambulance!
   to-long *pang*-gil *ahm*-boo-lahns!   *Tolong panggil ambulans!*
Call a doctor!
   pang-gil *dok*-tor!   *Panggil doktor!*

EMERGENCIES

Please take me/us to a hospital.
to-long *hahm*-tahr-kahn
sai-yuh/*kah*-mee ke *hos*-pi-tahl

Tolong hantarkan saya/kami ke hospital.

My blood group is
(A, B, O, AB) positive/negative.
koom-poo-lahn *dah*-ruh *sai*-yuh
ee-*ah*-lah(h) (ay, bee, oh, ay bee)
po-si-tif/*neh*-gah-tif

Kumpulan darah saya ialah (A, B, O, AB) positif/negatif.

My contact number is ...
nom-bor teh-*leh*-fon *sai*-yuh ...

Nombor telefon saya ...

The number of my next of kin is ...
nom-bor teh-*leh*-fon *oon*-tu(k)
ke-loo-*ahr*-guh *sai*-yuh
ee-*ah*-lah(h) ...

Nombor telefon untuk keluarga saya ialah ...

I have medical insurance.
sai-yuh *ah*-duh in-*soo*-rahns
ke-see-*hah*-tahn

Saya ada insurans kesihatan.

Please get medicine from
the chemist for me.
to-long be-*lee* oo-baht *oon*-tu(k)
sai-yuh dee *fahr*-mah-see

Tolong beli ubat untuk saya di farmasi.

ENGLISH – MALAY

A

> Root words are given in square brackets after verbs. (Root words are often used in place of active verbs by Malay speakers.) Verbs are preceeded by 'to' to distinguish them from nouns of similar spelling.
>
> to look   me-lee-haht *[lee-haht]*   melihat *[lihat]*
>
> Remember that nouns don't change their form according to whether they're singular or plural. When a word can be either a noun or an adjective, the adjective form is followed by the marking (adj).
>
> Bullets separate more than one alternative word and slashes words that are interchangeable.

A

to be able (can)	bo-*leh(h)*	boleh

> Can (may) I take your photo?
> bo-*leh(h)* ahm-bil fo-to ahn-duh?   Boleh ambil foto anda?
>
> Can you show me (on the map)?
> to-long toon-*joo(k)*-kahn (dee pe-*tuh*)?   Tolong tunjukkan (di peta)?

aboard	dee ah-*tahs*	di atas
abortion	peng-goo-goo-rahn	pengguguran
above	dee ah-*tahs*	di atas
to accept	me-ne-ree-muh *[te-ree-muh]*	menerima *[terima]*
accident	ke-mah-*lah*-ngahn	kemalangan
accommodation	pe-*ngee*-nah-pahn	penginapan
to accompany	me-ne-*mah*-nee	menemani
across	se-be-*rahng*	seberang
activist	ahk-ti-vis	aktivis
adaptor (electric)	a-*dap*-ter eh-*lehk*-trik	adapter elektrik
address (of house)	*ah*-lah-maht	alamat
admission (entry)	ke-mah-*su(k)*-kahn	kemasukan
adult	deh-*wah*-suh	dewasa
aeroplane	*kah*-pahl ter-bahng	kapal terbang
afraid	tah-*kut*	takut
after	se-le-*pahs* • se-te-*lah(h)* • se-soo-*dah(h)*	selepas • setelah • sesudah
afternoon	te-ngah-*hah*-ree • pe-*tahng*	tengahari • petang
in the afternoon	pah-*duh* wahk-too te-ngah-*hah*-ree/pe-*tahng*	pada waktu tengahari/petang
this afternoon	te-ngah-*hah*-ree/pe-*tahng* ee-nee	tengahari/petang ini
again	se-moo-luh	semula
against (opposed)	me-*nen*-tahng	menentang
age	oo-*mur*	umur
ago	le-*pahs*	lepas
(half an hour) ago	(se-te-*ngah(h)* jahm) le-*pahs*	(setengah jam) lepas
(three days) ago	(tee-*guh* hah-ree) le-*pahs*	(tiga hari) lepas

to agree	ber-se-*too*-joo [se-*too*-joo]	*bersetuju [setuju]*

I don't agree.
*sai-*yuh *tee-*dah(k) se-*too*-joo

Saya tidak setuju.

Agreed.
se-*too*-joo

Setuju.

ahead	dee de-*pahn*/hah-dah-*pahn*	*di depan/hadapan*
straight ahead	te-*rus* ke hah-dah-*pahn*	*terus ke hadapan*
AIDS	ehds	*AIDS*
air	oo-*dah*-ruh	*udara*
air-conditioner	pen-*dee*-ngin oo-*dah*-ruh	*pendingin udara*
airmail	mehl oo-*dah*-ruh	*mel udara*
airport	lah-*pah*-ngahn ter-bahng	*lapangan terbang*
airport tax	*choo*-kai pe-ner-*bah*-ngan	*cukai penerbangan*
alarm clock	jahm *lo*-chehng	*jam loceng*
alive	*hee*-dup	*hidup*
all	se-*moo*-uh	*semua*
allergy	*ah*-ler-jee • ah-lah-*hahn*	*alergi • alahan*
alley	lo-*rong*	*lorong*
to allow	mem-be-*nahr*-kahn •	*membenarkan •*
	me-*ngee*-zin-kahn	*mengizinkan*

It's (not) allowed.
dee-*lah*-rahng

Dilarang.

almost	*hahm*-pir • nyah-ris-*nyah*-ris	*hampir • nyaris-nyaris*
alone	ber-sen-dee-ree-ahn	*bersendirian*
already	*soo*-dah(h) • te-*lah(h)* • per-*nah(h)*	*sudah • telah • pernah*
also	*joo*-guh • pun	*juga • pun*
altitude	ke-*teeng*-gee-ahn	*ketinggian*
always	se-*lah*-loo • *sen*-tee-ah-sah	*selalu • sentiasa*
ambassador	doo-*tah*	*duta*
among	dee *ahn*-tah-ruh/kah-*lah*-ngahn	*di antara/kalangan*
anarchist	hoo-roo-hah-*ruh*	*huru-hara*
ancient	*pur*-buh • *koo*-no • *too*-uh	*purba • kuno • tua*
and	dahn	*dan*
angry	mah-*rah(h)*	*marah*
animal	bee-*nah*-tahng • *hai*-wahn	*binatang • haiwan*
to annoy	meng-*gahng*-goo [gahng-goo]	*mengganggu [ganggu]*
to answer	men-*jah*-wahb [jah-wahb]	*menjawab [jawab]*
ant	se-*mut*	*semut*
antibiotics	an-tai-bai-o-tik	*antibiotik*
antiques	*bah*-rahng ahn-tik	*barang antik*
antiseptic	pem-*bahs*-mee koo-*mahn*	*pembasmi kuman*
any	*ah*-puh pun • se-*bah*-rahng	*apa pun • sebarang*
anything	*ah*-puh-*ah*-puh	*apa-apa*
anytime	bee-luh-*bee*-luh	*bila-bila*
anywhere	mah-nuh-*mah*-nuh	*mana-mana*
apple	*eh*-pahl	*epal*

appointment	te-moo-*jahn*-jee	*temujanji*
appropriate	se-soo-ai	*sesuai*
approximately	kee-ruh-*kee*-ruh	*kira-kira*
archaeological	kah-jee-*pur*-buh • *ahr*-kee-o-lo-ji	*kajipurba • arkeologi*
architecture	se-nee-*bee*-nuh	*senibina*
to argue	mem-*bahn*-tah(h) *[bahn*-tah(h)]*	*membanta [bantah]*
arm (of body)	le-*ngahn*	*lengan*
to arrive	*dah*-tahng • *tee*-buh • sahm-*pai*	*datang • tiba • sampai*
arrivals	ke-dah-*tah*-ngahn *[dah*-tahng]* •	*kedatangan [datang] •*
	ke-*tee*-buh-an *[tee*-buh]*	*ketibaan [tiba]*
art	se-*nee*	*seni*
artist	se-nee-mahn/se-*nee*-wah-tee (m/f)	*seniman/seniwati*
artwork	ka-ri-*ah* se-*nee*	*karya seni*
ashtray	be-*kahs* ah-boo ro-ko(k)	*bekas abu rokok*
to ask for something	me-*min*-tuh *[min*-tuh]*	*meminta [minta]*
to ask a question	ber-*tah*-nyuh *[tah*-nyuh]*	*bertanya [tanya]*
asleep	*tee*-dur	*tidur*
assault	se-*rah*-ngahn	*serangan*
assistance	per-*to*-lo-ngan • *bahn*-too-ahn	*pertolongan • bantuan*
asthma	*sah*-kit le-*lah(h)*	*sakit lelah*
at (location)	dee • de-*kaht*	*di • dekat*
at (time)	pah-*duh*	*pada*
ATM	ay tee ehm	*ATM*
atmosphere (of place)	*swah*-sah-nuh	*suasana*
atmosphere (of planet)	*aht*-mos-fe-rah	*atmosfera*
aunt	e-*mah(k)* sow-*dah*-ruh	*emak saudara*
autumn	*moo*-sim *loo*-ru(h)	*musim luruh*
avenue	*jah*-lahn	*jalan*
avocado	ah-vo-*kah*-do	*avokado*

B

baby	*bah*-yee	*bayi*
babysitter	pen-*jah*-guh ah-*nah*(k)	*penjaga anak*
back (of body)	*ping*-gahng	*pinggang*
at the back (behind)	dee be-*lah*-kahng	*di belakang*
backpack	behg *sahn*-dahr	*beg sandar*
bad	boo-*ru*(k)	*buruk*
bad (attitude)	see-*kahp*	*sikap*
bad (weather)	coo-*ah*-chuh	*cuaca*
bag	behg	*beg*
baggage	bah-*gah*-see •	*bagasi •*
	bah-rahng-*bah*-rahng	*barang-barang*
baggage claim	*toon*-tu-tahn bah-*gah*-see	*tuntutan bagasi*
bakery	ke-*dai* ro-tee	*kedai roti*
ball (for sport)	*bo*-luh	*bola*
banana	*pee*-sahng	*pisang*
band (music)	*koom*-poo-lahn	*kumpulan*
bandage	kain *pem*-bah-lut	*kain pembalut*

bank	bank	bank
bank clerk	ke-*rah*-nee bank	kerani bank
bar (drinks)	bahr	bar
barber	peng-*gun*-ting *rahm*-but	penggunting rambut
to bargain	*tah*-wahr-me-*nah*-wahr [tah-wahr]	tawar-menawar [tawar]
basket	*bah*-kul	bakul
to bathe	*mahn*-dee	mandi
bathing suit	*bah*-joo re-*nahng*	baju renang
bathroom	*bee*-li(k) air	bilik air
battery	*bah*-te-ree	bateri
to be (see Grammar, page 29)		
beach	*pahn*-tai	pantai
bean	*kah*-chahng	kacang
beautiful (scenery)	*in*-dah(h)	indah
beautiful (woman or object)	chahn-*ti(k)*	cantik
because	se-*bahb* • ke-*rah*-nuh	sebab • kerana
bed	*kah*-til	katil
bedroom	*bee*-li(k) tee-dur	bilik tidur
beef	*dah*-ging *lem*-boo	daging lembu
beer	bir • ah-*ra(k)*	bir • arak
before	se-*be*-lum	sebelum
beggar	pe-*nge*-mis	pengemis
to begin	moo-*luh*-kahn	mulakan
behind	dee be-*lah*-kahng	di belakang
below	dee bah-*wah(h)*	di bawah
beside	dee te-*pee/sahm*-ping	di tepi/samping
best	ter-bai(k)	terbaik
bet	tah-*ru*-hahn	taruhan
better	le-*bi(h)* bai(k)	lebih baik
between	*ahn*-tah-ruh	antara
bicycle	bah-*see*-kahl	basikal
big	be-*sahr*	besar
bill (account)	bil	bil
binoculars	te-ro-pong	teropong
bird	boo-*rung*	burung
birth certificate	soo-*raht* be-rah-*nah(k)*	surat beranak
birthday (cake)	(kehk) *hah*-ree *jah*-dee/*lah*-hir	(kek) hari jadi/lahir
to bite	meng-*gee*-git [*gee*-git]	menggigit [gigit]
bite (dog, insect)	*gee*-gee-tahn	gigitan
black	*hee*-tahm	hitam
blanket	se-*lee*-mut	selimut
to bleed	ber-*dah*-rah(h) [*dah*-rah(h)]	berdarah [darah]
blood	*dah*-rah(h)	darah
blood group	*koom*-poo-lahn *dah*-rah(h)	kumpulan darah
blood pressure	te-*kah*-nahn *dah*-rah(h)	tekanan darah
blood test	*oo*-jee-ahn *dah*-rah(h)	ujian darah
blue	*bee*-roo	biru

English	Pronunciation	Malay
to board (ship, etc)	nai(k)	naik
boarding pass	pahs nai(k)	pas naik
boat	bot • pe-rah-hoo • sahm-pahn	bot • perahu • sampan
body	bah-dahn	badan
boiled water	air mah-sah(k)	air masak
bone	too-lahng	tulang
book	boo-koo	buku
to make a booking	mem-boo-aht tem-pah-hahn	membuat tempahan
bookshop	ke-dai boo-koo	kedai buku
boots	boot • kah-sut boot	but • kasut but
border	sem-pah-dahn	sempadan
bored	bo-sahn	bosan
to borrow	me-min-jahm [pin-jahm]	meminjam [pinjam]
both	ke-doo-uh-doo-uh	kedua-dua

Don't bother.	bee-ahr-lah(h)	Biarlah.

English	Pronunciation	Malay
bottle	bo-tol	botol
bottle opener	pem-boo-kuh bo-tol	pembuka botol
(at the) bottom	(dee) bah-hah-gee-ahn	(di) bahagian
	bah-wah(h) • dee dah-sahr	bawah • di dasar
box (package)	ko-tah(k)	kotak
boy	ah-nah(k) le-lah-kee	anak lelaki
boyfriend	te-mahn le-lah-kee • pah(k)-we	teman lelaki • pakwe (col)
brain	o-tah(k)	otak
bread	ro-tee	roti
break (fracture)	pe-chah	pecah
breakfast	sah-rah-pahn pah-gee	sarapan pagi
to bribe	me-rah-soo-ah(h)	merasuah
bridge	jahm-bah-tahn	jambatan
brilliant	bah-gus	bagus
to bring	mem-bah-wuh [bah-wuh]	membawa [bawa]
broken	pah-tah(h)	patah
older brother	ah-bahng	abang
brown	chok-laht	coklat
bruise	tahn-duh le-bahm	tanda lebam
bucket	bahl-dee	baldi
Buddhist	pe-ngah-nut boo-duh	penganut Buda
bug (insect)	se-rahng-guh	serangga
to build	mem-bee-nuh [bee-nuh]	membina [bina]
building	bah-ngoo-nahn	bangunan
burn	bah-kahr	bakar
... bus	bahs ...	bas ...
city	bahn-dahr	bandar
intercity	ahn-tah-ruh bahn-dahr	antara bandar
bus station	steh-sehn bahs	stesen bas
bus stop	per-hen-tee-ahn bahs	perhentian bas

business	per-nee-ah-*gah*-ahn	*perniagaan*
busker	peng-hi-bur *jah*-lah-nahn	*penghibur jalanan*
busy (place/party)	rah-*mai*	*ramai*
(time)	si-*bu(k)*	*sibuk*
but	te-*tah*-pee	*tetapi*
butter	men-*teh*-guh	*mentega*
butterfly	koo-poo-*koo*-poo	*kupu-kupu*
buttons	boo-*tahng*	*butang*
to buy	mem-be-*lee* [be-*lee*]	*membeli [beli]*

C

cabin	*bee*-li(k)	*bilik*
calm	te-*nahng*	*tenang*
camera (shop)	(ke-*dai*) ka-me-rah	*(kedai) kamera*
to camp	ber-*keh* mah(h) *[keh*-mah(h)]	*berkhema [khemah]*
campsite	kah-*wah*-sahn per-*keh*-mah-han	*kawasan perkhemahan*
can (able)	bo-*leh(h)* • *dah*-paht • *mahm*-poo	*boleh • dapat • mampu*

Can we camp here?
bo-*leh(h)* ta(k) *kah*-mee
ber-*keh*-mah(h) dee *see*-nee?

Boleh tak kami
berkhemah di sini?

to cancel	mem-bah-*tahl*-kah [bah-*tahl*]	*membatalka [batal]*
candle	*lee*-lin	*lilin*
can opener	pem-*boo*-kuh tin	*pembuka tin*
car (park)	tem-*paht* le-*tah(k)* ke-*reh*-tuh	*(tempat letak) kereta*
cards (playing)	down te-*rup*	*daun terup*
careful	ber-*hah*-tee-*hah*-tee	*berhati-hati*
to carry	mem-*bah*-wuh *[bah*-wuh]	*membawa [bawa]*
cash	wahng *too*-nai	*wang tunai*
cashier	joo-roo-*wahng*	*juruwang*
cassette	*kah*-seht	*kaset*
cat	koo-*ching*	*kucing*
cave	*goo*-uh	*gua*
CD	see dee	*CD*
to celebrate	me-*rah*-yuh-kahn *[rah*-yuh]	*merayakan [raya]*
chair	ke-*roo*-see	*kerusi*
chance	ke-*mung*-ki-nahn • pe-loo-*ahng*	*kemungkinan • peluang*
to change	me-noo-*kahr [too*-kahr]	*menukar [tukar]*
changing rooms	*bee*-li(k) too-*kahr* pah-kai-*ahn*	*bilik tukar pakaian*
to chat up	me-*ngoo*-ruht	*mengurat*
cheap	*moo*-rah(h)	*murah*

Cheat!
pe-nee-*poo*!

Penipu!

to check	me-me-*rik*-sah [pe-*rik*-sah]	*memeriksa [periksa]*

check-in (desk)	(kown-ter) pen-dahf-tah-rahn	(kaunter) pendaftaran
cheese	keh-joo	keju
chemist (pharmacy)	fahr-mah-see	farmasi
cheque	chehk	cek
chess	chah-tur	catur
chewing gum	gahm koo-nyah(h)	gam kunyah
chicken	ai-yahm	ayam
child	ah-nah(k)-ah-nah(k) • boo-dah(k)	anak-anak • budak
childminding	pen-jah-gah-ahn ah-nah(k)	penjagaan anak
chilli	chee-lee	cili
chocolate	chok-laht	coklat
to choose	me-mee-li(h) [pee-li(h)]	memilih [pilih]
Christmas Day	hah-ree kris-muhs	Hari Krismas
Christmas Eve	mah-lahm kris-muhs	Malam Krismas
church	ge-reh-juh	gereja
cigarette (papers)	(ker-tahs) ro-ko(k)	(kertas) rokok
clove cigarettes	kreh-teh(k)	kretek
cinema	pahng-gung wai-yahng	panggung wayang
citizenship	ke-wahr-guh-ne-gah-rah-ahn	kewarganegaraan
city	bahn-dahr	bandar
civil rights	ha(k) ah-sah-see mah-noo-see-uh	hak asasi manusia
(1st) class	ke-lahs (per-tah-muh)	kelas (pertama)
(2nd) class	ke-lahs (ke-doo-uh)	kelas (kedua)
to clean	mem-ber-si(h)-kahn [ber-si(h)]	membersihkan [bersih]
cliff	te-bing ting-gee	tebing tinggi
clock	jahm	jam
to close	me-noo-tup [too-tup]	menutup [tutup]
clothing (store)	(ke-dai) pah-kai-ahn	(kedai) pakaian
cloudy	men-dung • be-rah-wahn	mendung • berawan
(night)club	ke-lahb (mah-lahm)	kelab (malam)
coast	ping-gir lowt	pinggir laut
cocaine	ko-kehn	kokain
coconut	ke-lah-puh	kelapa
coffee	ko-pee	kopi
coins	shee-ling	syiling
cold	se-ju(k)	sejuk
(to have a) cold	ah-duh sel-se-muh	ada selsema

It's cold here.
se-ju(k) dee see-nee — *Sejuk di sini.*

---

cold water	air se-ju(k)	air sejuk
college	ko-lehj	kolej
colour	wahr-nuh	warna
to come (arrive)	dah-tahng • tee-buh	datang • tiba
to come from (origin)	be-rah-sahl [ah-sahl]	berasal [asal]

Come on! *joom!*		*Jum!*
comfortable	se-*leh*-suh	selesa
company (friends)	kah-*wahn*-kah-*wahn*	kawan-kawan
(business)	sha-ree-kaht	syarikat
compass	*kom*-pahs	kompas
to complain	me-*ngah*-doo [*ah*-doo]	mengadu [adu]
computer game	per-*mai*-nahn kom-*piu*-ter	permainan komputer
concert	kon-sert	konsert
condom	kon-dom	kondom
to confirm (a booking)	me-nge-*sah(h)*-kahn [sah(h)]	mengesahkan [sah]

Congratulations! *tah(h)-nee-ah(h)!*		*Tahniah!*
constipation	*sem*-be-lit • *kons*-tee-pah-see	sembelit • konstipasi
contraceptive	kon-trah-*sehp*-see	kontrasepsi
to cook	*mah*-sah(k)	masak
cool (temperature)	dee-*ngin*	dingin

Cool! bah-*gus*!		*Bagus!*
corner	soo-*dut* • *pen*-joo-roo	sudut • penjuru
corrupt (adj)	soo-kuh me-ne-*ree*-muh *rah*-soo-ah(h)	suka menerima rasuah
cost (of object/service)	*hahr*-guh • kos	harga • kos
cotton	*kah*-pahs	kapas
cough (n/v)	bah-tu(k)	batuk
to count	me-*ngee*-ruh [*kee*-ruh]	mengira [kira]
country	ne-*gah*-ruh	negara
countryside	kah-*wah*-sahn loo-ahr *bahn*-dahr	kawasan luar bandar
court (legal)	mah(h)-*kah*-mah(h)	mahkamah
(tennis)	*pah*-dahng teh-*nis*	padang tenis
cow	lem-boo	lembu
crab	ke-*tahm*	ketam
crazy	gee-luh	gila
credit card	kahd *kreh*-dit	kad kredit
crossroad	sim-*pahng* jah-lahn	simpang jalan
crowded	pe-*nuh(h)* se-*sa(k)*	penuh sesak
cucumber	tee-mun	timun
cup	chah-*wahn*	cawan
custom (tradition)	*ah*-daht	adat
customs (border)	kahs-tahm	kastam
to cut	me-*mo*-tong [*po*-tong]	memotong [potong]
cute (baby)	cho-*mehl*	comel

D

daily	hah-ree-*ahn*	harian
to dance	ber-*dahn*-sah [*dahn*-sah]	berdansa [dansa]
dangerous	bah-*hah*-yuh	bahaya
dark	ge-*lahp*	gelap
date (appointment)	te-*moo*-jahn-jee	temujanji
(time)	tah-*rikh*	tarikh
date of birth	tah-*rikh* lah-*hir*	tarikh lahir
daughter	ah-*nah*(k) pe-*rem*-pwahn	anak perempuan
dawn (sunrise)	fah-*jahr* (mah-tuh-*hah*-ree ter-*bit*)	fajar (matahari terbit)
day	*hah*-ree	hari
day after tomorrow	*loo*-suh	lusa
day before yesterday	kel-*mah*-rin •	kelmarin •
	doo-uh hah-ree le-*pahs*	dua hari lepas
in (six) days	dah-*lahm* (e-*nahm*) hah-ree	dalam (enam) hari
dead (battery/animal)	*mah*-tee	mati
dead (person)	me-*ning*-gahl *doo*-ni-uh	meninggal dunia
deaf	pe-*kah*(k) • *too*-lee	pekak • tuli
death	ke-*mah*-tee-ahn	kematian
to decide	me-moo-*tus*-kahn [poo-*tus*]	memutuskan [putus]
deep	dah-*lahm*	dalam
deer	*roo*-suh	rusa
deforestation	pe-ne-*bah*-ngahn hoo-*tahn*	penebangan hutan
delay	ke-*leh*-wah-tahn •	kelewatan •
	pe-*nahng*-gu-hahn	penangguhan
delicious	se-*dahp*	sedap
delirious	*gee*-luh	gila
democracy	deh-mo-*krah*-see	demokrasi
demonstration	toon-*ju*(k) pe-rah-*sah*-ahn	tunjuk perasaan
dentist	*dok*-tor *gee*-gee	doktor gigi
to deny	me-nah-*fee*-kahn [nah-*fee*]	menafikan [nafi]
deodorant	di-o-do-rahn	deodoran
depart	be-*rahng*-kaht [*ahng*-kaht]	berangkat [angkat]
department stores	poo-*saht* mem-be-*lee*-be-*lah*(h)	pusat membeli-belah
departure	pe-le-*pah*-sahn	pelepasan
desert	*goo*-run • *pah*-dahng *pah*-sir	gurun • padang pasir
destination	*dehs*-tee-nah-see	destinasi
develop (film)	men-*choo*-chee [*choo*-chee]	mencuci [cuci]
diabetes	*ken*-ching *mah*-nis	kencing manis
diarrhoea	*chi*-rit-bi-rit	cirit-birit
diary	*boo*-koo *chah*-tah-tahn	buku catatan
dictionary	*kah*-mus	kamus
to die (person)	me-*ning*-gahl [*ting*-gahl]	meninggal [tinggal]
different	ber-*beh*-zuh	berbeza
difficult	soo-*sah*(h) • soo-*kahr*	susah • sukar
dinner	*mah*-kahn *mah*-lahm	makan malam
director (of film)	pe-*ngah*-rah(h) (*fee*-lem)	pengarah (filem)

dirty	ko-tor	kotor
disabled	cha-chat	cacat
disco	dis-ko	disko
discount	dis-kown	diskaun
to discover	men-joom-pah-ee [joom-pah]	menjumpai [jumpa]
disease	pe-nyah-kit	penyakit
distance (length)	jah-rah(k)	jarak
to dive	me-nye-lahm [se-lahm]	menyelam [selam]
diving equipment	ah-laht se-lahm	alat selam
dizzy	pe-ning	pening
to do	me-lah-koo-kahn [lah-koo] •	melakukan [laku] •
	mem-boo-aht [boo-aht]	membuat [buat]

What are you doing?
boo-aht ah-puh?

Buat apa?

I didn't do it.
boo-kahn sai-yuh

Bukan saya.

doctor	dok-tor	doktor
documentary	do-kiu-men-tah-ree	dokumentari
dog	ahn-jing	anjing
door	peen-too	pintu
dope (drugs)	dah-dah(h)	dadah
double bed	kah-til ke-lah-min	katil kelamin
drama (arts)	(se-nee) drah-mah	(seni) drama
to dream	ber-mim-pee	bermimpi [mimpi]
dress	bah-joo gown	baju gaun
drink	mee-nu-mahn	minuman
to drink	mee-num	minum
to drive	me-mahn-doo	memandu [pandu]
drivers licence	leh-sehn me-mahn-doo	lesen memandu
drug (prescription)	oo-baht	ubat
(illegal)	dah-dah(h)	dadah
drug dealer	pen-joo-ahl dah-dah(h)	penjual dadah
drums	drahm • gen-dahng	dram • gendang
to be drunk	mah-bu(k)	mabuk
to dry	me-nge-ring-kahn [ke-ring]	mengeringkan [kering]
duck	ee-ti(k)	itik
dysentery	pe-nyah-kit beh-ra(k) dah-rah(h)	penyakit berak darah

E

each	se-tee-ahp • tee-ahp-tee-ahp	setiap • tiap-tiap
ear	te-lee-nguh	telinga
early	ah-wahl	awal

It's early.
mah-si(h) ah-wahl

Masih awal

to earn	men-dah-paht [dah-paht]	mendapat [dapat]

earrings	soo-*bahng* • *ahn*-ting-*ahn*-ting	subang • anting-anting
earth	boo-*mee*	bumi
east	*tee*-mur	timur
easy	se-*nahng* • moo-*dah(h)*	senang • mudah
eat	*mah*-kahn	makan
economy (class)	(ke-*lahs*) ee-ko-no-mee	(kelas) ekonomi
editor	pe-*nyun*-ting	penyunting
to educate	men-dee-*di(k)* [dee-*di(k)*]	mendidik [didik]
education	pen-dee-*di(k)*-kahn	pendidikan
egg	te-*lur*	telur
elections	pee-lee-*hahn*-rah-yuh	pilihanraya
electricity	eh-*lehk*-trik	elektrik
embarrassment	*mah*-loo	malu
embassy	ke-doo-tah-ahn	kedutaan
emergency	ke-che-*mah*-sahn • dah-roo-raht	kecemasan • darurat
employee	pe-*ker*-juh	pekerja
employer	mah-*ji(k)*-kahn	majikan
empty	ko-song	kosong
to end	me-ngah-*khi*-ree [ah-khir]	mengakhiri [akhir]
endangered species	bee-*nah*-tahng *hahm*-pir poo-*pus*	binatang hampir pupus
engine	*ehn*-jin	enjin
engineer	joo-*roo*-te-ruh	jurutera
English	*ing*-ge-ris	Inggeris
to enjoy (oneself)	me-*nik*-mah-tee [*nik*-maht]	menikmati [nikmat]

Enough!
dah(h) *choo*-kup!   Dah cukup!

to enter	mah-*su(k)*	masuk
entertaining	meng-hee-*bur*-kahn [hee-*bur*]	menghiburkan [hibur]
entrance	*jah*-lahn/*peen*-too mah-*su(k)*	jalan/pintu masuk
envelope	sahm-*pul* soo-raht	sampul surat
environment	soo-ah-sah-nuh	suasana
epilepsy	sah-*wahn* bah-bee • eh-pee-lehp-see	sawan babi • epilepsi
equal opportunity	hah(k) *sah*-muh tah-*rahf*	hak sama taraf
equipment	ke-*leng*-kah-pahn [*leng*-kahp]	kelengkapan [lengkap]
essential	pah-*ling pen*-ting	paling penting
European	o-rahng eh-ro-*pah(h)*	orang Eropah
evening	pe-*tahng* • *mah*-lahm	petang • malam
every	se-*tee*-ahp • *tee*-ahp-*tee*-ahp	setiap • tiap-tiap
everyone	se-*moo*-uh o-rahng	semua orang
every day	se-*tee*-ahp *hah*-ree	setiap hari
everything	se-moo-*uh*-nyuh	semuanya
example	chon-*to(h)* • mi-*sah*-lahn	contoh • misalan

For example ...
mi-*sahl*-nyuh .../chon-to(h)-nyuh ...   Misalnya ... /Contohnya ...

excellent	sa-*nghaht* bai(k)/*oo*-lung	sangat baik/ulung
exchange (rate)	(kah-*dahr*) per-too-*kah*-rahn	(kadar) pertukaran

F

| Excuse me. | mah-*ahf*-kahn *sai*-yuh | *Maafkan saya.* |

exhibition	pah-*meh*-rahn	*pameran*
exit	ke-*loo*-ahr	*keluar*
expensive	mah-*hahl*	*mahal*
exploitation	ehks-*ploy*-tah-see	*eksploitasi*
to export	me-*ngehks*-port [ehks-port]	*mengeksport [eksport]*
express mail	mehl *ehks*-prehs	*mel ekspres*
eye	*mah*-tuh	*mata*

F

face	*moo*-kuh	*muka*
factory	kee-*lahng*	*kilang*
to faint	*pehng*-sahn	*pengsan*
to fall	jah-*tuh(h)* • *goo*-gur	*jatuh • gugur*
family	ke-loo-*ahr*-guh	*keluarga*
famous	ter-ke-*nahl*	*terkenal*
fan (machine)	kee-*pahs*	*kipas*
(of a team)	pe-*nyo*-kong [*so*-kong]	*penyokong [sokong]*

| Fantastic! | bah-*gus!* | *Bagus!* |

| far | jow(h) | *jauh* |

| Is it far? | jow(h) tah(k) | *Jauh tak?* |

farm	lah-*dahng* • ke-*bun*	*lading • kebun*
farmer	pe-*tah*-nee	*petani*
fart	*ken*-tut	*kentut*
fast (quick)	che-*paht*	*cepat*
fat	ge-*mu(k)*	*gemuk*
father	ah-*yah(h)* • bah-*puh*	*ayah • bapa*
fault (someone's)	sah-*lah(h)*	*salah*
fear	ke-tah-*ku*-tahn	*ketakutan*
feelings	pe-*rah*-sah-ahn [*rah*-suh]	*perasaan [rasa]*
female (human)	pe-*rem*-pwahn	*perempuan*
(animal)	be-*tee*-nuh	*betina*
festival	pe-rah-*yah*-ahn • *pehs*-tah	*perayaan • pesta*
fever	de-*mahm*	*demam*
few	be-be-*rah*-puh	*beberapa*
fiance(e)	too-*nah*-ngahn	*tunangan*
fiction	*fik*-shen	*fiksyen*
fight	per-gah-*du(h)*-hahn	*pergaduhan*
to fight	ber-gah-*du(h)* [gah-*du(h)*]	*bergaduh [gaduh]*
to fill	me-*ngee*-see [*ee*-see]	*mengisi [isi]*
film (speed)	(ke-*lah*-joo-ahn) *fee*-lem	*(kelajuan) filem*
filtered	ber-*tah*-pis	*bertapis*

English	Pronunciation	Malay
to find	men-*joom*-pah-ee [*joom*-pah]	menjumpai [jumpa]
finger	*jah*-ree	jari
finished	*hah*-bis	habis
fire	ah-*pee*	api
first	per-*tah*-muh	pertama
first-aid kit	ko-*tah(k)* per-to-*lo*-ngahn	kotak pertolongan
	ke-che-*mah*-sahn	kecemasan
first name	*nah*-muh per-*tah*-muh	nama pertama
fish	ee-*kahn*	ikan
to fish	me-*mahn*-ching [*pahn*-ching]	memancing [pancing]
flag	ben-*deh*-ruh	bendera
flea	koo-*too*	kutu
flight	pe-ner-*bah*-ngahn	penerbangan
floor (of room)	*lahn*-tai	lantai
(storey)	*ting*-kaht	tingkat
flower (seller)	(pen-*joo*-ahl) *boo*-nguh	(penjual) bunga
fluent	*fah*-si(h)	fasih
fly	*lah*-laht	lalat
foggy	ber-*kah*-bus	berkabus
to follow (join in)	me-*ngee*-ku-tee [*ee*-kut]	mengikuti [ikut]
food	mah-*kah*-nahn	makanan
food stall	ge-*rai* • wah-*rung*	gerai • warung
foot	*kah*-kee	kaki
football (soccer)	*bo*-luh seh-*pah(k)*	bola sepak
footpath	*jah*-lahn pe-*jah*-lahn kah-*kee*	jalan pejalan kaki
for (purpose)	oon-*tu(k)* • *boo*-aht	untuk • buat
(length of time)	se-*lah*-muh	selama
foreigner	o-rahng *ah*-sing	orang asing
forest	hoo-*tahn*	hutan
forever	se-*lah*-muh-*lah*-muh-nyuh	selama-lamanya
to forget	*loo*-puh	lupa

I forget.
sai-yuh ter-*loo*-puh

Saya terlupa.

Forget about it!
tah(k) ah-puh!

Tak apa!

English	Pronunciation	Malay
to forgive	me-mah-*ahf*-kahn [mah-*ahf*]	memaafkan [maaf]
fork	*gahr*-foo	garfu
fortune teller	too-*kahng* te-*nung*/tee-*li(k)*	tukang tenung/tilik
free (not bound)	beh-*bahs*	bebas
(of charge)	per-*choo*-muh	percuma
to freeze	mem-be-koo [*be*-koo]	membeku [beku]
fresh	se-*gahr*	segar
Friday	*hah*-ree joo-mah-*aht*	hari Jumaat
fried	go-*rehng*	goreng
friend	kah-*wahn* • te-*mahn*	kawan • teman
frog	*kah*-tah(k) • *ko*-do(k)	katak • kodok
from	dah-*ree* • dah-ree-*pah*-duh	dari • daripada

fruit	boo-*ah(h)*-boo-*ah*-hahn	*buah-buahan*
full	pe-*nu(h)*	*penuh*
full (of food)	ke-*nyahng*	*kenyang*
fun	se-ro-no(k)	*seronok*
to have fun	oon-*tu(k)* ber-se-ro-no(k)	*untuk berseronok*
to make fun of	me-*ngeh*-jeh(k)	*mengejek*
funeral	pe-mah-*kah*-mahn	*pemakaman*
funny	lah-*wah(k)* • ke-*lah*-kahr • *loo*-choo	*lawak • kelakar • lucu*
future	mah-*suh* de-*pahn*	*masa depan*

G

game (boardgame)	per-*mai*-nahn	*permainan*
(sport)	per-*mai*-nahn	*permainan*
game show	kuiz	*kuiz*
garage	gah-*rahj*	*garaj*
garden	ke-*bun*	*kebun*
gardens (botanical)	ke-*bun* bo-*tah*-nee	*kebun botani*
garlic	*bah*-wahng poo-*ti(h)*	*bawang putih*
gay	geh	*gay*
general	oo-mum • ahm	*umum • am*
generous	moo-rah(h) hah-tee	*murah hati*
gentle	lem-*but*	*lembut*
geography	ji-o-grah-fee	*geografi*
gift	pem-be-*ree*-ahn [be-*ree*]	*pemberian [beri]*
girl	boo-*dah(k)*/ah-*nah(k)*	*budak/anak*
	pe-*rem*-pwahn	*perempuan*
girlfriend	te-*mahn* wah-*nee*-tah • *mah(k)*-we	*teman wanita • makwe*
give	mem-be-*ree* [be-*ree*]	*memberi [beri]*

Could you give me ...?	
to-long bah-*gee* ...?	Tolong bagi ...?

glass	kah-*chuh*	*kaca*
glasses (eye)	cher-*min* mah-*tuh*	*cermin mata*
glue	gahm	*gam*
to go	per-gee	*pergi*

Let's go.	
joom per-gee	Jum pergi.
We'd like to go to ...	
kah-mee nah(k) per-gee ke ...	Kami nak pergi ke ...
Go straight ahead.	
per-gee te-*rus*	Pergi terus.

to go home	poo-*lahng*	*pulang*
to go out with	ke-*loo*-ahr ber-*sah*-muh	*keluar bersama*
goal	gol	*gol*

goalkeeper	pen-jah-*guh* gol	*penjaga gol*
goat	*kahm*-bing	*kambing*
God (Muslim)	too-*hahn* • ahl-*luh*(h)	*Tuhan • Allah*
gold	e-*mahs*	*emas*
good	bai(k)	*baik*

Good afternoon.
se-*lah*-maht te-ngah-*hah*-ree/pe-*tahng*   *Selamat tengahari/petang*

Goodbye. (speaker leaving)
se-*lah*-maht *ting*-gahl   *Selamat tinggal.*

Goodbye. (speaker staying)
se-*lah*-maht *jah*-lahn   *Selamat jalan.*

Goodbye. (inf)
bai   *Bye.*

Good evening.
se-*lah*-maht pe-*tahng*   *Selamat petang.*

Good morning.
se-*lah*-maht *pah*-gee   *Selamat pagi.*

Good night.
se-*lah*-maht *mah*-lahm   *Selamat malam.*

government	ke-rah-*jah*-ahn	*kerajaan*
gram	grahm	*gram*
grammar	tah-tah-bah-*hah*-suh	*tatabahasa*
grandchild	choo-*choo*	*cucu*
grandfather	dah-*tu(k)* • ah-*tu(k)*	*datuk • atuk*
grandmother	neh-*neh(k)*	*nenek*
grape	*ahng*-gur	*anggur*
grass	*room*-put	*rumput*
grave	koo-*bur*	*kubur*

Great!
bah-*gus*!   *Bagus!*

green	*hee*-jow	*hijau*
grey	ke-*lah*-boo	*kelabu*
ground	tah-*na(h)*	*tanah*
group	*koom*-poo-lahn •	*kumpulan* •
	ke-*lom*-po(k)	*kelompok*
to guess	me-ne-*kuh* [te-*kuh*]	*meneka [teka]*
guest	te-*tah*-moo	*tetamu*
guide (person or audio)	pe-*mahn*-doo	*pemandu*
guidebook	*boo*-koo *pahn*-dwahn	*buku panduan*
guide dog	*ahn*-jing pe-*mahn*-doo	*anjing pemandu*
guided trek	trehk ber-*pahn*-doo	*trek perbandu*
guitar	gee-*tahr*	*gitar*

H

habit	ke-bee-ah-*sah*-ahn	*kebiasaan*
hair	*rahm*-but	*rambut*
hairbrush	be-*rus* rahm-but	*berus rambut*
half	se-te-*ngah(h)*	*setengah*
half a litre	se-te-*ngah(h)* lee-ter	*setengah liter*
to hallucinate	ber-*khah*-yahl [*khah*-yahl]	*berkhayal [khayal]*
ham	*dah*-ging bah-*bee*	*daging babi*
hammock	boo-*ai*-ahn	*buaian*
hand	tah-*ngahn*	*tangan*
handbag	behg tah-*ngahn*	*beg tangan*
handicrafts	*krahf*-tah-ngahn	*kraftangan*
handmade	boo-*ah*-tahn tah-*ngahn*	*buatan tangan*
handsome (male)	*hehnd*-sem • kah-*chah(k)*	*hendsem • kacak*
happy	gem-*bee*-ruh	*gembira*

Happy birthday!
se-*lah*-maht hah-ree jah-dee!   *Selamat hari jadi!*

harbour	pe-lah-*bu*-hahn	*pelabuhan*
hard (not soft)	ke-*rahs*	*keras*
(difficult)	soo-*sah(h)* • soo-*kahr*	*susah • sukar*
harassment	*gahng*-goo-ahn	*gangguan*
hashish	*gahn*-jah • *hah*-sis	*ganja • hasis*
hat	*to*-pee	*topi*
to have	ah-*duh* • mem-*poo*-nyah-ee [*poo*-nyah]	*ada • mempunyai [punya]*

Do you have ...?
ahn-dah ah-*duh* ... tah(k)   *Anda ada ... tak?*

I have ...
sai-yuh mem-*poo*-nyah-ee ...   *Saya mempunyai ...*

he	*dee*-uh	*dia*
head	ke-*pah*-luh	*kepala*
headache	*sah*-kit ke-*pah*-luh	*sakit kepala*
healthy	si-*haht*	*sihat*
to hear	men-de-*ngahr* [de-*ngahr*]	*mendengar [dengar]*
heart	*jahn*-tung	*jantung*
heat	hah-*buh* • *pah*-nahs	*haba • panas*
heavy	be-*raht*	*berat*

Hello.
heh-lo   *Helo.*

helmet	*to*-pee ke-leh-*dahr*	*topi keledar*
to help	me-*no*-long [*to*-long] • mem-*bahn*-too [*bahn*-too]	*menolong [tolong] • membantu [bantu]*

Tolong!

herbs	*her*-bah	*herba*
herbalist (person)	*sin*-seh(h)	*sinseh*
herbalist shop	ke-*dai* oo-*baht* chee-nuh	*kedai ubat Cina*
here	dee *see*-nee	*di sini*
heroin (addict)	(pe-*nah*-gi(h)) *heh*-ro-in	*(penagih) heroin*
high	*teeng*-gee	*tinggi*
high school	se-ko-*lah*(h) me-ne-*ngah*(h)	*sekolah menengah (SM)*
to hike	ber-*jah*-lahn kah-*kee*	*berjalan kaki*
hiking boots	boot *jah*-lahn	*but jalan*
hill	boo-*kit*	*bukit*
Hindu	hin-*doo*	*Hindu*
to hire (rent)	me-*nyeh*-wuh *[seh*-wuh]	*menyewa [sewa]*
historical ruins	run-*tu*-hahn ber-se-*jah*-rah(h)	*runtuhan bersejarah*
history	se-*jah*-rah(h)	*sejarah*
to hitchhike	me-*noom*-pahng	*menumpang*
HIV positive	ehch ai vee *po*-si-tif	*HIV positif*
holiday	coo-*tee*	*cuti*
homeless	pe-*ngahng*-gur	*penganggur*
homosexual	ho-mo-*sehk*-soo-ahl	*homoseksual*
honest	*joo*-jur	*jujur*
honeymoon	*boo*-lahn mah-*doo*	*bulan madu*
horny	gah-*tahl*	*gatal*
horrible	*dah*(h)-shaht • me-nge-*ree*-kahn	*dahsyat* • *mengerikan*
horse (riding)	(pe-*nung*-gah-ngahn) *koo*-duh	*(penunggangan) kuda*
hospital	hos-*pee*-tahl	*hospital*
hospitality	ke-rah-*mah*(h)-tah-*mah*(h)-hahn	*keramah-tamahan*
hot (temperature)	*pah*-nahs	*panas*
(spicy)	pe-*dahs*	*pedas*

It's hot here.
pah-nahs dee *see*-nee

Panas di sini.

to be hot	ke-*pah*-nahs-sahn *[pah*-nahs]	*kepanasan [panas]*
hotel	ho-*tehl*	*hotel*
hour	jahm	*jam*
house	roo-mah(h)	*rumah*
how	*mah*-chahm *mah*-nuh • *bah*-*gai*-mah-nuh	*macam mana* • *bagaimana*

How can I get to ...?
mah-chahm *mah*-nuh sai-yuh
bo-*leh*(h) per-gee ke ...?

Macam mana saya boleh pergi ke ...?

How do you say ... in Malay?
mah-chahm *mah*-nuh chah-*kahp* ...
ah-*lahm* bah-hah-suh me-*lah*-yoo?

Macam mana cakap ... alam bahasa Melayu?

D I C T I O N A R Y

225

How many? (animals) be-*rah*-puh *eh*-kor?	*Berapa ekor?*
How many? (goods) be-*rah*-puh *bah*-nya(k)?	*Berapa banyak?*
How much? be-*rah*-puh?	*Berapa?*

hug	pe-*lu(k)*	peluk
human rights	ha(k) ah-sah-*see* mah-*noo*-si-uh	hak asasi manusia
humid	*lem*-bahb	lembab
a hundred	se-*rah*-tus	seratus
hungry	*lah*-pahr	lapar
to hunt	ber-*boo*-roo [*boo*-roo]	berburu [buru]
husband	soo-*ah*-mee	suami

I

I	*sai*-yuh • *ah*-koo	saya • aku

I'm (Chris). *sai*-yuh (kris)	Saya (Chris).

ice	ais	ais
ice cream	ais krim	ais krim
idea	*ai*-deh-ah	idea
identification	pe-*nge*-nah-lahn	pengenalan
ID	kahd pe-*nge*-nah-lahn	kad pengenalan
idiot	bo-*do(h)*	bodoh
if	kah-*low*	kalau
imagine	mem-bah-*yahng*-kahn	membayangkan
immediately	de-*ngahn* ser-tah-mer-tah	dengan serta-merta
immigration	ee-mee-*greh*-sen	imigresen
important	pen-*ting*	penting

It's (not) important. (tah(k)) pen-*ting*	(Tak) penting.

in	dah-*lahm*	dalam
in a hurry	ter-boo-roo-boo-roo	terburu-buru
in front of	dee de-*pahn*	di depan
included	ter-*mah*-su(k)	termasuk
income tax	choo-kai pen-dah-*pah*-tahn	cukai pendapatan
indigenous	*ahs*-lee	asli
indigestion	sah-kit pe-*rut*	sakit perut
infection	*jahng*-ki-tahn	jangkitan
information	*mahk*-loo-maht • in-for-*mah*-see	maklumat • informasi
to inject	me-nyun-*ti(k)*-kahn	menyuntikkan [suntik]
injection	sun-*ti(k)*-kahn	suntika [suntik]
injury	ke-che-de-*rah*-ahn [che-de-*rah*]	kecederaan [cedera]
insect	se-*rahng*-guh	serangga

inside	dee dah-*lahm*	*di dalam*
instructor	joo-roo-*lah*-ti(h) • goo-*roo*	*jurulatih • guru*
insurance	in-soo-*rahns*	*insurans*
intense	*sah*-ngaht • men-*dah*-lahm	*sangat • mendalam*
interesting	me-*nah*-ri(k)	*menarik*
international	ahn-tah-rah-*bahng*-suh	*antarabangsa*
intersection	per-*sim*-pah-ngahn	*persimpangan*
interview	wah-wahn-*chah*-ruh	*wawancara*
island	poo-*low*	*pulau*
itch	gah-*tahl*	*gatal*
itinerary	jah-*doo*-ahl per-jah-*lah*-nahn	*jadual perjalanan*
ivory	gah-*ding*	*gading*

J

jacket	ja-*keht*	*jaket*
jail	pen-*jah*-ruh	*penjara*
jar	*bo*-tol	*botol*
jeans	jeen	*jean*
jeep	jeep	*jip*
jewellery	*bah*-rahng ke-*mahs*	*barang kemas*
job	pe-ker-*jah*-ahn	*pekerjaan*
joke	lah-*wah*(k) • ke-lah-*kahr*	*lawak • kelakar*
to joke	ber-lah-*wah*(k) [lah-*wah*(k)]	*berlawak [lawak]*
journalist	wahr-*tah*-wahn	*wartawan*
journey	per-jah-*lah*-nahn	*perjalanan*
judge (court)	hah-*kim*	*hakim*
juice	joos	*jus*
jump (across)	lom-*paht*	*lompat*
(high)	lon-*chaht*	*loncat*
jumper (sweater)	*bah*-joo se-*ju*(k)	*baju sejuk*
just one	sah-*too* sah-juh	*satu saja*
justice	ke-ah-*di*-lahn	*keadilan*

K

key	*koon*-chee	*kunci*
keyboard	pah-*pahn* ke-*koon*-chee	*papan kekunci*
kick	*ten*-dah-ngahn [ten-dahng]	*tendangan [tendang]*
kick off	me-moo-*lah*-ee [moo-*luh*]	*memulai [mula]*
to kill	mem-boo-*nuh*(h) [boo-*nuh*(h)]	*membunuh [bunuh]*
kilogram	kee-lo-*grahm*	*kilogram*
kilometre	*ki*-lo-mee-ter	*kilometer*
kind (adj)	bai(k) hah-*tee*	*baik hati*
kindergarten	tah-*dee*-kah	*tadika*
kiss	*chee*-um	*cium*
to kiss	men-*chee*-um [*chee*-um]	*mencium [cium]*
kitchen	dah-*pur*	*dapur*
knee	loo-*tut*	*lutut*

knife	*pee-sow*	*pisau*
to know (someone)	ke-*nahl*	*kenal*
(something)	*tah*-hoo	*tahu*

I (don't) know.
sai-yuh *(tee-dah*(k)) *tah*-hoo

Saya (tidak) tahu.

L

lake	tah-*si*(k)	*tasik*
lamb	*ah*-nah(k) bee-*ree*-bee-*ree*	*anak biri-biri*
land (ground)	tah-*nah(h)*	*tanah*
landscape	lahns-*kahp*	*lanskap*
language	bah-*hah*-suh	*bahasa*
large	loo-*ahs* • be-*sahr*	*luas • besar*
last (final)	te-rah-*khir*	*terakhir*
last month	boo-lahn le-*pahs*	*bulan lepas*
last night	mah-lahm se-*mah*-lahm	*malam semalam*
last week	ming-goo le-*pahs*	*minggu lepas*
last year	tah-hoon le-*pahs*	*tahun lepas*
late (not on time)	leh-*waht* • *lahm*-baht	*lewat • lambat*
later	ke-*moo*-dee-ahn • *nahn*-tee	*kemudian • nanti*
laugh	ge-*lah*(k) • ke-tah-*wuh*	*gelak • ketawa*
laundry (shop)	ke-*dai* do-bee	*kedai dobi*
law	oon-*dahng*-oon-*dahng*	*undang-undang*
lawyer	pe-*gwahm*	*peguam*
laxatives	oo-*baht* pen-*choo*-chee pe-*rut*	*ubat pencuci perut*
lazy	mah-*lahs*	*malas*
leader	pe-*meem*-pin [peem-pin]	*pemimpin [pimpin]*
leak	bo-*chor*	*bocor*
to learn	be-lah-jahr [ah-jahr]	*belajar [ajar]*
leather	koo-*lit*	*kulit*
lecture	koo-lee-*ah(h)* • *shah*-rah-hahn	*kuliah • syarahan*
lecturer	pen-shah-*rah(h)*	*pensyarah*
left, (behind/over)	dee-*ting*-gahl-kahn [ting-gahl]	*ditinggalkan [tinggal]*
left (not right)	ki-ree	*kiri*
left-handed	ki-dahl	*kidal*
left luggage	bah-*gah*-see yahng dee-*ting*-gahl-kahn	*bagasi yang ditinggalkan*
left-wing	sah-*yahp* ki-ree	*sayap kiri*
leg (body)	kah-kee	*kaki*
(in race)	poo-si-ngahn	*pusingan*
lemon	lee-mow nee-pis	*limau nipis*
length	pahn-jahng	*panjang*
lens	kahn-*tuh* • lehn-*sah*	*kanta • lensa*
lesbian	lehs-*bee*-uhn	*lesbian*
less	koo-*rahng*	*kurang*
letter	soo-*raht*	*surat*
library	per-poos-*tah*-kah-ahn	*perpustakaan*

English	Pronunciation	Malay
lice	*koo-*too	kutu
to lie	me-*nee-*poo *[tee-*poo]	menipu [tipu]
life	*hee-*dup	hidup
lift (elevator)	lif	lif
light (electric)	*lahm-*poo	lampu
(not dark)	te-*rahng*	terang
(not heavy)	ri-*ngahn*	ringan
light bulb	*mehn-*tul	mentul
lighter	pe-me-*ti(k)* ah-pee	pemetik api
to like	soo-kuh • *ge-*mahr	suka • gemar
lips	*bee-*bir	bibir
lipstick	*gin-*choo	gincu
to listen	men-*de-*ngahr *[de-*ngahr]	mendengar [dengar]
little (small)	ke-*chil*	kecil
(amount)	se-*dee-*kit	sedikit
to live (life)	*hee-*dup	hidup
(somewhere)	*ting-*gahl	tinggal
liver	*hah-*tee	hati
local	tem-*pah-*tahn	tempatan
local (city) bus	bahs *(bahn-*dahr) tem-*pah-*tahn	bas (bandar) tempatan
location	tem-*paht*	tempat
to lock	me-*ngun-*chee *[koon-*chee]	mengunci [kunci]
long (measurement)	*pahn-*jahng	panjang
(time)	*lah-*muh	lama
long distance	*jah-rah(k)* pahn-jahng	jarak panjang
long-distance bus	bahs *jah-rah(k)* jow(h)	bas jarak jauh
to look	me-*lee-*haht *[lee-*haht]	melihat [lihat]
to look after	men-*jah-*guh *[jah-*guh]	menjaga [jaga]
to look for	men-*chah-*ree *[chah-*ree]	mencari [cari]
loose	*long-*gahr	longgar
to lose (something)	meng-*hee-lahng-*kahn *[hee-lahng]*	menghilangkan [hilang]
loss	ke-kah-*lah-*hahn [kah-*lah(h)]*	kekalahan [kalah]
lost	ter-*se-*saht *[se-*saht]	tersesat [sesat]

Get lost!		
per-*gee-*lah(h)/be-*lah(h)-*lah(h)		Pergilah!/Belahlah!

a lot (quantity)	*bah-*nya(k)	banyak
loud	*bee-*sing	bising
lounge (room)	roo-*ahng tah-*moo	ruang tamu
love	kah-*si(h)* • *chin-*tuh • *sah-*yahng	kasih • cinta • sayang

I love you.		
*sai-*yuh me-nyin-*tah-ee* moo		Saya menyintai mu.

lover	ke-*kah-*si(h)	kekasih
low	ren-*dah(h)*	rendah
loyal	se-*tee-*uh	setia
luck	nah-*sib*	nasib
lucky	be-*roon-*tung	beruntung
luggage	bah-*gah-*see	bagasi

L

D
I
C
T
I
O
N
A
R
Y

luggage lockers	ahl-*mah*-ree bah-*gah*-see	*almari bagasi*
lunch	*mah*-kahn te-ngah-*hah*-ree	*makan tengahari*
lunchtime	*wak*-too mah-kahn te-ngah-*hah*-ree	*waktu makan tengahari*
luxury	ke-meh-*wah*-hahn	*kemewahan*

M

machine	me-*sin*	*mesin*
mad (angry)	*mah*-rah(h)	*marah*
made (of)	dee-per-*boo*-aht (dah-ree-*pah*-duh)	*diperbuat (daripada)*
magazine	mah-jah-*lah*(h)	*majalah*
mail	mehl	*mel*
main ...	... oo-*tah*-muh	*... utama*
road	jah-lahn	*jalan*
square	dah-*tah*-rahn	*dataran*
majority	mah-*jo*-ree-tee	*majoriti*
to make	mem-*boo*-aht *[boo*-aht]	*membuat [buat]*
make-up	*ah*-laht so-*leh*(k)-kahn	*alat solekan*
malaria	mah-lah-*ree*-ah	*malaria*
Malay	bah-*hah*-suh me-*lah*-yoo	*Bahasa Melayu*

I (don't) speak Malay.
sai-yuh (tee-dah(k)) *tah*-hoo *chah*-kahp
bah-*hah*-suh me-*lah*-yoo
Saya (tidak) tahu cakap bahasa Melayu

Malaysia	mah-*lay*-see-ah	*Malaysia*
male (person)	le-*lah*-kee	*lelaki*
(animal)	*jahn*-tahn	*jantan*
man	le-*lah*-kee	*lelaki*
manager	pe-*ngoo*-rus	*pengurus*
mango	*mang*-guh	*mangga*
many	bah-*nya*(k)	*banyak*
map	pe-*tuh*	*peta*

Can you show me ... on the map?
to-long toon-*joo*(k)-kahn ... dee pe-*tuh?*
Tolong tunjukkan ... di peta?

market (night)	pah-*sahr (mah*-lahm)	*pasar (malam)*
marriage	per-*kah*(h)-wi-nahn	*perkahwinan*
to marry	ber-*kah*(h)-win • ber-*nee*-kah(h)	*berkahwin • bernikah*
mask (face)	to-*pehng*	*topeng*
massage	oo-ru-tahn	*urutan*
to massage	me-*ngoo*-rut *[oo*-rut]	*mengurut [urut]*
mat	*tee*-kahr	*tikar*
matches	*mahn*-chis	*mancis*
material (for clothing)	kain	*kain*

It doesn't matter.
ta(k) *ah*-puh
Tak apa.

What's the matter?
ke-*nah*-puh be-*gee*-nee?
Kenapa begini?

mattress	tee-*lahm*	tilam
may (can)	bo-*leh*(h)	boleh
maybe	*moong*-kin	mungkin
meaning	*mahk*-nuh • *er*-tee	makna • erti
meat	*dah*-ging	daging
mechanic	me-*ka*-nik	mekanik
medicine	oo-*baht*	ubat
meditation	tah-*fah*-kur	tafakur
to meet	ber-*te*-moo [*te*-moo]	bertemu [temu]
meeting	per-te-*moo*-ahn • me-*shoo*-ah-raht	pertemuan • mesyuarat
menthol (cigarettes)	(*ro*-ko(k)) *mehn*-tol	(rokok) mentol
menu	*meh*-noo	menu
message	pe-*sah*-nahn	pesanan
metal	lo-*gahm*	logam
metre	*mee*-ter	meter
midnight	te-*ngah*(h) *mah*-lahm	tengah malam
migraine	*mai*-grehn	migraine
milk	soo-*soo*	susu
millimetre	*mi*-lee-*mee*-ter	milimeter
million	joo-*tuh*	juta
mineral water	air mi-*ne*-rahl	air mineral
(with/without gas)	(ber-*kar*-bo-naht/bee-*ah*-suh)	(berkarbonat/biasa)
minibus	bahs mee-*nee*	bas mini
minute	*mi*-nit	minit

Just a minute.
se-ke-*jahp*   Sekejap.

in (five) minutes
dah-*lahm* (*lee*-muh) *mi*-nit lah-*gee*   dalam (lima) minit lagi

mirror	*cher*-min	cermin
to miss (feel absence)	me-*rin*-doo-ee [*rin*-doo]	merindui [rindu]
Miss	chi(k)	Cik
mistake	ke-see-lah-*pahn* • ke-sah-*lah*-hahn	kesilapan • kesalahan
misunderstanding	sah-*lah*(h) fah-*hahm*	salah faham
to mix	men-cham-*pur*-kahn [chahm-*pur*]	mencampurkan [campur]
mobile phone	teh-*leh*-fon *bim*-bit	telefon bimbit
modem	mo-*dem*	modem
moisturising cream	krim pe-*lem*-bahb	krim pelembab
monastery	bee-*ah*-ruh	biara
Monday	hah-ree ees-*nin*	hari Isnin
money	*doo*-it • *wahng*	duit • wang
monk	bee-*ah*-rah-wahn	biarawan
monkey	mo-*nyeht* • ke-*ruh*	monyet • kera
month (this)	boo-*lahn* (ee-*nee*)	bulan (ini)
moon	boo-*lahn*	bulan
more	le-*bi*(h)	lebih
morning	*pah*-gee	pagi
Moslem	o-*rahng* ees-*lahm*	orang Islam

mosque	*mahs*-jid	*masjid*
mosquito (net)	nyah-mu(k) (ke-*lahm*-boo)	*nyamuk (kelambu)*
most (the)	(yahng) *pah*-ling	*(yang) paling*
mother	e-*mah(k)* • ee-boo	*emak/ibu*
mother-in-law	ee-boo mer-*too*-uh	*ibu mertua*
motorboat	bot ber-*mo*-tor	*bot bermotor*
motorcycle	mo-to-see-kahl	*motosikal*
motorway (tollway)	*jah*-lahn *ber*-tol	*jalan bertol*
mountain	*goo*-nung	*gunung*
mountain bike	bah-see-kahl goo-nung	*basikal gunung*
mountaineering	men-*dah*-kee goo-nung	*mendaki gunung*
mountain hut	pon-*do(k)*	*pondok*
mountain path	*jah*-lahn goo-nung	*jalan gunung*
mountain range	per-goo-*nu*-ngahn	*pergunungan*
mouth	*moo*-lut	*mulut*
movie	*fee*-lem	*filem*
Mr	en-*chi(k)* • *too*-ahn	*Encik • Tuan*
Mrs	pwahn	*Puan*
much	*bah*-nya(k)	*banyak*
mud	*loom*-pur	*lumpur*
muscle	o-*tot*	*otot*
museum	moo-*zee*-um	*muzium*
music	*moo*-zik	*muzik*
musician	pe-*main moo*-zik	*pemain muzik*
Muslim	o-rahng ees-lahm	*orang Islam*
must	*mes*-tee • *hah*-rus	*mesti • harus*

N

name	*nah*-muh	*nama*

> **What's your name?**
> see-*ah*-puh *nah*-muh *ahn*-dah
>
> *Siapa nama anda?*

nappy	kain *lahm*-pin	*kain lampin*
nappy rash	roo-*ahm bah*-yee	*ruam bayi*
nationality	*bahng*-suh	*bangsa*
national park	tah-*mahn* ne-*gah*-ruh	*taman negara*
nature	ah-*lahm* se-moo-luh-*jah*-dee	*alam semulajadi*
nausea	moo-*ahl*	*mual*
near	de-*kaht*	*dekat*

> **Is it near here?**
> de-*kaht*-kuh dah-*ree* see-*nee*?
>
> *Dekatkah dari sini?*

necessary	per-*loo*	*perlu*
necklace	*rahn*-tai	*rantai*
need	per-*loo*	*perlu*
needle	*jah*-rum	*jarum*
(sewing, syringe)		

English	Pronunciation	Malay
neighbour	*jee-rahn*	*jiran*
nervous	*che-mahs* • *coo-ah(k)*	*cemas* • *cuak*
never	*tee-dah(k) per-nah(h)*	*tidak pernah*
never mind	*ta(k) ah-puh*	*tak apa*
new	*bah-roo*	*baru*
news	*be-ree-tuh*	*berita*
newspaper	*soo-raht kah-bahr*	*surat khabar*
next	*yahng be-ree-kut-nyah* • *de-pahn*	*yang berikutnya* • *depan*

Next time.
lain kah-lee

Lain kali.

next to	*dee se-be-lah(h)*	*di sebelah*
nickname	*nah-muh pang-gi-lahn*	*nama panggilan*
night	*mah-lahm*	*malam*
Saturday night	*sab-too mah-lahm*	*Sabtu malam*
no	*tee-dah(k)*	*tidak*
noise	*boo-nyee*	*bunyi*
noisy	*bee-sing*	*bising*
none	*tee-ah-duh*	*tiada*
noodles	*mee*	*mee*
noon	*te-ngah-hah-ree*	*tengahari*
north	*oo-tah-ruh*	*utara*
nose	*hee-dung*	*hidung*
not	*boo-kahn*	*bukan*
not yet	*be-lum lah-gee*	*belum lagi*
notebook	*boo-koo chah-tah-tahn*	*buku catatan*
nothing	*tee-dah(k) ah-puh-ah-puh*	*tidak apa-apa*
novel (book)	*no-vel*	*novel*
now	*se-kah-rahng*	*sekarang*
nuclear energy	*te-nah-guh noo-klee-er*	*tenaga nuklear*
nuclear testing	*oo-jee-ahn noo-klee-er*	*ujian nuklear*
nude	*bo-gehl* • *te-lah-njahng*	*bogel* • *telanjang*
number	*nom-bor*	*nombor*
nun	*bee-ah-rah-wah-tee*	*biarawati*
nurse	*joo-roo-rah-waht*	*jururawat*
nut (food)	*kah-chahng*	*kacang*

O

occupation	*pe-ker-jah-ahn*	*pekerjaan*
ocean	*low-tahn*	*lautan*
offer	*tah-wah-rahn*	*tawaran*
office worker	*pe-ker-juh pe-jah-baht*	*pekerja pejabat*
offside	*of-said*	*offside*
often	*se-ring* • *ke-rahp*	*sering* • *kerap*
oil (cooking)	*min-ya(k) mah-sah(k)*	*minyak masak*

OK.		
oh-kay/bai(k)		OK./Baik.

old (person)	*too*-uh	tua
(building)	*lah*-muh	lama
older sister	kah-*kah(k)*	kakak
older brother	ah-*bahng*	abang
Olympic Games	ke-*soo*-kah-nahn o-*lim*-pik	Kesukanan Olimpik
on (location)	dee	di
on time	te-*paht* pah-duh mah-*sah*-nyuh	tepat pada masanya
once	se-*kah*-lee	sekali
once again	se-*kah*-lee lah-*gee*	sekali lagi
one-way (ticket)	(tee-*keht*) se-*hah*-luh	(tiket) sehala
onion	*bah*-wahng	bawang
only	hah-*nyuh*	hanya
open	*boo*-kuh	buka
to open	mem-*boo*-kuh *[boo*-kuh]	membuka [buka]
operation	o-pe-*rah*-see	operasi
(telephone) operator	o-pe-*ray*-tor (teh-*leh*-fon)	operator (telefon)
opinion	pen-*dah*-paht	pendapat
opposite	lah-*wahn*	lawan
or	ah-*tow*	atau
oral	lee-*sahn*	lisan
orange (colour)	o-*rehn* • *jeeng*-gah	oren • jingga
(food)	o-*rehn*	oren
orchestra	or-*kehs*-truh	orkestra
to order	me-*nehm*-pah(h) *[tehm*-pah(h)]	menempah [tempah]
to organise	me-*ngah*-tur *[ah*-tur]	mengatur [atur]
orgasm	or-*gahs*-mah	orgasma
original	*ahs*-lee	asli
other	lain	lain
outgoing	rah-*mah(h)*-tah-*mah(h)*	ramah-tamah
outside	*loo*-ahr	luar
over (above)	dee ah-*tahs*	di atas
overdose	ter-*lah*-loo bah-*nyu*(k)	terlalu banyak
	mah-kahn oo-baht	makan ubat
over here	dee *see*-nee	di sini
over there	dee *sah*-nuh	di sana
to we	ber-*hoo*-tahng	berhutang
owner	pe-*mee*-li(k)	pemilik
oxygen	ok-*see*-jen	oksigen

P

package	*boong*-ku-sahn	bungkusan
padlock	me-*mahng*-guh •	memangga •
	mang-guh	mangga (col)
pain	*sah*-kit	sakit
pain in the neck	me-nyoo-*sah(h)*-kahn	menyusahkan

painful	me-nyah-*kit*-kahn	menyakitkan
painkillers	oo-*baht* tah-*hahn sah*-kit	ubat tahan sakit
painter (artist)	pe-*loo*-kis • *ahr*-tis • se-*nee*-mahn	pelukis • artis • seniman
painting (activity)	me-*loo*-kis	melukis
(picture)	loo-*ki*-sahn	lukisan
pair (a couple)	se-*pah*-sahng	sepasang
palace	ees-tah-nuh	istana
pap smear	smir	smir
paper	ker-*tahs*	kertas
paraplegic	*loom*-pu(h) kah-kee	lumpuh kaki
parents	ee-boo bah-puh • o-rahng *too*-uh	ibu bapa • orang tua
parliament	*pahr*-lee-men	parlimen
part (n)	bah-*hah*-gee-ahn	bahagian
party (fiesta)	*pehs*-tuh	pesta
(political)	*pahr*-tee	parti
to pass (give)	mem-*be*-ree [be-ree]	memberi [beri]
passenger	pe-*noom*-pahng	penumpang
passport (number)	(*nom*-bor) *pahs*-port	(nombor) pasport
past (before)	dah-*hoo*-loo • yahng *lah*-loo	dahulu • yang lalu
path	*jah*-lahn ke-*chil* • lo-*rong*	jalan keci • lorong
patient (adj)	sah-*bahr*	sabar
to pay	mem-*bah*-yahr [bah-yahr]	membayar [bayar]
payment	bah-*yah*-rahn	bayaran
peace	ah-*mahn* • dah-*mai*	aman • damai
peak (of mountain)	*pun*-chah(k)	puncak
pedestrian	pe-*jah*-lahn *kah*-kee	pejalan kaki
pen	pehn	pen
penalty	hoo-*koo*-mahn	hukuman
penis	zah-*kahr*	zakar
penknife	*pee*-sow *lee*-paht	pisau lipat
pensioner	pe-*sah*-ruh	pesara
people	o-rahng	orang
perfect	sem-*pur*-nuh	sempurna
performance	per-toon-*ju(k)*-kahn	pertunjukan
perhaps	*moong*-kin	mungkin
period pain	*sah*-kit haid	sakit haid
permission	ee-zin	izin
permit	per-*mit*	permit
person	o-rahng	orang
personality	pe-ree-*bah*-dee	peribadi
to perspire	ber-pe-*lu(h)* [pe-*lu(h)*]	berpeluh [peluh]
petrol	*peh*-trol • *min*-yah(k)	petrol • minyak
pharmacy	fahr-*mah*-see	farmasi
phone book	*boo*-koo teh-*leh*-fon	buku telefon
phone box	teh-*leh*-fon ah-wahm	telefon awam
phonecard	kahd teh-*leh*-fon	kad telefon
photograph	*gahm*-bahr • *fo*-to	gambar • foto

May I take a photograph?
bo-leh(h) sai-yuh ahm-bil
gahm-bahr/fo-to?

Boleh saya ambil
gambar/foto?

photograph	*gahm-bahr • fo-to*	gambar • foto
photographer	joo-roo-*gahm*-bahr	jurugambar
photography	se-*nee fo*-to	senifoto
to pick up	me-*ngahm*-bil [*ahm*-bil]	mengambil [ambil]
pickpocket	pe-nye-*lu(k)* sah-*koo*	penyeluk saku
picture	*gahm*-bahr	gambar
piece	*po*-tong	potong
pig	*bah*-bee	babi
pill	pil	pil
the Pill	oo-*baht* pen-che-*gah(h)* hah-mil	ubat pencegah hamil
pillow	*bahn*-tahl	bantal
pillowcase	sah-*rung bahn*-tahl	sarung bantal
pineapple	*nah*-nahs • *neh*-nahs	nanas • nenas
pink	meh-*rah(h) jahm*-boo	merah jambu
pipe (plumbing)	paip	paip
piss	ken-*ching*	kencing
to piss	boo-*ahng* air ke-*chil*	buang air kecil
place	tem-*paht*	tempat
place of birth	tem-*paht* ke-la-*hi*-rahn	tempat kelahiran
plain (adj)	se-*der*-hah-nuh	sederhana
plan	pe-*lahn*	pelan
planet	plah-*neht*	planet
plant	tah-*nah*-mahn	tanaman
plastic	*plahs*-tik	plastik
plate	*peeng*-gahn	pinggan
plateau	dah-*tah*-rahn *teeng*-gee	dataran tinggi
play (theatre)	*drah*-mah	drama
to play (a game, music)	ber-*main* [main]	bermain [main]
(cards)	main kahd • main down te-*rup*	main kad • main daun terup
player	pe-*main*	pemain
please	see-*lah*-kahn • *to*-long	silakan • tolong
plug (electricity)	pluhg	plug
plus	*tahm*-bah(h)	tambah
pocket	po-*keht* • sah-*koo* • ko-*cheh(k)*	poket • saku • kocek
poetry	sah-*jah(k)* • poo-ee-*see*	sajak • puisi
poisonous	be-*rah*-chun	beracun
poker (the game)	*po*-ker	poker
police	*po*-lis	polis
political speech	oo-*chah*-pahn • pee-*dah*-to po-*lee*-tik	ucapan/pidato politik
politicians	*ah*-lee po-*lee*-tik	ahli politik
pollen	de-*boo*-nguh	debunga
pollution	pen-che-*mah*-rahn	pencemaran
pool (swimming)	ko-*lahm* re-*nahng*	kolam renang
(game)	per-*mai*-nahn bee-*lee*-uhrd	permainan biliard

poor	mis-kin	miskin
popular	po-piu-luhr	popular
pork	dah-ging bah-bee	daging babi
port (harbour)	pe-lah-bu-hahn	pelabuhan
portrait sketcher	pe-loo-kis po-treht	pelukis potret
possible	bo-leh(h)	boleh

It's not possible.
tee-dah(k) bo-leh(h)/dee-lah-rahng   Tidak boleh./Dilarang.

postage	bah-yah-rahn pos	bayaran pos
postcard	pos-kahd	poskad
postcode	pos-kod	poskod
poster	pos-ter	poster
post office	pe-jah-baht pos	pejabat pos
pot (cooking)	pe-ree-u(k)	periuk
(dope)	gahn-jah	ganja
potato	ken-tahng	kentang
pottery	se-nee tem-bee-kahr	seni tembikar
poverty	ke-mees-ki-nahn	kemiskinan
power	koo-ah-suh	kuasa
prayer	do-ah • sem-bah-yahng	doa • sembahyang
prayer book	boo-koo do-ah	buku doa
to prefer	le-bi(h) soo-kuh	lebih suka
pregnant	hah-mil • me-ngahn-dung	hamil • mengandung
prehistoric art	se-nee prah-se-jah-rah(h)	seni prasejarah
premenstrual tension	pee em es	PMS
to prepare	me-nye-dee-ah-kahn [se-dee-uh]	menyediakan [sedia]
prescription	ah-rah-hahn dok-tor ber-too-lis	arahan doktor bertulis
present (time)	se-kah-rahng • kee-nee	sekarang • kini
(gift)	pem-be-ree-ahn [be-ree] • hah-dee-ah(h)	pemberian [beri]• hadiah
presentation	pe-nyahm-pai-ahn [sahm-pai]	penyampaian [sampai]
presenter (TV, etc)	pe-nyahm-pai	penyampai
president	preh-see-den	presiden
pressure	te-kah-nahn	tekanan
pretty (adj)	chahn-ti(k) • een-dah(h) • lah-wah	cantik • indah • lawa
to prevent	men-che-gah(h)	mencegah
price (of goods or service)	hahr-guh	harga
pride	ke-bahng-gah-ahn [bahng-guh]	kebanggaan [bangga]
priest (Catholic, Protestant)	pah-de-ree	paderi
prime minister	per-dah-nuh men-te-ree	perdana menteri
print (artwork)	cheh-ta(k)-kahn (kar-yah se-nee)	cetakan (karya seni)
prison	pen-jah-ruh	penjara
prisoner	bahn-doo-ahn	banduan
private	per-sen-dee-ree-ahn • pe-ree-bah-dee	persendirian • peribadi
private hospital	hos-pee-tahl swahs-tah	hospital swasta
problem	mah-sah-ah-lah(h)	masalah

to produce	meng-*hah*-sil-kahn *[hah*-sil]	menghasilkan [hasil]
producer (film)	pe-*ner*-bit [ter-*bit*] (*fee*-lem)	penerbit [terbit] (filem)
profession	pe-ker-*jah*-ahn	pekerjaan
program (TV)	rahn-*chah*-ngahn	rancangan
projector	pro-*jehk*-tor	projektor
promise	*jahn*-jee	janji
proposal	chah-*dah*-ngahn • *ahn*-joo-rahn	cadangan • anjuran
prostitute	pe-*lah*-chur • soon-*dahl*	pelacur • sundal
to protect	me-*lin*-du-ngee *[lin*-dung]	melindungi [lindung]
protected forest	hoo-*tahn* sim-*pahn*	hutan simpan
protected species	hai-*wahn* ter-*leen*-dung	haiwan terlindung
to protest	mem-bahn-*tah(h)* [bahn-*tah(h)*]	membantah [bantah]
public toilet	tahn-*dahs* ah-*wahm*	tandas awam
to pull	me-*nah*-ri(k) *[tah*-ri(k)]	menarik [tarik]
pump	pahm	pam
puncture	ke-bo-*cho*-rahn	kebocoran
to punish	meng-*hoo*-kum *[hoo*-kum]	menghukum [hukum]
puppet (leather)	*(koo*-lit) bo-neh-kah	(kulit) boneka
(wooden)	*pah*-tung kah-yoo	patung kayu
puppy	*ah*-nah(k) *ahn*-jing	anak anjing
pure	*moor*-nee • soo-*chee* • too-*lehn*	murni • suci • tulen
purple	oo-*ngoo*	ungu
purse	*dom*-peht • puhrs	dompet • purse
to push	me-no-*lah(k)* [to-*lah(k)*]	menolak [tolak]
to put	me-le-*tah(k)*-kahn [le-*tah(k)*]	meletakkan [letak]

Q

qualifications	ke-lah-*yah(k)*-kahn	kelayakan
quality	moo-*too* • kwah-lee-*tee*	mutu • kualiti
quantity	joom-*lah(h)*	jumlah
quarantine	kwah-*rahn*-teen	kuarantin
quarter	soo-*koo*	suku
question	per-*tah*-nyuh-ahn • so-*ah*-lahn	pertanyaan • soalan
to question	ber-*tah*-nyuh [tah-*nyuh*]	bertanya [tanya]
queue	be-*rah*-tur	beratur
quick	che-*paht* • pahn-*tahs*	cepat • pantas
quickly	de-*ngahn* che-*paht*/pahn-*tahs*	dengan cepat/pantas
quiet	se-*nyahp* • soo-*nyee* • se-*pee*	senyap • sunyi • sepi
quinine	kui-*nin*	kuinin
to quit	ber-*hen*-tee *[hen*-tee]	berhenti [henti]

R

race (breed)	*bahng*-suh • kowm	bangsa • kaum
(sport)	per-*loom*-bah-ahn	perlumbaan
racism	rah-*sis*-mah	rasisme
racquet	rah-*keht*	raket
radiator	rah-*dee*-ah-tor	radiator

English	Pronunciation	Malay
railroad	*jah*-lahn ke-reh-tah-*ah*-pee	jalan keretapi
railway station	*steh*-sehn ke-reh-tah-*ah*-pee	stesen keretapi
rain	*hoo*-jahn	hujan

It's raining heavily.

hoo-*jahn* le-*baht*   Hujan lebat.

English	Pronunciation	Malay
rally (demonstration)	per-*him*-pu-nahn	perhimpunan
rape	pe-ro-go-lahn [ro-*gohl*]	perogolan [rogol]
rare (uncommon)	jah-*rahng*	jarang
rash	roo-*ahm*	ruam
rat	tee-*kus*	tikus
rate of pay	kah-*dahr* pem-bah-*yah*-rahn	kadar pembayaran
raw (food)	men-*tah(h)*	mentah
razor	pee-sow *choo*-kur	pisau cukur
to read	mem-*bah*-chuh [*bah*-chuh]	membaca [baca]
ready	se-dee-*uh* • see-*ahp*	sedia • siap
to realise	me-nye-*dah*-ree [se-*dahr*]	menyedari [sedar]
reason	se-*bahb* • ah-lah-sahn	sebab • alasan
receipt	re-*sit*	resit
to receive	me-ne-*ree*-muh [te-ree-muh]	menerima [terima]
recent	bah-*roo* ber-*lah*-koo	baru berlaku
to recognise	ke-*nahl* • me-ngah-*koo*-ee [ah-*koo*-ee]	kenal • mengakui [akui]
to recommend	me-nge-*shor*-kahn [shor]	mengesyorkan [syor]
recording	rah-*kah*-mahn	rakaman
to recycle	meng-goo-*nah*-kahn kem-*bah*-lee	menggunakan kembali
red	meh-*rah(h)*	merah
referee	pe-*ngah*-dil	pengadil
reforestation	pe-nah-*nah*-mahn hoo-*tahn* se-*moo*-luh	penanaman hutan semula
refrigerator	pe-*tee* se-*ju(k)*	peti sejuk
refugee	pe-lah-*ree*-ahn	pelarian
to refund	pe-ngem-*bah*-lee-ahn wahng	pengembalian wang
to refuse	me-no-*la(k)* [to-*la(k)*] • eng-*gahn*	menolak[tolak] • enggan
region	kah-*wah*-sahn • dah-eh-rah(h)	kawasan • daerah
registered mail	soo-*raht* ber-*dahf*-tahr	surat berdaftar
to regret	me-nye-*sahl* [se-*sahl*]	menyesal [sesal]
relationship	hoo-*bu*-ngahn	hubungan
to relax	be-reh-*haht* [reh-*haht*]	berehat [rehat]
religion	ah-*gah*-muh	agama
religious	ke-ah-*gah*-mah-ahn • be-ree-*mahn*	keagamaan • beriman
to remember	ee-*ngaht*	ingat
remote	jow(h) • ter-pen-*chil*	jauh • terpencil
to rent	me-*nyeh*-wuh [*seh*-wuh]	menyewa [sewa]
to repair	mem-per-*bai*-kee	memperbaiki [baik]
repeat	me-ngoo-*lah*-ngee [oo-*lahng*]	mengulangi [ulang]
reply	jah-*wah*-pahn • bah-lah-*sahn*	jawapan • balasan
to reply	men-jah-*wahb* [jah-*wahb*]	menjawab [jawab]

to report	me-lah-*por*-kahn [lah-*por*]	melaporkan [lapor]
republic	ree-*puhb*-lik	republik
reservation	tem-*pah(h)*-hahn	tempahan
to reserve	me-nem-*pah(h)* [tem-*pah(h)*]	menempah [tempah]
respect	hor-*maht*	hormat
responsibility	tang-gung-*jah*-wahb	tanggungjawab
rest (relaxation)	reh-*haht*	rehat
(what's left)	*see*-suh	sisa
to rest	be-reh-*haht* [reh-*haht*]	berehat [rehat]
restaurant	rehs-*to*-rahn	restoran
result	*hah*-sil • ah-*kee*-baht	hasil • akibat
resumé	reh-siu-*meh* • see-vee	resume • CV
return	kem-*bah*-lee	kembali
return ticket	ti-*keht* per-gee *bah*-li(k)	tiket pergi balik
review	pe-me-*rik*-sah-ahn kem-*bah*-lee	pemeriksaan kembali
rheumatism	pe-*nyah*-kit se-*ngahl*-se-*ngahl* too-*lahng*	penyakit sengal-sengal tulang
rhythm	ren-*tah(k)*	rentak
rice (cooked)	nah-*see*	nasi
(uncooked)	be-*rahs*	beras
rich (food)	sah-*ngaht* le-*mah(k)*	sangat lemak
(wealthy)	kah-*yuh*	kaya
to ride (bike, horse)	me-*nai(k)*-kee [nai(k)]	menaiki [naik]
(bus, car,	me-*noong*-gahng	menunggang
plane, train)	*[toong*-gahng]	[tunggang]
right (not left)	kah-*nahn*	kanan
(correct)	be-*tul*	betul

You're right.
ahn-dah be-*tul*   Anda betul.

right now	se-*kah*-rahng *joo*-guh	sekarang juga
right-wing	sah-*yahp kah*-nahn	sayap kanan
ring (on finger)	*chin*-chin	cincin
(sound)	boo-*nyee*	bunyi

I'll give you a ring.
sai-yuh teh-*leh*-fon *ahn*-dah nahn-*tee*   Saya telefon anda nanti.

ripe	*mah*-sah(k)	masak
rip-off	ter-*lah*-loo mah-*hahl*	terlalu mahal
risk	ree-*see*-ko	risiko
river	soo-*ngai*	sungai
road	*jah*-lahn	jalan
road map	pe-*tuh jah*-lahn	peta jalan
roasted	*pahng*-gahng	panggang
to rob	me-rom-*pa(k)* [rom-*pa(k)*]	merompak [rompak]
rock	bah-*too*	batu
rock climbing	pen-dah-*kee*-ahn te-*bing* bah-*too*	pendakian tebing batu
rock group	koom-*pu*-lahn rok	kumpulan rock
rolling	ber-goo-*ling*	berguling

romance	per-*chin*-tah-ahn	*percintaan*
roof	ah-*tahp* • *boom*-bung	*atap* • *bumbung*
room (number)	(*nom*-bor) *bee*-li(k)	*(nombor) bilik*
rope	tah-*lee*	*tali*
rotten	boo-*su(k)* • ro-*sah(k)*	*busuk* • *rosak*
round (shape)	boo-*laht*	*bulat*
(at the) roundabout	(dee) boo-*lah*-tahn	*(di) bulatan*
to row	men-*dah*-yung	*mendayung*
rubbish	sahm-*pah(h)*	*sampah*
rug	per-*mai*-dah-nee	*permaidani*
ruins	run-*tu*-hahn	*runtuhan*
rules	pe-*rah*-tu-rahn	*peraturan*
run	lah-*ree*	*lari*

S

sad	se-*di(h)*	*sedih*
safe (secure)	se-*lah*-maht	*selamat*
safe (vault)	pe-*tee* be-*see*	*peti besi*
safe sex	sehks se-*lah*-maht	*seks selamat*
sail	lah-*yahr*	*layar*
sailor	ah-*nah(k) kah*-pahl	*anak kapal*
saint	o-rahng soo-*chee*	*orang suci*
(on) sale	joo-ah-*lahn* moo-*ra(h)*	*jualan murah*
sales department	bah-*hah*-gee-ahn pen-joo-ah-lahn	*bahagian penjualan*
salt	gah-*rahm*	*garam*
salty	*mah*-sin	*masin*
same	*sah*-muh	*sama*
sand	*pah*-sir	*pasir*
sandals	se-*lee*-pahr	*selipar*
sanitary napkins	too-*ah*-luh wah-*nee*-tah	*tuala wanita*
Saturday	*hah*-ree *sab*-too	*hari Sabtu*
to save	me-nye-*lah*-maht-kahn [se-*lah*-maht]	*menyelamatkan [selamat]*
to say	ber-*kah*-tuh [*kah*-tuh]	*berkata [kata]*
scared	tah-*kut*	*takut*
scenery	pe-*mahn*-dah-ngahn	*pemandangan*
school	se-ko-*lah(h)*	*sekolah*
science	sains	*sains*
scientist	*sain*-tis	*saintis*
scissors	*goon*-ting	*gunting*
scoreboard	pah-*pahn mah*-tuh/mahr-*kah(h)*	*papan mata/markah*
screen (film)	lah-*yahr* pe-*rah(k)*	*layar perak*
script	mah-*niu*-skrip • nahs-*kah(h)*	*manuskrip* • *naskhah*
sculpture	se-*nee* oo-*kir*	*seni ukir*
sea	lowt	*laut*
to search	men-*chah*-ree [*chah*-ree]	*mencari [cari]*
seasick	mah-*bu(k)* lowt	*mabuk laut*
seaside	te-*pee* lowt	*tepi laut*

season	moo-sim	musim
seat	tem-paht doo-du(k)	tempat duduk
seat belt	tah-lee peeng-gahng ke-leh-dahr	tali pinggang keledar
second (unit of time)	sah-aht	saat
(in order)	ke-doo-uh	kedua
secretary	se-tee-uh-oo-suh-huh	setiausaha
to see	lee-haht	lihat

> **I see. (understand)**
> sai-yuh fah-hahm
> **Saya faham.**
>
> **See you later.**
> joom-puh lah-gee
> **Jumpa lagi.**
>
> **See you tomorrow.**
> joom-puh eh-so(k)
> **Jumpa esok.**

self-employed	be-ker-juh sen-dee-ree	bekerja sendiri
selfish	me-mee-kir-kahn dee-ree	memikirkan diri
	sen-dee-ree sah-juh	sendiri saja
self-service	lah-yahn dee-ree	layan diri
to sell	men-joo-ahl [joo-ahl]	menjual [jual]
to send	meng-hahn-tahr [hahn-tahr]	menghantar [hantar]
sensible	ah-rif • moo-nah-sah-bah(h)	arif • munasabah
sentence (words)	ah-yaht	ayat
(prison)	hoo-ku-mahn	hukuman
to separate	me-mee-sah(h)-kahn [pee-sah(h)]	memisahkan [pisah]
serious	see-ree-uhs	serius
servant	o-rahng gah-jee	orang gaji
to serve	me-lah-yah-nee [lah-yahn]	melayani [layan]
service (assistance)	khid-maht • jah-suh	khidmat • jasa
several	be-be-rah-puh	beberapa
to sew	jah-hit	jahit
sex	sehks	seks
sexism	sehk-sis-muh	seksisme
sexy	mem-be-rah-hee-kahn [be-rah-hee]	memberahikan [berahi]
shade	te-du(h)	teduh
to shampoo	men-shehm-poo [shem-poo]	mensyempu [syempu]
shape	ben-tu(k)	bentuk
to share (with)	ber-kong-see (de-ngahn)	berkongsi (dengan)
to share a dorm	ber-kong-see bee-li(k)/dorm	berkongsi bilik/dorm
to shave	choo-kur	cukur
she	dee-uh	dia
sheet (bed)	chah-dahr	cadar
(of paper)	he-lai	helai
shell (sea)	koo-lit	kulit
ship	kah-pahl	kapal
shirt	bah-joo • ke-meh-juh	baju • kemeja
shit	tai(k)	tahi

to shit	boo-*ahng* air be-*sahr*	*buang air besar*
shoelaces	tah-*lee* kah-sut	*tali kasut*
shoes	*kah*-sut	*kasut*
to shoot	me-*nehm*-ba(k) *[tehm*-ba(k)]	*menembak [tembak]*
shop	ke-*dai*	*kedai*
to go shopping	mem-*be*-*lee*-be-*lah(h)* [be-*lee*]	*membeli-belah [beli]*
short (length, height)	*pehn*-deh(k)	*pendek*
short film	*fee*-lem pehn-deh(k)	*filem pendek*
short story	cher-*pehn*	*cerpen*
shortage	ke-koo-*rah*-ngahn	*kekurangan*
shorts (clothes)	se-loo-*ahr* pehn-*de(k)*	*seluar pendek*
shoulders	bah-*hoo*	*bahu*
to shout	men-je-*rit* [je-*rit*]	*menjerit [jerit]*
show	per-toon-*joo(k)*-kahn [toon-*joo(k)*]	*pertunjukan [tunjuk]*
to show	me-noon-*joo(k)*-kahn [toon-*joo(k)*]	*menunjukkan [tunjuk]*

Please show me (on the map).
to-long toon-*joo(k)*-kahn (dee pe-*tuh*)   *Tolong tunjukkan (di peta).*

to shower	*mahn*-dee	*mandi*
shrimp	oo-*dahng*	*udang*
shrine	tem-*paht* soo-*chee*	*tempat suci*
shut	*too*-tup	*tutup*
shy	*mah*-loo • se-*gahn*	*malu • segan*
sick	*sah*-kit	*sakit*
sickness	pe-nyah-*kit*	*penyakit*
side (of a street)	te-*pee* (*jah*-lahn)	*tepi (jalan)*
sign	*tahn*-duh	*tanda*
to sign	me-nahn-duh-*tah*-ngah-nee [tahn-duh-*tah*-ngahn]	*menandatangani [tandatangan]*
signature	tahn-duh-*tah*-ngahn	*tandatangan*
silk	soo-*te*-ruh	*sutera*
silver	peh-*ra(k)*	*perak*
of silver	dah-ree-*pah*-duh peh-*ra(k)*	*daripada perak*
similar	se-*mah*-chahm • se-*roo*-puh	*semacam • serupa*
simple	se-der-*hah*-nuh	*sederahana*
sin	do-*suh*	*dosa*
since	se-*jah(k)*	*sejak*
to sing	me-nyah-*nyee* [nyah-nyee]	*menyanyi [nyanyi]*
singer	pe-*nyah*-nyee	*penyanyi*
single room	bee-li(k) se-o-*rahng*	*bilik seorang*
to sit	*doo*-du(k)	*duduk*
size	saiz	*saiz*
skin	koo-*lit*	*kulit*
skinny	koo-*rus*	*kurus*
sky	lah-*ngit*	*langit*
sleazy (person)	ko-*tor* • tee-*dah(k)* ke-*mahs*	*kotor • tidak kemas*
to sleep	*tee*-dur	*tidur*
sleeping bag	kahn-*tung* tee-dur	*kantung tidur*

sleeping pills	oo-*baht* tee-dur	ubat tidur
sleepy	me-*ngahn*-tu(k)	mengantuk
to slice	meng-*hee*-ris	menghiris [hiris]
slide (film)	ge-*lahn*-sahr fee-*lem*	gelansar filem
slow	per-*lah*-hahn	perlahan
small	ke-*chil*	kecil
smell	bow	bau
to smell	meng-*hee*-doo [hee-doo]	menghidu [hidu]
to smile	se-*nyum*	senyum
smoke	ah-*sahp*	asap
to smoke	me-ro-ko(k) [ro-ko(k)]	merokok [rokok]
snake	oo-*lahr*	ular
soap	sah-*bun*	sabun
soap opera	*drah*-mah sah-bun	drama sabun
soccer	*bo*-luh seh-pah(k)	bola sepak
social welfare	ke-bah-*ji(k)*-kahn so-see-*ahl*	kebajikan sosial
socialist	so-see-*ah*-lis	sosialis
society	mah-*shah*-rah-kaht	masyarakat
socks	*sto*-king	stoking
soft	*lem*-but	lembut
some	be-be-*rah*-puh	beberapa
someone	se-se-o-rahng	seseorang
something	se-soo-*ah*-too	sesuatu
sometimes	kah-*dahng*-kah-*dahng*	kadang-kadang
son	*ah*-nah(k) le-lah-*kee*	anak lelaki
song	lah-*goo*	lagu
soon	se-ke-*jahp* lah-*gee*	sekejap lagi
sorry	mah-*ahf*	maaf

I'm sorry.		
mah-*ahf*		Maaf.

sound	boo-*nyee*	bunyi
sour	*mah*-sahm	masam
south	se-lah-*tahn*	selatan
souvenir	chen-de-ruh-*mah*-tuh	cenderamata
souvenir shop	ke-*dai* chen-de-ruh-*mah*-tuh	kedai cenderamata
soy sauce	kee-*chahp*	kicap
space (area)	roo-*ahng*	ruang
speak	chah-*kahp*	cakap
to speak (Malay)	ber-bah-*hah*-suh me-*lah*-yoo	berbahasa Melayu
special	ees-tee-*meh*-wuh • khahs	istimewa • khas
specialist	pah-*kahr*	pakar
speed (limit)	(hahd) lah-*joo*	(had) laju
spicy	pe-*dahs*	pedas
spoon	soo-*doo*	sudu
sport	soo-*kahn*	sukan
sportsplayer	pe-*main* soo-*kahn*	pemain sukan
sprain	ter-se-*lee*-uh(h)	terseliuh

spring (season)	moo-sim boo-nguh	musim bunga
(coil)	pe-gahs • spring	pegas • spring
square (shape)	se-gee-em-paht	segiempat
(plaza)	dah-tah-rahn	dataran
stadium	stah-dee-um	stadium
stage	pen-tahs	pentas
stairs	tahng-guh	tangga
stale	bah-see	basi
stamp	se-tehm	setem
standard (adj)	stahn-dahrd • tah-rahf	standard • taraf
standard of living	tah-rahf ke-hee-du-pahn	taraf kehidupan
starfruit	be-lim-bing	belimbing
stars (in the sky)	bin-tahng	bintang
to start	me-moo-luh-kahn [moo-luh]	memulakan [mula]
station	steh-sehn	stesen
stationmaster	pe-gah-wai pe-ngah-wahs	pegawai pengawas
	steh-sehn ke-reh-tah-ah-pee	stesen keretapi
statue	pah-tung	patung
to stay (remain)	ting-gahl	tinggal
(overnight)	ber-mah-lahm [mah-lahm]	bermalam [malam]
to steal	men-choo-ree [choo-ree]	mencuri [curi]
steam	wahp	wap
steep (hill)	choo-rahm	curam
step	lang-kah(h)	langkah
still (yet)	mah-si(h)	masih
stomach	pe-rut	perut
stomachache	sah-kit pe-rut	sakit perut
stone	bah-too	batu
stoned (drugged)	mah-bu(k)	mabuk
to stop	ber-hen-tee [hen-tee]	berhenti [henti]

Stop!		
ber-hen-tee!		Berhenti!

storm	ree-but	ribut
story	che-ree-tuh	cerita
stove	dah-pur	dapur
straight (line)	(gah-ri-sahn) loo-rus	(garisan) lurus
strange	pe-li(k) • gahn-jil • ah-neh(h)	pelik • ganjil • aneh
stranger	o-rahng yahng tee-dah(k)	orang yang tidak
	dee-ke-nah-lee	dikenali
stream (small river)	soo-ngai	sungai
street	jah-lahn	jalan
strength	ke-koo-ah-tahn	kekuatan
(on) strike	mo-go(k)	mogok
string	tah-lee	tali
stroll	jah-lahn-jah-lahn • see-ahr-see-ahr	jalan-jalan • siar-siar
strong	koo-ah(t)	kuat
student (school)	pe-lah-jahr • moo-rid	pelajar • murid
student (university)	mah-hah-sis-wah • pe-lah-jahr	mahasiswa • pelajar

studio	stoo-*dee*-o	*studio*
stupid	bo-*do(h)*	*bodoh*
style	*gah*-yuh	*gaya*
subtitles	tehks	*teks*
suburb	*ping*-gir *bahn*-dahr	*pinggir bandar*
suburbs of Kuala Lumpur	*ping*-gir *bahn*-dahr koo-*ah*-luh *loom*-pur	*pinggir bandar Kuala Lumpur*
success	ke-jah-*yah*-ahn	*kejayaan*
to suffer	men-de-*ree*-tuh [de-*ree*-tuh]	*menderita [derita]*
sugar	*goo*-luh	*gula*
summer	*moo*-sim *pah*-nahs	*musim panas*
sun	mah-tuh-*hah*-ree	*matahari*
sunblock	krim pe-*leen*-dung chah-*hah*-yuh mah-tuh-*hah*-ree	*krim pelindung cahaya matahari*
sunburnt	koo-lit ter-bah-*kahr*	*kulit terbakar*
Sunday	*hah*-ree ah-*hahd*	*hari Ahad*
sunglasses	cher-*min* mah-tuh hee-tahm	*cermin mata hitam*
sunny	che-*rah(h)*	*cerah*
sunrise	mah-tuh-*hah*-ree ter-*bit*	*matahari terbit*
sunset	mah-tuh-*hah*-ree ter-be-*nahm*	*matahari terbenam*
supermarket	pah-sah-*rah*-yuh	*pasaraya*

Sure. bo-*leh(h)*	*Boleh.*

surface mail	mehl bee-*ah*-suh	*mel biasa*
to surf	ber-se-*lahn*-chahr [se-*lahn*-chahr]	*berselancar [selancar]*
surfboard	pah-*pahn* se-*lahn*-chahr	*papan selancar*
surname	*nah*-muh ke-loo-*ahr*-guh	*nama keluarga*
surprise	ke-joo-*tahn*	*kejutan*
to survive	hee-*dup*	*hidup*
to sweat	ber-pe-*lu(h)* [pe-*lu(h)*]	*berpeluh [peluh]*
sweet (adj)	mah-*nis*	*manis*
sweets	goo-luh-*goo*-luh	*gula-gula*
to swim	be-re-*nahng* [re-*nahng*]	*berenang [renang]*
swimming pool	ko-*lahm* re-*nahng*	*kolam renang*
swimsuit	bah-joo re-*nahng*	*baju renang*
sword	pe-*dahng*	*pedang*
sympathetic	ber-sim-*pah*-tee	*bersimpati*
synagogue	ge-reh-juh yah-*hoo*-dee	*gereja Yahudi*
synthetic	sin-*teh*-tik	*sintetik*
syringe	*jah*-rum soon-*ti(k)*	*jarum suntik*

T

table	*meh*-juh	*meja*
tablet	bee-*jee* oo-*baht*	*biji ubat*
table tennis	ping-*pong*	*ping-pong*
tail (of animal)	*eh*-kor	*ekor*
tailor	too-*kahng* jah-*hit*	*tukang jahit*

to take (away)	me-*ngahm*-bil *[ahm*-bil]	mengambil [ambil]
(train)	me-*nai(k)*-kee	menaiki [naik]
to take off (depart)	ber-le-*pahs* [le-*pahs]* • be-*rahng*-kaht [*ahng*-kaht]	berlepas [lepas] • berangkat [angkat]
to take photographs	me-*ngahm*-bil fo-to/ gahm-bahr	mengambil foto/ gambar
to talk (chat)	ber-*chah*-kahp [*chah*-kahp]	bercakap [cakap]
tall	*ting*-gee	tinggi
tampon	*tahm*-pon	tampon
taste	*rah*-suh	rasa
tasty	se-*dahp* • eh-nah(k)	sedap • enak
tax	*choo*-kai	cukai
taxi (stand)	(steh-sehn) *tehk*-see	(stesen) teksi
tea	teh(h)	teh
teacher	*goo*-roo • *chi(k)*-goo	guru • cikgu (col)
teaching	me-*ngah*-jahr	mengajar
team (sport)	pah-*su(k)*-kahn	pasukan
tear (crying)	air mah-*tuh*	air mata
teeth	*gee*-gee	gigi
telegram	teh-leh-*grahm*	telegram
telephone	teh-*leh*-fon	telefon
to telephone	me-neh-*leh*-fon [teh-*leh*-fon]	menelefon [telefon]
television	teh-leh-*vee*-shen	televisyen
to tell (inform)	mem-be-ree-*tah*-hoo [*tah*-hoo]	memberitahu [tahu]
teller	teh-ler	teler (col)
temperature (fever)	soo-*hoo* bah-*dahn*	suhu badan
(weather)	soo-*hoo* oo-dah-ruh	suhu udara
temple		
(Buddhist)	to-*kong* boo-dah	tokong Buda
(Chinese)	to-*kong* chee-nuh	tokong Cina
(Hindu)	*koo*-il	kuil
tennis (court)	(pah-*dahng*) teh-*nis*	(padang) tenis
tent	kheh-*mah(h)*	khemah
tent pegs	pah-*koo* kah-yoo • pahn-*chahng* kheh-*mah(h)*	paku kayu • pancang khemah
tenth	ke-se-*poo*-lu(h)	kesepuluh
terrible	me-nge-*ree*-kahn [nge-*ree]*	mengerikan [ngeri]
test (exam)	oo-*jee*-ahn (pe-pe-*rik*-sah-ahn)	ujian (peperiksaan)
to thank	ber-te-*ree*-muh kah-si(h)	berterima kasih

Thank you. te-*ree*-muh kah-si(h)	Terima kasih.

that	ee-too	itu
theatre (play)	*pahng*-gung sahn-dee-*wah*-rah	panggung sandiwara
there (distant)	dee *sah*-nuh	di sana
(nearby)	dee *see*-too	di situ

there is/are ... dee *sah*-nuh/*see*-too ah-duh ...	di sana/situ ada ...

they	me-*reh*-kuh	*mereka*
thief	pen-choo-*ree*	*pencuri*
thin	*nee*-pis • *ti*-pis	*nipis • tipis*
to think	ber-*fee*-kir *[fee*-kir]	*berfikir [fikir]*
third	ke-*tee*-guh	*ketiga*
thirsty	hows • dah-*hah*-guh	*haus • dahaga*
this	ee-*nee*	*ini*
thought	fee-ki-*rahn*	*fikiran*
thread	be-*nahng*	*benang*
throat	te-*kah(k)* • ke-*rong*-kong	*tekak • kerongkong*
Thursday	hah-ree kah-*mis*	*hari Khamis*
ticket	tee-*keht*	*tiket*
ticket collector	pe-moo-*ngut* tee-*keht*	*pemungut tiket*
ticket office	pe-*jah*-baht tee-*keht*	*pejabat tiket*
tide (low/high)	air (*soo*-rut/pah-*sahng*)	*air (surut/pasang)*
tiger	hah-*ree*-mow	*harimau*
tight	ke-*taht* • sem-*pit*	*ketat • sempit*
time	mah-*suh*	*masa*

What time is it?	
poo-kul be-*rah*-puh?	*Pukul berapa?*

timetable	jah-doo-*ahl wak*-too	*jadual waktu*
tin opener	pem-*boo*-kuh tin	*pembuka tin*
tired	pe-*naht*	*penat*
tissues	ti-*soo*	*tisu*
to	ke	*ke*
toad	*kah*-tah(k) • *ko*-do(k)	*katak • kodok*
toast (bread)	(ro-tee) *bah*-kahr	*(roti) bakar*
tobacco	tem-*bah*-kow	*tembakau*
today	hah-ree ee-*nee*	*hari ini*
together	ber-*sah*-muh	*bersama*
toilet paper	tee-*soo*	*tisu*
toilet	*tahn*-duhs	*tandas*
tomorrow	*eh*-so(k)	*esok*
tomorrow afternoon	te-ngah-*hah*-ree/pe-*tahng eh*-so(k)	*tengahari/petang esok*
tomorrow morning	*eh*-so(k) *pah*-gee	*pagi esok*
tongue	lee-*dah(h)*	*lidah*
tonight	mah-*lahm* ee-*nee*	*malam ini*
too (excessive)	ter-*lah*-loo	*terlalu*
too (as well)	*joo*-guh • pun	*juga • pun*

Too expensive!	
ter-*lah*-loo mah-*hahl!*	*Terlalu mahal!*
Too many/much!	
ter-*lah*-loo bah-*nya(k)!*	*Terlalu banyak!*

tool	*ah*-laht	*alat*
tooth	*gee*-gee	*gigi*

tooth (front/back)	*gee*-gee (de-*pahn*/be-*lah*-kahng)	gigi (depan/belakang)
toothache	*sah*-kit *gee*-gee	sakit gigi
toothbrush	be-*rus gee*-gee	berus gigi
toothpaste	oo-*baht gee*-gee	ubat gigi
torch (flashlight)	*lahm*-poo soo-*lu(h)*	lampu suluh
to touch	me-nyen-*tu(h)*[sen-*tu(h)]*	menyentuh [sentuh]
tour	ber-ke-*lee*-ling	berkeliling
tourist	pe-*lahn*-chong *[lahn*-chong]	pelancong [lancong]
tourist information	pe-*jah*-baht	pejabat
office	*mah(k)*-loo-maht pe-*lahn*-chong	maklumat pelancong
toward	ke ah-*rah(h)*	ke arah
towel	*too*-ah-luh	tuala
tower	me-*nah*-ruh	menara
toxic waste	*see*-suh boo-ah-*ngahn tok*-sik	sisa buangan toksik
track (footprints)	ke-*sahn* je-*ja(k)*	kesan jejak
(sports)	o-*lah(h)*-rah-guh	olahraga
(path)	*jah*-lahn ke-*chil* • lo-*rong*	jalan kecil • lorong
traffic	lah-loo-*lin*-tahs	lalulintas
traffic jam	ke-se-*sah*-tahn lah-loo-*lin*-tahs	kesesatan lalu lintas
traffic lights	*lahm*-poo ee-*shah*-raht	lampu isyarat
trail (route)	*jah*-lahn	jalan
train	ke-reh-tuh-*ah*-pee	keretapi
train station	steh-sehn ke-reh-tuh-*ah*-pee	stesen keretapi
to translate	men-ter-je-*mah(h)*-kahn	menterjemahkan
	[ter-je-*mah(h)]*	[terjemah]
to travel	me-ngem-*bah*-ruh	mengembara
travel agency	eh-jen-*see* pe-*lahn*-cho-ngahn	agensi pelancongan
travel book	*boo*-koo kem-*bah*-ruh	buku kembara
travellers cheque	chehk kem-*bah*-ruh	cek kembara
travel sickness	mah-*bu(k)* jah-lahn	mabuk jalan
tree	*po*-ko(k) • *po*-hon	pokok • pohon
to trek	per-jah-*lah*-nahn *[jah*-lahn] •	perjalanan [jalan] •
	pe-ngem-*bah*-ruh-ahn	pengembaraan
	[kem-*bah*-ruh]	[kembara]
trip (journey)	per-jah-*lah*-nahn	perjalanan
trousers	se-loo-*ahr* pahn-*jahng*	seluar panjang
truck	lo-*ree*	lori
true	be-*nahr*	benar

It's true.		
be-*nahr*		Benar.

to trust	per-*chah*-yuh	percaya
truth	ke-be-*nah*-rahn	kebenaran
to try (attempt)	men-*choo*-buh *[choo*-buh]	mencuba [cuba]
T-shirt	*bah*-joo tee	baju T
Tuesday	hah-ree se-*lah*-suh	hari Selasa
tune (song)	lah-*goo* • *nah*-duh	lagu • nada
turn	be-*lo(k)* • *poo*-sing	belok • pusing

Turn left/right.		
beh-lo(k) ki-ree/kah-nahn		*Belok kiri/kanan.*

TV	teh-leh-*vee*-shen	*televisyen*
twice	*doo*-uh kah-lee	*dua kali*
twin beds	*kah*-til *kem*-bahr	*katil kembar*
twins	*kem*-bahr	*kembar*
type (of product)	je-*nis*	*jenis*
to type	me-*naip* (taip)	*menaip [taip]*
typhoid	tai-*foid*	*tifoid*
typical	bee-*ah*-suh	*biasa*
tyre	*tai*-yahr	*tayar*

U

umbrella	*pah*-yung	*payung*
under	*bah*-wah(h)	*bawah*
to understand	fah-*hahm*	*faham*

I (don't) understand.		
sai-yuh (*tee*-dah(k)) fah-*hahm*		*Saya (tidak) faham.*

underwear	se-loo-*ahr* dah-*lahm*	*seluar dalam*
unemployed	pe-*ngahng*-gur	*penganggur*
unions	per-sah-*too*-ahn se-*ker*-juh	*persatuan sekerja*
universe	ah-*lahm* se-mes-tah	*alam semesta*
university	yoo-ni-*ver*-si-tee	*universiti*
unripe	be-*lum* mah-sah(k)	*belum masak*
unsafe	*tee*-dah(k) se-*lah*-maht	*tidak selamat*
until (June)	se-*hing*-guh (joon)	*sehingga (Jun)*
unusual	*loo*-ahr bee-*ah*-suh	*luar biasa*
up	ah-*tahs*	*atas*
uphill (road)	(*jah*-lahn) nai(k) boo-*kit*	*(jalan) naik bukit*
urgent	men-de-*sah(k)* • *pen*-ting	*mendesak • penting*
useful	ber-*goo*-nuh	*berguna*
usual	bee-*ah*-suh	*biasa*

V

vacant	*ko*-song	*kosong*
vacation	*choo*-tee	*cuti*
vaccination	pen-chah-*chah*-rahn	*pencacaran*
valley	*lem*-bah(h)	*lembah*
valuable	ber-*har*-guh	*berharga*
value (price)	nee-*lai*	*nilai*
van	vahn	*van*
vegetables	*sai*-yur-*sai*-yu-rahn	*sayur-sayuran*
vegetarian (food)	*sai*-yu-rahn *sah*-juh	*sayuran saja*
(person)	(*o*-rahng yahng)	*(orang yang)*
	mah-kahn *sai*-yur *sah*-juh	*makan sayur saja*

I'm vegetarian.
*sai-yuh mah-*kahn *sai-yur sah-hah-juh*   *Saya makan sayur sahaja.*

vegetation	toom-*bu(h)*-toom-*bu(h)*-hahn	*tumbuh-tumbuhan*
vein	oo-*raht dah-*rah(h)	*urat darah*
venereal disease	pe-*nyah*-kit ke-*lah*-min	*penyakit kelamin*
very	sah-*ngaht* • ah-*maht*	*sangat • amat*
video cassette	*kah-*seht *vi*-dee-o	*kaset video*
view	pe-*mahn*-dah-ngahn [*pahn*-dahng]	*pemandangan [pandang]*
village	*kahm*-pung • deh-*suh*	*kampung • desa*
virus	vi-*rus*	*virus*
visa	*vee*-sah	*visa*
to visit	me-lah-*waht* [lah-*waht*] • me-*ngoon*-ju-ngee [*koon*-jung]	*melawat [lawat] • mengunjungi [kunjung]*
vitamin	vi-*tah*-min	*vitamin*
voice	soo-*ah*-ruh	*suara*
volcano	*goo*-nung be-*rah*-pee	*gunung berapi*
volume (sound)	soo-*ah*-ruh	*suara*
vomit (n/v)	moon-*tah(h)*	*muntah*
to vote	me-*ngun*-dee [*un*-dee]	*mengundi [undi]*
vulgar	bee-*ah*-dahb • kah-*sahr*	*biadab • kasar*

W

wait	*toong*-goo	*tunggu*
waiter	pe-*lah*-yahn	*pelayan*
waiting room	*bee*-li(k) me-*noong*-goo	*bilik menunggu*
to wake up	bah-*ngun* • *bahng*-kit	*bangun • bangkit*
to walk	ber-*jah*-lahn kah-*kee*	*berjalan kaki*
wall (inside)	*deen*-ding	*dinding*
(outside)	tehm-*bo(k)*	*tembok*
to want	hen-*da(k)* • ee-ngin • mow	*hendak • ingin • mahu*
war	pe-*rahng*	*perang*
wardrobe	*ahl*-mah-ree	*almari*
warm	soo-*ahm*	*suam*
to wash (yourself)	*mahn*-dee	*mandi*
(something)	men-*choo*-chee [*choo*-chee]	*mencuci [cuci]*
washing machine	me-*sin* bah-*su(h)*	*mesin basuh*
watch (for wrist)	jahm tah-*ngahn*	*jam tangan*
to watch	me-*non*-ton (*ton*-ton)	*menonton [tonton]*

Watch out!
ber-*hah*-tee-*hah*-tee!/ah-*wahs*!   *Berhati-hati!/Awas!*

water	air ...	*air*
boiled	... *mah*-sah(k)	*masak*
mineral	... ee-*ne*-ruhl	*mineral*
purified	... u-*lehn*	*tulen*

water bottle	bo-*tol* air	*botol air*
waterfall	air *ter*-jun	*air terjun*
watermelon	tem-*bee*-kai	*tembikai*
waves	om-*bah(k)*	*ombak*
way	*jah*-lahn	*jalan*

Please tell me the way to ...
to-long be-ree-*tah*-hoo *sai*-yuh
jah-lahn ke ...?

Tolong beritahu saya
jalan ke ...?

Which way?
jah-lahn *mah*-nuh?

Jalan mana?

Way Out.
jah-lahn ke-*loo*-ahr

Jalan keluar.

we (incl)	*kee*-tuh	*kita*
(excl)	*kah*-mee	*kami*
weak	le-*mah(h)*	*lemah*
wealthy	kah-*yuh*	*kaya*
to wear	me-mah-*kai* [pah-*kai*]	*memakai [pakai]*
weather	choo-*ah*-chuh	*cuaca*
wedding	per-kah-*wi*-nahn •	*perkahwinan* •
	per-nee-*kah(h)*-hahn	*pernikahan*
wedding cake	kehk per-kah-*wi*-nahn	*kek perkahwinan*
wedding present	hah-dee-*ah(h)* per-kah-*wi*-nahn	*hadiah perkahwinan*
Wednesday	hah-ree rah-*boo*	*hari Rabu*
(this) week	*ming*-goo (ee-*nee*)	*minggu ini*
weekend	hoo-*jung* *meeng*-goo	*hujung minggu*
to weigh	me-*nim*-bahng [*tim*-bahng]	*menimbang [timbang]*
weight	be-*raht*	*berat*

Welcome.
se-lah-*maht* dah-*tahng*

Selamat datang.

You're welcome.
sah-*muh*-sah-*muh*

Sama-sama.

welfare	ke-bah-*ji(k)*-kahn •	*kebajikan* •
	ke-se-*jah(h)*-te-rah-ahn	*kesejahteraan*
well (healthy)	si-*haht*	*sihat*
west	bah-*raht*	*barat*
Westerner (col)	o-rahng bah-*raht*	*orang barat*
wet	bah-*sah(h)*	*basah*
what	*ah*-puh	*apa*

What?
ah-puh?

Apa?

What's he saying?
dee-*uh* chah-*kahp* *ah*-puh?

Dia cakap apa?

What is that?
ah-puh too?   *Apa tu?*

What's your name?
see-*ah*-puh *nah*-muh *ahn*-dah?   *Siapa nama anda?*

What time is it?
poo-kul be-*rah*-puh se-*kah*-rahng?   *Pukul berapa sekarang?*

wheel	ro-*duh*	roda
wheelchair	ke-*roo*-see be-*ro*-duh	kerusi beroda
when (past, future)	*bee*-luh	bila

When?
bee-luh?   *Bila?*

When does (the train) leave?
bee-luh (ke-reh-tah-*ah*-pee) ber-to-*la(k)*?   *Bila (keretapi) bertolak?*

Where?
mah-*nuh*?   *Mana?*

Where's the bank?
bank dee mah-*nuh*?   *Bank di mana?*

which	*yahng*	yang
while (currently)	*sahm*-bil	sambil
white	poo-ti (h)	putih
who	see-*ah*-puh	siapa

Who?
see-*ah*-puh?   *Siapa?*

Who's calling?
see-*ah*-puh yahng teh-*leh*-fon?   *Siapa yang telefon?*

Who is it?
see-*ah*-puh nee?   *Siapa ni?*

Who are they?
see-*ah*-puh me-*reh*-kuh?   *Siapa mereka?*

| whole (all) | se-loo-*ru(h)* | seluruh |
| why | ke-*nah*-puh • me-*ngah*-puh | kenapa • mengapa |

Why is the bank closed?
ke-*nah*-puh bank too-tup?   *Kenapa bank tu tutup?*

wide	leh-*bahr*	lebar
wife	ees-te-ree	isteri
wild animal	bee-*nah*-tahng lee-*yahr*/boo-ahs	binatang liar/buas
to win	me-*nahng*	menang
wind	*ah*-ngin	angin
window	*ting*-kahp	tingkap

to go window-shopping	me-*lee*-haht-*lee*-haht sah-juh [*lee*-haht]	melihat-lihat saja [lihat]
windscreen	*kah*-chuh de-*pahn*	kaca depan
wine	wain	wain
wings	sah-*yahp*	sayap
winner	joo-*ah*-ruh • *jo*-hahn • pe-me-*nahng*	juara • johan • pemenang
winter	*moo*-sim se-*joo(k)*	musim sejuk
wire	wah-*yahr*	wayar
wise	bee-ja(k)-*sah*-nuh • *ah*-rif	bijaksana • arif
to wish	hah-*jaht* • *hahs*-raht • ke-*ee*-ngi-nahn [*ee*-ngin]	hajat • hasrat • keinginan [ingin]
with	de-*ngahn* • ber-*sah*-muh	dengan • bersama
within	dee dah-*lahm*	di dalam
within an hour	dah-*lahm* se-*jahm*	dalam sejam
without	*tahn*-puh	tanpa
without filter	*tahn*-puh fil-ter	tanpa filter
woman	wah-*nee*-tah • o-rahng pe-*rem*-pwahn	wanita • orang perempuan
wonderful	bah-*gus* se-kah-*lee* • meng-kah-*gum*-kahn	bagus sekali • mengkagumkan
wood (timber)	kah-*yoo* (bah-*la(k)*)	kayu (balak)
woodcarving	oo-ki-*rahn* kah-yoo	ukiran kayu
wool	boo-*loo* bee-*ree*-bee-*ree*	bulu biri-biri
word	per-kah-*tah*-ahn	perkataan
work	*ker*-juh	kerja
to work	be-*ker*-juh [*ker*-juh]	bekerja [kerja]
workout (sport)	lah-*ti(h)*-hahn (soo-*kahn*)	latihan (sukan)
work permit	*per*-mit *ker*-juh	permit kerja
world	doo-nee-*uh*	dunia
World Cup	pee-*ah*-luh doo-ni-*uh*	Piala Dunia
worried	ree-*sow* • beem-*bahng* • khoo-*ah*-tir	risau • bimbang • khuatir
worship	pe-nyem-*bah(h)*-hahn	penyembahan
worth	nee-*lai* • *hahr*-guh	nilai • harga
wound (injury)	loo-*kuh* (ke-che-de-*rah*-ahn)	luka (kecederaan)
wristwatch	jahm tah-*ngahn*	jam tangan
to write	me-*noo*-lis [*too*-lis]	menulis [tulis]
writer	pe-*noo*-lis	penulis
writing paper	*ker*-tahs *too*-lis	kertas tulis
wrong	sah-*lah(h)*	salah

I'm wrong. (my fault)	
sai-yuh sah-*lah(h)*	Saya salah.

Y

year (this)	tah-hoon (ee-nee)	tahun (ini)
yellow	koo-ning	kuning
yes	yah	ya
yesterday	se-mah-lahm	semalam
yesterday afternoon	te-ngah-hah-ree/pe-tahng se-mah-lahm	tengahari/petang semalam
yesterday morning	pah-gee se-mah-lahm	pagi semalam
yet	be-lum	belum
not yet	be-lum lah-gee	belum lagi
you (inf)	kah-moo • eng-kow	kamu • engkau
(pol)	ahn-dah	anda
(pl)	kah-lee-ahn	kalian
young	moo-duh	muda
younger (sibling)	ah-di(k)	adik
youth (collective)	be-lee-uh	belia
youth hostel	ahs-rah-mah be-lee-uh	asrama belia

Z

zebra	zeh-brah	zebra
zodiac	bin-tahng ke-lah-hi-rahn	bintang kelahiran
zoo	zoo	zoo

A

ada	ah-duh	to have
abang	ah-*bahng*	older brother
ada selsema	ah-duh sel-*se*-muh	(to have a) cold
adapter elektrik	a-*dap*-ter eh-*lehk*-trik	adaptor (electric)
adat	ah-*daht*	custom (tradition)
adik	ah-*di(k)*	younger (sibling)
agama	ah-*gah*-muh	religion
agensi pelancongan	ah-jen-*see* pe-*lahn*-cho-ngahn	travel agency
ahli politik	ah-lee po-*lee*-tik	politicians
AIDS	ayds	AIDS
air	air	water
air (surut/pasang)	air (soo-rut/pah-*sahng*)	(low/high) tide
air masak	air mah-sah(k)	boiled water
air mata	air mah-tuh	tear (crying)
air mineral (berkarbonat/biasa)	air mi-*ne*-rahl (ber-*kar*-bo-naht/ bee-*ah*-suh)	mineral water (with/without gas)
air sejuk	air se-*ju(k)*	cold water
air terjun	air *ter*-jun	waterfall
air tulen	air tu-*lehn*	purified water
ais	ais	ice
ais krim	ais krim	ice cream
akibat	ah-*kee*-baht	result
aktivis	*ahk*-ti-vis	activist
aku	ah-koo	I
alahan	ah-lah-hahn	allergy
alam semesta	ah-*lahm* se-*mes*-tah	universe
alam semulajadi	ah-*lahm* se-moo-luh-*jah*-dee	nature
alamat	ah-lah-maht	address (of house)
alasan	ah-lah-sahn	reason
alat	ah-laht	tool
alat selam	ah-laht se-*lahm*	diving equipment
alat solekan	ah-laht so-*leh(k)*-kahn	make-up
alergi	ah-ler-jee	allergy
Allah	ahl-*luh(h)*	God (Muslim)
almari	ahl-*mah*-ree	wardrobe
almari bagasi	ahl-*mah*-ree bah-*gah*-see	luggage lockers
am	ahm	general
aman	ah-*mahn*	peace
amat	ah-*maht*	very
anak anjing	ah-nah(k) *ahn*-jing	puppy
anak biri-biri	ah-nah(k) bee-*ree*-bee-*ree*	lamb
anak kapal	ah-nah(k) *kah*-pahl	sailor
anak lelaki	ah-nah(k) le-*lah*-kee	boy • son
anak perempuan	ah-nah(k) pe-*rem*-pwahn	girl • daughter

anak-anak	*ah*-nah(k)-*ah*-nah(k)	child
anda	*ahn*-dah	you (pol)
aneh	ah-*neh(h)*	strange
anggur	*ahng*-gur	grape
angin	*ah*-ngin	wind
anjing	*ahn*-jing	dog
anjing pemandu	*ahn*-jing pe-*mahn*-doo	guide dog
anjuran	*ahn*-joo-rahn	proposal
antara	*ahn*-tah-ruh	between
antara bandar	*ahn*-tah-ruh *bahn*-dahr	intercity
antarabangsa	ahn-tah-rah-*bahng*-suh	international
antibiotik	an-tai-bai-o-tik	antibiotics
anting-anting	*ahn*-ting-*ahn*-ting	earrings
apa	*ah*-puh	what
apa-apa	*ah*-puh-*ah*-puh	anything
apa pun	*ah*-puh pun	any
api	ah-*pee*	fire
arahan doktor bertulis	ah-rah-*hahn* *dok*-tor ber-*too*-lis	prescription
arak	ah-*rah(k)*	beer
arif	ah-*rif*	sensible • wise
arkeologi	*ahr*-kee-o-lo-ji	archaeological
artis	*ahr*-tis	painter (artist)
asap	ah-*sahp*	smoke
asli	*ahs*-lee	indigenous • original
asrama belia	as-*rah*-mah be-*lee*-uh	youth hostel
atap	ah-*tahp*	roof
atas	ah-*tahs*	up
atau	ah-*tow*	or
ATM	ay tee ehm	ATM
atmosfera	*aht*-mos-fe-rah	atmosphere (of planet)
avokado	ah-vo-*kah*-do	avocado
awal	ah-*wahl*	early
ayah	ah-*yah(h)*	father
ayam	ai-*yahm*	chicken
ayat	ah-*yaht*	sentence (words)

B

babi	*bah*-bee	pig
badan	*bah*-dahn	body
bagaimana	bah-*gai*-mah-nuh	how
bagasi	bah-*gah*-see	luggage • baggage
bagasi yang ditinggalkan	bah-*gah*-see yahng dee-ting-*gahl*-kahn	left luggage
bagus	bah-*gus*	brilliant • cool • fantastic
bagus sekali	bah-*gus* se-kah-*lee*	wonderful
bahagian	bah-*hah*-gee-ahn	part

(di) bahagian bawah	(dee) bah-*hah*-gee-ahn bah-*wah(h)*	(at the) bottom
bahagian penjualan	bah-*hah*-gee-ahn pen-joo-*ah*-lahn	sales department
bahasa	bah-*hah*-suh	language
Bahasa Melayu	bah-*hah*-suh me-*lah*-yoo	Malay
bahaya	bah-*hah*-yuh	dangerous
bahu	bah-*hoo*	shoulders
baik	bai(k)	good • OK
baik hati	bai(k) *hah*-tee	kind (adj)
baju	bah-joo	shirt
baju gaun	bah-joo gown	dress
baju renang	bah-joo re-*nahng*	bathing suit • swimsuit
baju sejuk	bah-joo se-*ju(k)*	jumper (sweater)
baju T	bah-joo tee	T-shirt
bakar	bah-*kahr*	burn
bakul	bah-kul	basket
balasan	bah-lah-*sahn*	reply
baldi	*bahl*-dee	bucket
bandar	*bahn*-dahr	city
banduan	bahn-*doo*-ahn	prisoner
bangkit	*bahng*-kit	to wake up
bangsa	*bahng*-suh	nationality • race (breed)
bangun	bah-*ngun*	to wake up
bangunan	bah-ngoo-nahn	building
bank	bank	bank
bantal	*bahn*-tahl	pillow
bantuan	*bahn*-too-ahn	assistance
banyak	bah-*nya*(k)	many • much
bapa	bah-*puh*	father
bar	bahr	bar (drinks)
barang antik	bah-rahng *ahn*-tik	antiques
barang kemas	bah-rahng ke-*mahs*	jewellery
barang-barang	bah-rahng-*bah*-rahng	baggage
barat	bah-*raht*	west
baru	bah-*roo*	new
baru berlaku	bah-*roo* ber-*lah*-koo	recent
bas	bahs	bus
bas jarak jauh	bahs jah-*rah(k)* jow(h)	long-distance bus
bas mini	bahs mee-*nee*	minibus
bas (bandar) tempatan	bahs *(bahn*-dahr) tem-*pah*-tahn	local (city) bus
basah	bah-*sah(h)*	wet
basi	bah-*see*	stale
basikal	bah-*see*-kahl	bicycle
basikal gunung	bah-*see*-kahl goo-nung	mountain bike
bateri	bah-te-ree	battery
batu	bah-*too*	rock • stone
batuk	bah-tu(k)	cough • to cough

D
I
C
T
I
O
N
A
R
Y

bau	bow	smell
bawah	*bah*-wah(h)	under
bawang	*bah*-wahng	onion
bawang putih	*bah*-wahng poo-*ti*(h)	garlic
bayaran	bah-*yah*-rahn	payment
bayaran pos	bah-*yah*-rahn pos	postage
bayi	*bah*-yee	baby
bebas	beh-*bahs*	free (not bound)
beberapa	be-be-*rah*-puh	few • several • some
beg	behg	bag
beg sandar	behg *sahn*-dahr	backpack
beg tangan	behg tah-*ngahn*	handbag
bekas abu rokok	be-*kahs* ah-*boo* ro-ko(k)	ashtray
bekerja [kerja]	be-*ker*-juh [*ker*-juh]	to work
bekerja sendiri	be-*ker*-juh sen-*dee*-ree	self-employed

Belahlah! be-*la*(h)-la(h)!		Get lost!

belajar [ajar]	be-*lah*-jahr [*ah*-jahr]	to learn
belia	be-*lee*-uh	youth (collective)
belimbing	be-*lim*-bing	starfruit
belok	be-*lo*(k)	turn
belum	be-*lum*	yet
belum lagi	be-*lum* lah-gee	not yet
belum masak	be-*lum* mah-sah(k)	unripe
benang	be-*nahng*	thread
benar	be-*nahr*	true
bendera	ben-*deh*-ruh	flag
bentuk	ben-*tu*(k)	shape
beracun	be-*rah*-chun	poisonous
berangkat [angkat]	be-*rahng*-kaht [*ahng*-kaht]	depart

Berapa? be-*rah*-puh?		How much?

Berapa banyak? be-*rah*-puh *bah*-nya(k)?		How many? (goods)

Berapa ekor? be-*rah*-puh eh-kor?		How many? (animals)

beras	be-*rahs*	rice (uncooked)
berasal [asal]	be-*rah*-sahl [*ah*-sahl]	to come from (origin)
berat	be-*raht*	weight • heavy
beratur	be-*rah*-tur	queue
berawan	be-*rah*-wahn	cloudy
berbahasa (Melayu)	ber-bah-*hah*-suh (me-*lah*-yoo)	to speak (Malay)
berangkat [angkat]	be-*rahng*-kaht [*ahng*-kaht]	to take off (depart)
berbeza	ber-*beh*-zuh	different

B

berburu [buru]	ber-*boo*-roo [*boo*-roo]	to hunt
bercakap [cakap]	ber-*chah*-kahp [*chah*-kahp]	to talk (chat)
berdansa [dansa]	ber-*dahn*-sah [*dahn*-sah]	to dance
berdarah [darah]	ber-*dah*-rah(h) [*dah*-rah(h)]	to bleed
berehat [rehat]	be-reh-*haht* [reh-*haht*]	to relax • to rest
berenang [renang]	be-re-*nahng* [re-*nahng*]	to swim
berfikir [fikir]	ber-*fee*-kir [*fee*-kir]	to think
bergaduh [gaduh]	ber-gah-*du*(h) [gah-*du*(h)]	to fight
berguling	ber-goo-*ling*	rolling
berguna	ber-*goo*-nuh	useful
berharga	ber-*har*-guh	valuable
berhati-hati	ber-*hah*-tee-*hah*-tee	careful
berhenti [henti]	ber-*hen*-tee [*hen*-tee]	to quit • to stop
berhutang	ber-*hoo*-tahng	to owe
beriman	be-ree-mahn	religious
berita	be-ree-tuh	news
berjalan kaki	ber-*jah*-lahn kah-*kee*	to walk • to hike
berkabus	ber-*kah*-bus	foggy
berkahwin	ber-*kah*(h)-win	marry
berkata [kata]	ber-*kah*-tuh [*kah*-tuh]	to say
berkeliling	ber-ke-*lee*-ling	tour
berkhayal [khayal]	ber-*khah*-yahl [*khah*-yahl]	to hallucinate
berkhema [khemah]	ber-*keh*-mah(h) [*keh*-mah(h)]	to camp
berkongsi (dengan)	ber-*kong*-see (de-*ngahn*)	to share (with)
berkongsi bilik/dorm	ber-*kong*-see *bee*-li(k)/dorm	to share a dorm
berlawak [lawak]	ber-lah-*wah(k)* [lah-*wah(k)*]	to joke
berlepas [lepas]	ber-le-*pahs* [le-*pahs*]	to take off (depart)
bermain [main]	ber-*main* [main]	to play (a game, music)
bermalam [malam]	ber-*mah*-lahm [*mah*-lahm]	to stay (overnight)
bermimpi [mimpi]	ber-*mim*-pee [*mim*-pee]	to dream
bernikah	ber-*nee*-kah(h)	to marry
berpeluh [peluh]	ber-pe-*lu*(h) [pe-*lu*(h)]	to perspire
bersama	ber-*sah*-muh	together • with
berselancar [selancar]	ber-se-*lahn*-chahr [se-*lahn*-chahr]	to surf
bersendirian	ber-*sen*-dee-ree-ahn	alone
bersetuju [setuju]	ber-se-*too*-joo [se-*too*-joo]	to agree
bersimpati	ber-sim-*pah*-tee	sympathetic
bertanya [tanya]	ber-*tah*-nyuh [*tah*-nyuh]	to ask a question
bertapis	ber-*tah*-pis	filtered
bertemu [temu]	ber-te-*moo* [te-*moo*]	to meet
berterima kasih	ber-te-ree-muh kah-si(h)	to thank
beruntung	be-*roon*-tung	lucky
berus gigi	be-*rus gee*-gee	toothbrush
berus rambut	be-*rus* rahm-but	hairbrush

D I C T I O N A R Y

besar	be-*sahr*	big • large
betina	be-*tee*-nuh	female (animal)
betul	be-*tul*	right (correct)
biadab	bee-*ah*-dahb	vulgar
biara	bee-*ah*-ruh	monastery
biarawan	bee-ah-ruh-*wahn*	monk
biarawati	bee-ah-ruh-*wah*-tee	nun

| **Biarlah.** | | |
| bee-*ahr*-lah(h) | | Don't bother. |

Biarlah.	bee-*ahr*-lah(h)	Don't bother.
biasa	bee-*ah*-suh	usual • typical
bibir	bee-bir	lips
bijaksana	bee-ja(k)-*sah*-nuh	wise
biji ubat	bee-jee oo-*baht*	tablet
bil	bil	bill (account)
bila	bee-luh	when
bila-bila	bee-luh-bee-luh	anytime
bilik	bee-li(k)	cabin • room
bilik air	bee-li(k) air	bathroom
bilik menunggu	bee-li(k) me-*noong*-goo	waiting room
bilik seorang	bee-li(k) se-o-rahng	single room
bilik tidur	bee-li(k) *tee*-dur	bedroom
bilik tukar pakaian	bee-li(k) too-*kahr* pah-kai-*ahn*	changing rooms
bimbang	beem-bahng	worried
binatang	bee-*nah*-tahng	animal
binatang hampir pupus	bee-*nah*-tahng hahm-pir poo-*pus*	endangered species
binatang liar/buas	bee-*nah*-tahng lee-*yahr*/boo-ahs	wild animal
bintang	bin-*tahng*	stars (in the sky)
bintang kelahiran	bin-*tahng* ke-lah-*hi*-rahn	zodiac
bir	bir	beer
biru	bee-roo	blue
bising	bee-sing	loud • noisy
bocor	bo-*chor*	leak
bodoh	bo-*do(h)*	idiot • stupid
bogel	bo-*gehl*	nude
bola	bo-luh	ball (for sport)
bola sepak	bo-luh seh-pah(k)	football (soccer)
boleh	bo-*leh(h)*	to be able (can)

| **Boleh.** | | |
| bo-*leh(h)* | | Sure. |

(kulit) boneka	(koo-lit) bo-neh-*kah*	puppet (leather)
bosan	bo-sahn	bored
bot bermotor	bot ber-*mo*-tor	motorboat
bot	bot	boat
botol	bo-*tol*	bottle • jar

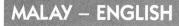

C

botol air	bo-*tol* air	water bottle
buah-buahan	boo-*ah(h)*-boo-*ah*-hahn	fruit
buaian	boo-*ai*-ahn	hammock
buang air besar	boo-*ahng* air be-*sahr*	to shit
buang air kecil	boo-*ahng* air ke-*chil*	to piss
buat	boo-*aht*	for (purpose)
buatan tangan	boo-*ah*-tahn tah-*ngahn*	handmade
budak	boo-*dah(k)*	child
budak perempuan	boo-*dah(k)* pe-*rem*-pwahn	girl
buka	boo-kuh	open
bukan	boo-*kahn*	not
bukit	boo-*kit*	hill
buku	boo-koo	book
buku catatan	boo-koo *chah*-tah-tahn	diary • notebook
buku doa	boo-koo do-ah	prayer book
buku kembara	boo-koo kem-*bah*-ruh	travel book
buku panduan	boo-koo *pahn*-dwahn	guidebook
buku telefon	boo-koo teh-*leh*-fon	phone book
bulan	boo-*lahn*	moon
bulan (ini)	boo-*lahn (ee*-nee)	(this) month
bulan depan	boo-*lahn* de-*pahn*	next month
bulan lepas	boo-*lahn* le-*pahs*	last month
bulan madu	boo-*lahn* mah-*doo*	honeymoon
bulat	boo-*laht*	round (shape)
(di) bulatan	(dee) boo-*lah*-tahn	(at the) roundabout
bulu biri-biri	boo-*loo* bee-*ree*-bee-*ree*	wool
bumbung	boom-bung	roof
bumi	boo-*mee*	earth
bunga	boo-*nguh*	flower
bungkusan	boong-ku-sahn	package
bunyi	boo-nyee	noise • sound
buruk	boo-*ru(k)*	bad
burung	boo-*rung*	bird
busuk	boo-*su(k)*	rotten
but	boot	boots
but jalan	boot *jah*-lahn	hiking boots
butang	boo-*tahng*	buttons

Bye.	bai	Goodbye. (inf)

C

cacat	chah-*chaht*	disabled
cadangan	chah-*dah*-ngahn	proposal
cadar	chah-dahr	sheet (bed)
cakap	chah-*kahp*	speak
cantik	chahn-*ti(k)*	beautiful • pretty
catur	chah-tur	chess

DICTIONARY

cawan	chah-wahn	cup
CD	see dee	CD
cek	chehk	cheque
cek kembara	chehk kem-bah-ruh	travellers cheque
cemas	che-mahs	nervous
cenderamata	chen-de-ruh-mah-tuh	souvenir
cepat	che-paht	fast (quick)
cerah	che-rah(h)	sunny
cerita	che-ree-tuh	story
cermin	cher-min	mirror
cermin mata	cher-min mah-tuh	glasses (eye)
cermin mata hitam	cher-min mah-tuh hee-tahm	sunglasses
cerpen	cher-pehn	short story
cetakan (karya seni)	cheh-ta(k)-kahn (kar-yah se-nee)	print (artwork)
Cik	chi(k)	Miss
cikgu (col)	chi(k)-goo	teacher
cili	chee-lee	chilli
cincin	chin-chin	ring (on finger)
cinta	chin-tuh	love
cirit-birit	chi-rit-bi-rit	diarrhoea
cium	chee-um	kiss
coklat	chok-laht	chocolate • brown
comel	cho-mehl	cute (baby)
contoh	chon-to(h)	example
cuaca	choo-ah-chuh	weather
cuak	choo-ah(k)	nervous
cucu	choo-choo	grandchild
cukai	choo-kai	tax
cukai pendapatan	choo-kai pen-dah-pah-tahn	income tax
cukai penerbangan	choo-kai pe-ner-bah-ngahn	airport tax
cukur	choo-kur	to shave
curam	choo-rahm	steep (hill)
cuti	choo-tee	vacation • holiday
CV	see vee	resumé

D

dadah	dah-dah(h)	drug (illegal)
daerah	dah-eh-rah(h)	region
daging	dah-ging	meat
daging babi	dah-ging bah-bee	pork • ham
daging lembu	dah-ging lem-boo	beef

D

Dah cukup!	dah(h) *choo*-kup!	Enough!

dahaga	dah-*hah*-guh	thirsty
dahsyat	*dah(h)*-shaht	horrible
dahulu	dah-*hoo*-loo	past (before)
dalam	dah-*lahm*	deep • in
damai	dah-*mai*	peace
dan	dahn	and
dapat	*dah*-paht	can (able)
dapur	dah-*pur*	kitchen • stove
darah	*dah*-rah(h)	blood
dari	dah-*ree*	from
daripada	dah-ree-*pah*-duh	from
daripada perak	dah-ree-*pah*-duh peh-*ra(k)*	of silver
darurat	dah-roo-raht	emergency
(di) dasar	(dee) dah-*sahr*	(at the) bottom
datang	*dah*-tahng	to come (arrive)
dataran	dah-*tah*-rahn	square
dataran tinggi	dah-*tah*-rahn *teeng*-gee	plateau
datuk	dah-*tu(k)*	grandfather
daun terup	down te-*rup*	playing cards
debunga	de-*boo*-nguh	pollen
dekat	de-*kaht*	near • at
demam	de-*mahm*	fever
demokrasi	deh-mo-*krah*-see	democracy
dengan	de-*ngahn*	with
dengan cepat	de-*ngahn* che-*paht*	quickly
dengan serta-merta	de-*ngahn* ser-*tah*-mer-*tah*	immediately
deodoran	di-o-do-rahn	deodorant
desa	deh-*suh*	village
destinasi	*dehs*-tee-nah-see	destination
dewasa	deh-*wah*-suh	adult
di	dee	at • on (location)
di antara	dee *ahn*-tah-ruh	among
di atas	dee *ah*-tahs	aboard • above • over
di bawah	dee bah-*wah(h)*	below
di belakang	dee be-*lah*-kahng	at the back (behind)
di dalam	dee dah-*lahm*	inside
di depan	dee de-*pahn*	in front of • ahead
di hadapan	dee hah-dah-*pahn*	ahead
di kalangan	dee kah-*lah*-ngahn	among
di samping	dee *sahm*-ping	beside
di sana	dee *sah*-nuh	over there
di sana ada ...	dee *sah*-nuh *ah*-duh ...	there is/are ...
di sebelah	dee se-be-*lah(h)*	next to
di seberang	dee se-be-*rahng*	over

di sini	dee see-nee	here
di situ	dee see-too	there (nearby)

Di situ ada ...		
dee see-too ah-duh ...		There is/are ...

di tepi	dee te-pee	beside
dia	dee-uh	he • she
dinding	deen-ding	wall (inside)
dingin	dee-ngin	cool (temperature)
diperbuat (daripada)	dee-per-boo-aht (dah-ree-pah-duh)	made (of)
diskaun	dis-kown	discount
disko	dis-ko	disco
ditinggalkan [tinggal]	dee-ting-gahl-kahn [ting-gahl]	to be left (behind, over)
doa	do-ah	prayer
doktor	dok-tor	doctor
doktor gigi	dok-tor gee-gee	dentist
dokumentari	do-kiu-men-tah-ree	documentary
dompet	dom-peht	purse
dosa	do-suh	sin
dram	drahm	drums
drama	drah-mah	play (theatre)
(seni) drama	(se-nee) drah-mah	drama (arts)
drama sabun	drah-mah sah-bun	soap opera
dua hari lepas	doo-uh hah-ree le-pahs	day before yesterday
dua kali	doo-uh kah-lee	twice
duduk	doo-du(k)	to sit
duit	doo-it	money
dunia	doo-nee-uh	world
duta	doo-tah	ambassador

E

(kelas) ekonomi	(ke-lahs) ee-ko-no-mee	economy (class)
ekor	eh-kor	tail (of animal)
eksploitasi	ehks-ploy-tah-see	exploitation
elektrik	eh-lehk-trik	electricity
emak saudara	e-mah(k) sow-dah-ruh	aunt
emak	e-mah(k)	mother
emas	e-mahs	gold
enak	eh-nah(k)	tasty
Encik	en-chi(k)	Mr
enggan	eng-gahn	to refuse
engkau	eng-kow	you (inf)
enjin	ehn-jin	engine
epal	eh-puhl	apple

epilepsi	eh-*pee*-lehp-see	epilepsy
erti	er-tee	meaning
esok	eh-so(k)	tomorrow
esok pagi	eh-so(k) *pah*-gee	tomorrow morning

F

faham	fah-*hahm*	to understand
fajar (matahari terbit)	fah-*jahr* (mah-tuh-*hah*-ree ter-*bit*)	dawn (sunrise)
farmasi	*fahr*-mah-see	chemist (pharmacy)
fasih	fah-si(h)	fluent
fikiran	fee-ki-*rahn*	thought
fiksyen	*fik*-shen	fiction
filem	fee-lem	movie • film (camera)
filem pendek	fee-lem pehn-*deh(k)*	short film
foto	*fo*-to	photograph

G

gading	gah-*ding*	ivory
gam	gahm	glue
gam kunyah	gahm koo-*nyah(h)*	chewing gum
gambar	*gahm*-bahr	picture • photograph
gangguan	*gahng*-goo-ahn	harassment
ganja	*gahn*-jah	marijuana
ganjil	*gahn*-jil	strange
garaj	gah-*rahj*	garage
garam	gah-*rahm*	salt
garfu	*gahr*-foo	fork
gatal	gah-*tahl*	itch • horny (col)
gay	geh	gay
gaya	*gah*-yuh	style
gelak	ge-*lah(k)*	laugh
gelansar filem	ge-*lahn*-sahr *fee*-lem	slide (film)
gelap	ge-*lahp*	dark
gemar	ge-mahr	to like
gembira	gem-*bee*-ruh	happy
gemuk	ge-*mu(k)*	fat
gendang	gen-*dahng*	drums
geografi	ji-o-grah-fee	geography
gerai	ge-*rai*	food stall
gereja	ge-*reh*-juh	church
gereja Yahudi	ge-*reh*-juh yah-*hoo*-dee	synagogue
gigi	*gee*-gee	tooth • teeth
gigitan	*gee*-gee-tahn	bite (dog, insect)
gila	*gee*-luh	crazy • delirious

gincu	gin-choo	lipstick
gitar	gee-tahr	guitar
gol	gol	goal
goreng	go-rehng	fried
gram	grahm	gram
gua	goo-uh	cave
gugur	goo-gur	to fall
gula	goo-luh	sugar
gula-gula	goo-luh-goo-luh	sweets
gunting	goon-ting	scissors
gunung	goo-nung	mountain
gunung berapi	goo-nung be-rah-pee	volcano
guru	goo-roo	teacher
gurun pasir	goo-run pah-sir	desert

H

haba	hah-buh	heat
habis	hah-bis	finished
hadiah	hah-dee-ah(h)	present (gift)
hadiah perkahwinan	hah-dee-ah(h) per-kah-wi-nahn	wedding present
haiwan	hai-wahn	animal
haiwan terlindung	hai-wahn ter-leen-dung	protected species
hajat	hah-jaht	to wish
hak asasi manusia	ha(k) ah-sah-see mah-noo-see-uh	civil rights • human rights
hak sama taraf	hah(k) sah-muh tah-rahf	equal opportunity
hakim	hah-kim	judge (court)
hamil	hah-mil	pregnant
hanya	hah-nyuh	only
harga	hahr-guh	price • cost
hari	hah-ree	day
hari Ahad	hah-ree ah-hahd	Sunday
hari ini	hah-ree ee-nee	today
hari Isnin	hah-ree ees-nin	Monday
hari jadi/lahir	hah-ree jah-dee/lah-hir	birthday
hari Jumaat	hah-ree joo-mah-aht	Friday
hari Khamis	hah-ree kah-mis	Thursday
hari Krismas	hah-ree kris-muhs	Christmas Day
hari Rabu	hah-ree rah-boo	Wednesday
hari Sabtu	hah-ree sahb-too	Saturday
hari Selasa	hah-ree se-lah-suh	Tuesday
harian	hah-ree-ahn	daily
harimau	hah-ree-mow	tiger
harus	hah-rus	must
hasil	hah-sil	result
hasis	hah-sis	hashish

I

hasrat	hahs-raht	to wish
hati	hah-tee	liver
haus	hows	thirsty
helai	he-*lai*	sheet (of paper)
hendak	hen-*da(k)*	to want
hendsem	hehnd-sem	handsome (male)
herba	her-bah	herbs
(penagih) heroin	(pe-*nah*-gi(h)) heh-ro-in	heroin (addict)
hidung	hee-dung	nose
hidup	hee-dup	to live (life) • alive
hijau	hee -jow	green
Hindu	hin-*doo*	Hindu
hitam	hee-tahm	black
HIV positif	ehch ai vee *po*-si-tif	HIV positive
homoseksual	ho-mo-*sehk*-soo-ahl	homosexual
hormat	hor-*maht*	respect
hospital	hos-*pee*-tahl	hospital
hospital swasta	hos-*pee*-tahl *swahs*-tah	private hospital
hotel	ho-*tehl*	hotel
hubungan	hoo-bu-ngahn	relationship
hujan	hoo-jahn	rain
hujung minggu	hoo-*jung* meeng-goo	weekend
hukuman	hoo-ku-mahn	sentence (prison)
huru-hara	hoo-*roo*-hah-*ruh*	anarchist
hutan	hoo-*tahn*	forest
hutan simpan	hoo-*tahn* sim-*pahn*	protected forest

I

ibu	ee-boo	mother
ibu bapa	ee-boo *bah*	parents
ibu mertua	ee-boo mer-*too*-uh	mother-in-law
idea	*ai*-deh-ah	idea
ikan	ee-*kahn*	fish
imigresen	ee-mee-*greh*-sen	immigration
indah	*in*-dah(h)	beautiful (scenery) • pretty
informasi	in-for-*mah*-see	information
ingat	ee-*ngaht*	to remember
Inggeris	ing-ge-ris	English
ingin	ee-ngin	to want
ini	ee-nee	this
insurans	in-soo-*rahns*	insurance
istana	ees-tah-nuh	palace
isteri	ees-te-ree	wife
istimewa	ees-tee-*meh*-wuh	special
itik	ee-*ti(k)*	duck
itu	ee-too	that
izin	ee-zin	permission

J

jadual perjalanan	jah-*doo*-ahl per-jah-*lah*-nahn	itinerary
jadual waktu	jah-doo-*ahl wak*-too	timetable
jahit	jah-*hit*	to sew
jaket	ja-*keht*	jacket
jalan	jah-lahn	avenue • road • street • trail • way
jalan bertol	jah-lahn ber-tol	motorway (tollway)
jalan gunung	jah-lahn goo-nung	mountain path
jalan-jalan	jah-lahn-jah-lahn	stroll
jalan kecil	jah-lahn ke-chil	path • track
jalan keretapi	jah-lahn ke-reh-tah-*ah*-pee	railroad
jalan masuk	jah-lahn mah-*su(k)*	entrance
jalan pejalan kaki	jah-lahn pe-*jah*-lahn kah-*kee*	footpath
jalan utama	jah-lahn oo-*tah*-muh	road
jam	jahm	clock • hour • watch
jam loceng	jahm *lo*-chehng	alarm clock
jam tangan	jahm tah-*ngahn*	wristwatch
jambatan	*jahm*-bah-tahn	bridge
jangkitan	*jahng*-ki-tahn	infection
janji	*jahn*-jee	promise
jantan	*jahn*-tahn	male (animal)
jantung	*jahn*-tung	heart
jarak	jah-*rah(k)*	distance (length)
jarak panjang	jah-*rah(k)* pahn-jahng	long distance
jarang	jah-*rahng*	rare (uncommon)
jari	jah-ree	finger
jarum	jah-rum	needle (sewing, syringe)
jarum suntik	jah-rum soon-*ti(k)*	syringe
jasa	jah-suh	service (assistance)
jatuh	jah-*tuh(h)*	to fall
jauh	jah-*uh(h)*	far
jawapan	jah-*wah*-pahn	reply
jean	jeen	jeans
jenis	je-*nis*	type (of product)
jingga	*jeeng*-gah	orange (colour)
jip	jeep	jeep
jiran	*jee*-rahn	neighbour
johan	*jo*-hahn	winner
jualan murah	joo-*ah*-lahn moo-*ra(h)*	(on) sale
juara	joo-*ah*-ruh	winner
juga	joo-guh	also • too
jujur	joo-jur	honest

Jum!	joom!	Come on!

270

MALAY – ENGLISH

jumlah	joom-*lah(h)*	quantity
jurugambar	joo-roo-*gahm*-bahr	photographer
jurulatih	joo-roo-*lah*-ti(h)	instructor
jururawat	joo-roo-*rah*-waht	nurse
jurutera	joo-roo-te-ruh	engineer
juruwang	joo-roo-*wahng*	cashier
jus	joos	juice
juta	joo-*tuh*	million

K

kaca	*kah*-chuh	glass
kaca depan	*kah*-chuh de-*pahn*	windscreen
kacak	kah-*chah(k)*	handsome (male)
kacang	*kah*-chahng	bean • nut (food)
kad kredit	kahd *kreh*-dit	credit card
kad pengenalan	kahd pe-*nge*-nah-lahn	ID
kad telefon	kahd teh-*leh*-fon	phonecard
kadang-kadang	*kah*-dahng-kah-*dahng*	sometimes
kadar pembayaran	kah-*dahr* pem-bah-*yah*-rahn	rate of pay
kain	kain	material (clothing)
kain lampin	kain *lahm*-pin	nappy
kain pembalut	kain *pem*-bah-lut	bandage
kajipurba	kah-jee-*pur*-buh	archaeological
kakak	kah-*kah(k)*	older sister
kaki	kah-*kee*	foot • leg
kalau	kah-*low*	if
kalian	kah-*lee*-ahn	you (pl)
kambing	*kahm*-bing	goat
(kedai) kamera	(ke-*dai*) ka-me-rah	camera (shop)
kami	*kah*-mee	we (excl)
kampung	*kahm*-pung	village
kamu	kah-*moo*	you (inf)
kamus	*kah*-mus	dictionary
kanan	kah-*nahn*	right (not left)
kanta	kahn-*tuh*	lens
kantung tidur	kahn-*tung tee*-dur	sleeping bag
kapal	*kah*-pahl	ship
kapal terbang	*kah*-pahl ter-*bahng*	aeroplane
kapas	*kah*-pahs	cotton
karya seni	ka-ri-*ah* se-*nee*	artwork
kasar	kah-*sahr*	vulgar
kaset	kah-*seht*	cassette
kaset video	kah-*seht vi*-dee-o	video cassette
kasih	kah-*si(h)*	love
kastam	*kahs*-tahm	customs (border)
kasut	*kah*-sut	shoes
kasut but	*kah*-sut boot	boots

katak	*kah*-tah(k)	frog • toad
katil	*kah*-til	bed
katil kelamin	*kah*-til ke-*lah*-min	double bed
katil kembar	*kah*-til *kem*-bahr	twin beds
kaum	kowm	race (breed)
kawan	kah-*wahn*	friend
kawan-kawan	kah-*wahn*-kah-*wahn*	company (friends)
kawasan	kah-*wah*-sahn	region
kawasan luar bandar	kah-*wah*-sahn *loo*-ahr *bahn*-dahr	countryside
kawasan perkhemahan	kah-*wah*-sahn per-*keh*-mah-han	campsite
kaya	kah-*yuh*	rich (wealthy)
kayu	kah-*yoo*	puppet (wooden) • wood
ke	ke	to
ke arah	ke ah-*rah(h)*	toward
keadilan	ke-ah-*di*-lahn	justice
keagamaan	ke-ah-*gah*-mah-ahn	religious
kebajikan	ke-bah-*ji(k)*-kahn	welfare
kebajikan sosial	ke-bah-*ji(k)*-kahn so-see-*ahl*	social welfare
kebanggaan [bangga]	ke-*bahng*-gah-ahn [*bahng*-guh]	pride
kebenaran	ke-be-*nah*-rahn	truth
kebiasaan	ke-bee-ah-*sah*-ahn	habit
kebocoran	ke-bo-*cho*-rahn	puncture
kebun	ke-*bun*	garden • farm
kebun botani	ke-*bun* bo-*tah*-nee	gardens (botanical)
kecederaan [cedera]	ke-che-de-*rah*-ahn [che-de-*rah*]	injury
kecemasan	ke-che-*mah*-sahn	emergency
kecil	ke-*chil*	little (small)
kedai	ke-*dai*	shop
kedai buku	ke-*dai* boo-koo	bookshop
kedai cenderamata	ke-*dai* chen-de-ruh-*mah*-tuh	souvenir shop
kedai dobi	ke-*dai* do-bee	laundry (shop)
kedai roti	ke-*dai* ro-tee	bakery
kedai ubat Cina	ke-*dai* oo-baht *chee*-nuh	herbalist shop
kedatangan [datang]	ke-dah-*tah*-ngahn [*dah*-tahng]	arrivals
kedua	ke-*doo*-uh	second (in order)
kedua-dua	ke-*doo*-uh-*doo*-uh	both
kedutaan	ke-*doo*-tah-ahn	embassy
keinginan [ingin]	ke-ee-ngi-nahn [ee-ngin]	to wish
kejayaan	ke-jah-*yah*-ahn	success
keju	*keh*-joo	cheese
kejutan	ke-joo-*tahn*	surprise
kek hari jadi	kehk *hah*-ree *jah*-dee	birthday cake

kek lahir	kehk lah-*hir*	birthday cake
kek perkahwinan	kehk per-kah-*wi*-nahn	wedding cake
kekalahan [kalah]	ke-kah-*lah*-hahn [kah-*lah(h)*]	loss
kekasih	ke-*kah*-si(h)	lover
kekuatan	ke-koo-*ah*-tahn	strength
kekurangan	ke-koo-*rah*-ngahn	shortage
kelab (malam)	ke-*lahb* (*mah*-lahm)	(night)club
kelabu	ke-*lah*-boo	grey
(kelajuan) filem	(ke-*lah*-joo-ahn) *fee*-lem	film (speed)
kelakar	ke-*lah*-kahr	joke • funny
kelapa	ke-*lah*-puh	coconut
kelas kedua	ke-*lahs* ke-*doo*-uh	2nd class
kelas pertama	ke-*lahs* per-*tah*-muh	1st class
kelayakan	ke-lah-*yah(k)*-kahn	qualifications
kelompok	ke-*lom*-po(k)	group
kelengkapan [lengkap]	ke-*leng*-kah-pahn [*leng*-kahp]	equipment
kelewatan	ke-*leh*-wah-tahn	delay
kelmarin lepas	kel-*mah*-rin le-*pahs*	day before yesterday
keluar	ke-*loo*-ahr	exit
keluar bersama	ke-*loo*-ahr ber-*sah*-muh	to go out with
keluarga	ke-*loo*-ahr-guh	family
kemalangan	ke-mah-*lah*-ngahn	accident
kemasukan	ke-mah-*su(k)*-kahn	admission (entry)
kematian	ke-*mah*-tee-ahn	death
kembali	kem-*bah*-lee	return
kembar	kem-bahr	twins
kemeja	ke-*meh*-juh	shirt
kemewahan	ke-meh-*wah*-hahn	luxury
kemiskinan	ke-*mees*-ki-nahn	poverty
kemudian	ke-*moo*-dee-ahn	later
kemungkinan	ke-*mung*-ki-nahn	chance
kenal	ke-*nahl*	to know (someone) • to recognise
kenapa	ke-*nah*-puh	why
kencing	ken-ching	piss
kencing manis	ken-ching *mah*-nis	diabetes
kentang	ken-*tahng*	potato
kentut	ken-tut	fart
kenyang	ke-*nyahng*	full (of food)
kepala	ke-*pah*-luh	head
kepanasan [panas]	ke-*pah*-nahs-sahn [*pah*-nahs]	to be hot
kera	ke-ruh	monkey
kerajaan	ke-rah-*jah*-ahn	government
keramah-tamahan	ke-rah-*mah(h)*-tah-*mah(h)*-hahn	hospitality
kerana	ke-*rah*-nuh	because

kerani bank	ke-*rah*-nee bank	bank clerk
kerap	ke-*rahp*	often
keras	ke-*rahs*	hard (not soft)
(tempat letak) kereta	(tem-*paht* le-*tah(k)*) ke-*reh*-tuh	car (park)
keretapi	ke-reh-tuh-*ah*-pee	train
kerja	*ker*-juh	work
kerongkong	ke-*rong*-kong	throat
kertas	ker-*tahs*	paper
kertas rokok	ker-*tahs* ro-ko(k)	cigarette papers
kertas tulis	ker-*tahs* too-lis	writing paper
kerusi	ke-roo-see	chair
kerusi beroda	ke-roo-see be-ro-duh	wheelchair
kesejahteraan	ke-se-*jah(h)*-te-rah-ahn	welfare
kesalahan	ke-sah-*lah*-hahn	mistake
kesan jejak	ke-*sahn* je-*ja(k)*	track (footprints)
kesepuluh	ke-se-*poo*-lu(h)	tenth
kesesatan lalu lintas	ke-se-*sah*-tahn lah-loo-*lin*-tahs	traffic jam
kesilapan	ke-see-lah-*pahn*	mistake
Kesukanan Olimpik	ke-soo-kah-nahn o-*lim*-pik	Olympic Games
ketakutan	ke-tah-*ku*-tahn	fear
ketam	ke-*tahm*	crab
ketat	ke-*taht*	tight
ketawa	ke-tah-*wuh*	laugh
ketibaan [tiba]	ke-*tee*-buh-an [*tee*-buh]	arrivals
ketiga	ke-*tee*-guh	third
ketinggian	ke-*teeng*-gee-ahn	altitude
kewarganegaraan	ke-*wahr*-guh-ne-gah-rah-ahn	citizenship
khas	khahs	special
khemah	keh-*mah(h)*	tent
khidmat	*khid*-maht	service (assistance)
khuatir	khoo-*ah*-tir	worried
kicap	kee-*chahp*	soy sauce
kidal	*ki*-dahl	left-handed
kilang	kee-*lahng*	factory
kilogram	*ki*-lo-grahm	kilogram
kilometer	*ki*-lo-mee-ter	kilometre
kini	*kee*-nee	present (time)
kipas	kee-*pahs*	fan (machine)
kira-kira	*kee*-ruh-*kee*-ruh	approximately
kiri	*ki*-ree	left (not right)
kita	*kee*-tuh	we (incl)
kocek	ko-*cheh(k)*	pocket
kodok	ko-do(k)	frog • toad

kokain	ko-*kehn*	cocaine
kolam renang	ko-*lahm* re-*nahng*	swimming pool
kolej	ko-*lehj*	college
komik	ko-mik	comics
kompas	kom-pahs	compass
kondom	kon-dom	condom
konsert	kon-sert	concert
konstipasi	kons-tee-pah-see	constipation
kontrasepsi	kon-trah-*sehp*-see	contraceptive
kopi	ko-pee	coffee
kos	kos	cost
kosong	ko-song	empty • vacant
kotak	ko-*tah(k)*	box (package)
kotak pertolongan	ko-*tah(k)* per-to-*lo*-ngahn	first-aid kit
kotor	ko-tor	dirty
kotor kemas	ko-tor ke-*mahs*	sleazy (person)
kraftangan	*krahf*-tah-ngahn	handicrafts
kretek	*kreh*-teh(k)	clove cigarettes
krim pelembab	krim pe-*lem*-bahb	moisturising cream
krim pelindung cahaya matahari	krim pe-*leen*-dung chah-*hah*-yuh mah-tah-*hah*-ree	sunblock
kualiti	kwah-lee-*tee*	quality
kuarantin	kwah-*rahn*-teen	quarantine
kuasa	koo-ah-*suh*	power
kuat	koo-*aht*	strong
kubur	koo-*bur*	grave
kucing	koo-*ching*	cat
(penunggangan) kuda	(pe-*nung*-gah-ngahn) koo-duh	horse (riding)
kuil	koo-il	temple (Hindu)
kuinin	kui-*nin*	quinine
kuiz	kuiz	game show
kuliah	koo-lee-*ah(h)*	lecture
kulit	koo-lit	skin • leather
kulit terbakar	koo-lit ter-bah-*kahr*	sunburnt
kumpulan	koom-poo-lahn	group (music) • band (music)
kumpulan darah	koom-poo-lahn dah-rah(h)	blood group
kumpulan rock	koom-poo-lahn rok	rock group
kuno	koo-no	ancient
kunci	koon-chee	key
kuning	koo-ning	yellow
kupu-kupu	koo-poo-koo-poo	butterfly
kurang	koo-rahng	less
kurus	koo-rus	skinny
kutu	koo-too	flea • lice

L

ladang	lah-*dahng*	farm
lagu	lah-*goo*	song • tune
lain	lain	other

Lain kali.		
lain *kah*-lee		Next time.

(had) laju	(hahd) lah-*joo*	speed (limit)
lalat	*lah*-laht	fly
lalulintas	lah-loo-*lin*-tahs	traffic
lama	lah-*muh*	long (time) • old
lambat	*lahm*-baht	late (not on time)
lampu	*lahm*-poo	light (electric)
lampu isyarat	*lahm*-poo ee-*shah*-raht	traffic lights
lampu suluh	*lahm*-poo soo-*lu(h)*	torch (flashlight)
langit	lah-*ngit*	sky
langkah	lang-*kah(h)*	step
lanskap	lahns-*kahp*	landscape
lantai	*lahn*-tai	floor (of room)
lapangan terbang	lah-*pah*-ngahn ter-bahng	airport
lapar	lah-*pahr*	hungry
lari	lah-*ree*	run
latihan (sukan)	lah-*ti(h)*-hahn (soo-*kahn*)	workout (sport)
laut	lowt	sea
lautan	low-tahn	ocean
lawa	lah-*wah*	pretty (adj)
lawak	lah-*wah(k)*	joke • funny
lawan	lah-*wahn*	opposite
layan diri	lah-*yahn* dee-ree	self-service
layar	lah-*yahr*	sail
layar perak	lah-*yahr* pe-*rah(k)*	screen (film)
lebar	leh-*bahr*	wide
lebih	le-*bi(h)*	more
lebih baik	le-*bi(h)* bai(k)	better
lebih suka	le-*bi(h)* soo-kuh	to prefer
lelaki	le-*lah*-kee	male • man
lemah	le-*mah(h)*	weak
lembab	lem-bahb	humid
lembah	lem-bah(h)	valley
lembu	lem-boo	cow
lembut	lem-but	gentle • soft
lengan	le-*ngahn*	arm (of body)
lensa	lehn-*sah*	lens
lepas	le-*pahs*	ago
lesbian	lehs-*bee*-uhn	lesbian
lesen memandu	leh-*sehn* me-*mahn*-doo	drivers licence
lewat	leh-*waht*	late (not on time)

lidah	lee-*dah(h)*	tongue
lif	lif	lift (elevator)
lihat	lee-*haht*	to see
lilin	lee-lin	candle
limau nipis	lee-mow *nee*-pis	lemon
lisan	lee-*sahn*	oral
logam	lo-*gahm*	metal
lompat	lom-*paht*	jump (across)
loncat	lon-*chaht*	jump (high)
longgar	long-gahr	loose
lori	lo-*ree*	truck
lorong	lo-*rong*	alley • path
luar	loo-ahr	outside
luar biasa	loo-ahr bee-*ah*-suh	unusual
luas	loo-*ahs*	large
luka (kecederaan)	loo-*kuh* (ke-che-de-*rah*-ahn)	wound (injury)
lukisan	loo-*ki*-sahn	painting (picture)
lucu	loo-choo	joke • funny
lumpuh kaki	loom-pu(h) kah-*kee*	paraplegic
lumpur	loom-pur	mud
lupa	loo-*puh*	to forget
(garisan) lurus	(gah-*ri*-sahn) loo-*rus*	straight (line)
lusa	loo-suh	day after tomorrow
lutut	loo-*tut*	knee

M

| maaf | mah-*ahf* | sorry |

| *Maafkan saya.* mah-*ahf*-kahn *sai*-yuh | | Excuse me. |

mabuk	mah-*bu(k)*	to be drunk
mabuk jalan	mah-*bu(k)* jah-lahn	travel sickness
mabuk laut	mah-*bu(k)* lowt	seasick
macam mana	mah-chahm mah-nuh	how
mahal	mah-*hahl*	expensive
mahasiswa	mah-*hah*-sis-wah	student (university)
mahkamah	*mah(h)*-kah-mah(h)	court (legal)
mahu	mow	to want
main daun terup	main down te-*rup*	to play cards
main kad	main kahd	to play cards
majalah	mah-jah-*lah(h)*	magazine
majikan	mah-*ji(k)*-kahn	employer
majoriti	mah-*jo*-ree-tee	majority
makan	mah-kahn	eat
makan malam	mah-kahn mah-lahm	dinner

makan sayur saja	*mah*-kahn sah-*yur sah*-juh	vegetarian
makan tengahari	*mah*-kahn te-ngah-*hah*-ree	lunch
makanan	mah-*kah*-nahn	food
maklumat	*mahk*-loo-maht	information
makna	*mahk*-nuh	meaning
maksud	*mahk*-sud	wish
malam	*mah*-lahm	night • evening
malam ini	*mah*-lahm ee-nee	tonight
Malam Krismas	*mah*-lahm *kris*-muhs	Christmas Eve
malam semalam	*mah*-lahm se-*mah*-lahm	last night
malaria	mah-lah-*ree*-ah	malaria
malas	mah-*lahs*	lazy
Malaysia	mah-*lay*-see-ah	Malaysia
malu	*mah*-loo	embarrassment • shy
mampu	*mahm*-poo	can (able)

Mana?		
mah-*nuh*?		Where?

mana-mana	mah-*nuh*-mah-*nuh*	anywhere
mancis	*mahn*-chis	matches
mandi	*mahn*-dee	to bathe/shower • to wash (yourself)
mangga	*mang*-guh	mango • padlock (col)
manis	mah-*nis*	sweet (adj)
manuskrip	mah-*niu*-skrip	script
marah	mah-*rah(h)*	angry
masa	mah-*suh*	time
masa depan	mah-*suh* de-*pahn*	future
masak	mah-*sah(k)*	to cook • ripe
masalah	mah-sah-ah-*lah(h)*	problem
masam	mah-*sahm*	sour
masih	mah-*si(h)*	still (yet)
masin	mah-*sin*	salty
masjid	*mahs*-jid	mosque
masuk	mah-*su(k)*	to enter
masyarakat	mah-*shah*-rah-kaht	society
mata	mah-*tuh*	eye
matahari	mah-tuh-*hah*-ree	sun
matahari terbenam	mah-tuh-*hah*-ree ter-be-*nahm*	sunset
matahari terbit	mah-tuh-*hah*-ree ter-*bit*	sunrise
mati	mah-*tee*	dead (battery, animal)
mee	mee	noodles

meja	meh-juh	table
mekanik	me-ka-nik	mechanic
mel	mehl	mail
mel biasa	mehl bee-ah-suh	surface mail
mel ekspres	mehl ehks-prehs	express mail
mel udara	mehl oo-dah-ruh	airmail
melakukan [laku]	me-lah-koo-kahn [lah-koo]	to do
melaporkan [lapor]	me-lah-por-kahn [lah-por]	to report
melawat [lawat]	me-lah-waht [lah-waht]	to visit
melayani [layan]	me-lah-yah-nee [lah-yahn]	to serve
meletakkan [letak]	me-le-tah(k)-kahn [le-tah(k)]	to put
melihat [lihat]	me-lee-haht [lee-haht]	to look
melihat-lihat saja [lihat]	me-lee-haht-lee-haht sah-juh [lee-haht]	to go window-shopping
melindungi [lindung]	me-lin-du-ngee [lin-dung]	to protect
melukis	me-loo-kis	painting (activity)
memaafkan [maaf]	me-mah-ahf-kahn [mah-ahf]	to forgive
memakai [pakai]	me-mah-kai [pah-kai]	to wear
memancing [pancing]	me-mahn-ching [pahn-ching]	to fish
memandu [pandu]	me-mahn-doo	to drive
memangga (col)	me-mahng-guh	padlock
membaca [baca]	mem-bah-chuh [bah-chuh]	to read
membantah [bantah]	mem-bahn-tah(h) [bahn-tah(h)]	to argue • to protest
membantu [bantu]	mem-bahn-too [bahn-too]	to help
membatalka [batal]	mem-bah-tahl-kah [bah-tahl]	to cancel
membawa [bawa]	mem-bah-wuh [bah-wuh]	to carry • to bring
membayangkan	mem-bah-yahng-kahn	imagine
membayar [bayar]	mem-bah-yahr [bah-yahr]	to pay
membeku [beku]	mem-be-koo [be-koo]	to freeze
membeli [beli]	mem-be-lee [be-lee]	to buy
membeli-belah [beli]	mem-be-lee-be-lah(h) [be-lee]	to go shopping
membenarkan	mem-be-nahr-kahn	to allow
memberahikan [berahi]	mem-be-rah-hee-kahn [be-rah-hee]	sexy
memberi [beri]	mem-be-ree [be-ree]	to give
memberitahu [tahu]	mem-be-ree-tah-hoo [tah-hoo]	to tell (inform)
membersihkan [bersih]	mem-ber-si(h)-kahn [ber-si(h)]	to clean
membina [bina]	mem-bee-nuh [bee-nuh]	to build
membuat [buat]	mem-boo-aht [boo-aht]	to make • to do
membuat tempahan	mem-boo-aht tem-pah-hahn	to make a booking
membuka [buka]	mem-boo-kuh [boo-kuh]	to open
membunuh [bunuh]	mem-boo-nuh(h) [boo-nuh(h)]	to kill
memeriksa [periksa]	me-me-rik-sah [pe-rik-sah]	to check
memikirkan diri sendiri saja	me-mee-kir-kahn dee-ree sen-dee-ree sah-juh	selfish

memilih [pilih]	me-mee-li(h) [pee-li(h)]	to choose
meminjam [pinjam]	me-min-jahm [pin-jahm]	to borrow
meminta [minta]	me-min-tuh [min-tuh]	to ask for something
memisahkan [pisah]	me-mee-sah(h)-kahn [pee-sah(h)]	to separate
memotong [potong]	me-mo-tong [po-tong]	to cut
memperbaiki [baik]	mem-per-bai-kee	to repair
memulai [mula]	me-moo-lah-ee [moo-luh]	to kick off
memulakan [mula]	me-moo-lah-kahn [moo-luh]	to start
mempunyai [punya]	mem-poo-nyah-ee [poo-nyah]	to have
memutuskan [putus]	me-moo-tus-kahn [poo-tus]	to decide
menafikan [nafi]	me-nah-fee-kahn [nah-fee]	to deny
menaiki [naik]	me-nai(k)-kee [nai(k)]	to ride (horse, bus, bike)
menaip [taip]	me-naip (taip)	to type
menandatangani [tandatangan]	me-nahn-duh-tah-ngah-nee [tahn-duh-tah-ngahn]	to sign
menang	me-nahng	to win
menara	me-nah-ruh	tower
menarik	me-nah-ri(k)	interesting
menarik [tarik]	me-nah-ri(k) [tah-ri(k)]	to pull
mencampurkan [campur]	men-cham-pur-kahn [chahm-pur]	to mix
mencari [cari]	men-chah-ree [chah-ree]	to look for • to search
mencegah	men-che-gah(h)	prevent
mencium [cium]	men-chee-um [chee-um]	to kiss
mencuba [cuba]	men-choo-buh [choo-buh]	to try (attempt)
mencuci [cuci]	men-choo-chee [choo-chee]	to wash (something) • to develop (film)
mencuri [curi]	men-choo-ree [choo-ree]	to steal
mendaki gunung	men-dah-kee goo-nung	mountaineering
mendalam	men-dah-lahm	intense
mendapat [dapat]	men-dah-paht [dah-paht]	to earn
mendayung	men-dah-yung	to row
mendengar [dengar]	men-de-ngahr [de-ngahr]	to hear • to listen
menderita [derita]	men-de-ree-tuh [de-ree-tuh]	to suffer
mendesak	men-de-sah(k)	urgent
mendidik [didik]	men-dee-di(k) [dee-di(k)]	to educate
mendung	men-dung	cloudy
meneka [teka]	me-ne-kuh [te-kuh]	to guess
menelefon [telefon]	me-neh-leh-fon [teh-leh-fon]	to telephone
menemani	me-ne-mah-nee	to accompany
menembak [tembak]	me-nehm-bah(k) [tehm-bah(k)]	to shoot
menempah [tempah]	me-nehm-pah(h) [tehm-pah(h)]	to order
menentang	me-nen-tahng	against (opposed)
menerima [terima]	me-ne-ree-muh [te-ree-muh]	to accept • to receive

M

mengadu [adu]	me-ngah-doo [ah-doo]	to complain
mengajar	me-ngah-jahr	teaching
mengakhiri [akhir]	me-ngah-khi-ree [ah-khir]	to end
mengambil [ambil]	me-ngahm-bil [ahm-bil]	to pick up • to take away
mengambil foto/gambar	me-ngahm-bil fo-to/gahm-bahr	to take photographs
mengandung	me-ngahn-dung	to be pregnant
mengantuk	me-ngahn-tu(k)	sleepy
mengapa	me-ngah-puh	why
mengatur [atur]	me-ngah-tur [ah-tur]	to organise
mengejek	me-ngeh-jeh(k)	to make fun of
mengeksport [eksport]	me-ngehks-port [ehks-port]	to export
mengakui [akui]	me-ngah-koo-ee [ah-koo-ee]	to recognise
mengembara	me-ngem-bah-ruh	to travel
mengerikan [ngeri]	me-nge-ree-kahn [nge-ree]	terrible • horrible
mengeringkan [kering]	me-nge-ring-kahn [ke-ring]	to dry
mengesahkan [sah]	me-nge-sah(h)-kahn [sah(h)]	to confirm (a booking)
mengesyorkan [syor]	me-nge-shor-kahn [shor]	to recommend
mengganggu [ganggu]	meng-gahng-goo [gahng-goo]	to annoy
menggigit [gigit]	meng-gee-git [gee-git]	to bite
menggunakan kembali	meng-goo-nah-kahn kem-bah-lee	to recycle
menghantar [hantar]	meng-hahn-tahr [hahn-tahr]	to send
menghasilkan [hasil]	meng-hah-sil-kahn [hah-sil]	to produce
menghiburkan [hibur]	meng-hee-bur-kahn [hee-bur]	entertaining
menghidu [hidu]	meng-hee-doo [hee-doo]	to smell
menghilangkan [hilang]	meng-hee-lahng-kahn [hee-lahng]	to lose (something)
menghiris [hiris]	meng-hee-ris [hee-ris]	to slice
menghukum [hukum]	meng-hoo-kum [hoo-kum]	to punish
mengikuti [ikut]	me-ngee-ku-tee [ee-kut]	to follow (join in)
mengira [kira]	me-ngee-ruh [kee-ruh]	to count
mengisi [isi]	me-ngee-see [ee-see]	to fill
mengizinkan	me-ngee-zin-kahn	to allow
mengkagumkan	meng-kah-gum-kahn	wonderful
mengulangi [ulang]	me-ngoo-lah-ngee [oo-lahng]	repeat
mengunci [kunci]	me-ngun-chee [koon-chee]	to lock
mengundi [undi]	me-ngun-dee [un-dee]	to vote
mengunjungi [kunjung]	me-ngoon-ju-ngee [koon-jung]	to visit
mengurat	me-ngoo-rut	to chat up
mengurut [urut]	me-ngoo-rut [oo-rut]	to massage
menikmati [nikmat]	me-nik-mah-tee [nik-maht]	to enjoy (oneself)

D I C T I O N A R Y

menimbang [timbang]	me-*nim*-bahng [*tim*-bahng]	to weigh
meninggal [tinggal]	me-*ning*-gahl [*ting*-gahl]	to die (person)
meninggal dunia	me-*ning*-gahl doo-ni-uh	dead (person)
menipu [tipu]	me-*nee*-poo [*tee*-poo]	to lie
menjaga [jaga]	men-*jah*-guh [*jah*-guh]	to look after
menjawab [jawab]	men-*jah*-wahb [*jah*-wahb]	to reply • to answer
menjerit [jerit]	men-je-*rit* [je-*rit*]	to shout
menjual [jual]	men-joo-*ahl* [joo-*ahl*]	to sell
menjumpai [jumpa]	men-*joom*-pah-ee [*joom*-pah]	to find
menolak [tolak]	me-no-*lah(k)* [to-*lah(k)*]	to refuse
menolong [tolong]	me-no-long [to-long]	to help
menonton [tonton]	me-non-ton [ton-ton]	to watch
mensyempu [syempu]	men-shehm-*poo* [shem-*poo*]	to shampoo
mentah	men-*tah(h)*	raw (food)
mentega	men-*teh*-guh	butter
menterjemahkan [terjemah]	men-ter-je-*mah(h)*-kahn [ter-je-*mah(h)*]	to translate
(rokok) mentol	(ro-ko(k)) mehn-tol	menthol (cigarettes)
mentul	*mehn*-tul	light bulb
menu	*meh*-noo	menu
menukar [tukar]	me-*noo*-kahr [*too*-kahr]	to change
menulis [tulis]	me-*noo*-lis [*too*-lis]	to write
menumpang	me-*noom*-pahng	to hitchhike
menunggang [tunggang]	me-*noong*-gahng [*toong*-gahng]	to ride (bus, car, plane, train)
menunjukkan [tunjuk]	me-*noon*-joo(k)-kahn [*toon*-joo(k)]	to show
menutup [tutup]	me-*noo*-tup [*too*-tup]	to close
menyakitkan	me-nyah-*kit*-kahn	painful
menyanyi [nyanyi]	me-*nyah*-nyee [*nyah*-nyee]	to sing
menyedari [sedar]	me-nye-*dah*-ree [se-*dahr*]	to realise
menyediakan [sedia]	me-nye-dee-*ah*-kahn [se-dee-*uh*]	to prepare
menyelam [selam]	me-nye-*lahm* [se-*lahm*]	to dive
menyelamatkan [selamat]	me-nye-*lah*-maht-kahn [se-*lah*-maht]	to save
menyentuh [sentuh]	me-nyen-*tu(h)* [sen-*tu(h)*]	to touch
menyesal [sesal]	me-nye-*sahl* [se-*sahl*]	to regret
menyewa [sewa]	me-*nyeh*-wuh [*seh*-wuh]	to hire (rent)
menyuntikkan [suntik]	me-nyun-*ti(k)*-kahn [sun-*ti(k)*]	to inject
merah	*meh*-rah(h)	red
merah jambu	*meh*-rah(h) jahm-boo	pink
merasuah	me-rah-soo-*ah(h)*	to bribe
merayakan [raya]	me-*rah*-yuh-kahn [*rah*-yuh]	to celebrate
mereka	me-*reh*-kuh	they

merindui [rindu]	me-*rin*-doo-ee [*rin*-doo]	to miss (feel absence)
merokok [rokok]	me-*ro*-ko(k) [*ro*-ko(k)]	to smoke
merompak [rompak]	me-rom-*pa(k)* [rom-*pa(k)*]	to rob
mesin	me-*sin*	machine
mesin basuh	me-*sin* bah-*su(h)*	washing machine
mesti	mes-tee	must
mesyuarat	me-*shoo* ah-raht	meeting
meter	mee-ter	metre
migraine	mai-grehn	migraine
milimeter	mi-li-*mee*-ter	millimetre
minggu	ming-goo	week
minggu depan	ming-goo de-*pahn*	next week
minggu ini	ming-goo ee-nee	this week
minggu lepas	ming-goo le-*pahs*	last week
minit	mi-nit	minute
minum	mee-num	to drink
minuman	mee-nu-*mahn*	drink
minyak	*min*-yah(k)	petrol
minyak masak	*min*-yah(k) *mah*-sah(k)	oil (cooking)
misalan	mi-*sah*-lahn	example
miskin	mis-kin	poor
modem	mo-*dem*	modem
mogok	mo-*go(k)*	(on) strike
monyet	mo-*nyeht*	monkey
motosikal	mo-to-*see*-kahl	motorcycle
mual	moo-ahl	nausea
muda	moo-duh	young
mudah	moo-*dah(h)*	easy
muka	moo-kuh	face
mulakan	moo-*luh*-kahn	to begin
mulut	moo-lut	mouth
munasabah	moo-*nah*-sah-bah(h)	sensible
mungkin	moong-kin	maybe • perhaps
muntah	moon-*tah(h)*	vomit • to vomit
murah	moo-rah(h)	cheap
murah hati	moo-rah(h) hah-tee	generous
murid	moo-*rid*	student (school)
murni	moor-nee	pure
musim	moo-sim	season
musim bunga	moo-sim boo-nguh	spring (season)
musim luruh	moo-sim *loo*-ru(h)	autumn
musim panas	moo-sim *pah*-nahs	summer
musim sejuk	moo-sim se-*joo(k)*	winter
mutu	moo-*too*	quality
muzik	moo-zik	music
muzium	moo-zee-um	museum

N

naik	nai(k)	to board (ship, etc)
(jalan) naik bukit	(jah-lahn) nai(k) boo-kit	uphill (road)
nama	nah-muh	name
nama keluarga	nah-muh ke-loo-ahr-guh	surname
nama panggilan	nah-muh pang-gi-lahn	nickname
nama pertama	nah-muh per-tah-muh	first name
nanas	nah-nahs	pineapple
nanti	nahn-tee	later
naskhah	nahs-kah(h)	script
nasi	nah-see	rice (cooked)
nasib	nah-sib	luck
negara	ne-gah-ruh	country
nenas	neh-nahs	pineapple
nenek	neh-neh(k)	grandmother
nilai	nee-lai	value (price) • worth
nipis	nee-pis	thin
nombor	nom-bor	number
novel	no-vel	novel (book)
nyamuk (kelambu)	nyah-mu(k) (ke-lahm-boo)	mosquito (net)
nyaris-nyaris	nyah-ris-nyah-ris	almost

O

offside	of-said	offside
OK	oh-kay	OK
oksigen	ok-see-jen	oxygen
olahraga	o-lah(h)-rah-guh	track (sports)
ombak	om-bah(k)	waves
operasi	o-pe-rah-see	operation
operator (telefon)	o-pe-rah-tor (teh-leh-fon)	(telephone) operator
orang	o-rahng	person • people
orang asing	o-rahng ah-sing	foreigner
orang barat	o-rahng bah-raht	Westerner (col)
orang Eropah	o-rahng eh-ro-pah(h)	European
orang gaji	o-rahng gah-jee	servant
orang Islam	o-rahng ees-lahm	Muslim
orang suci	o-rahng soo-chee	saint
orang tua	o-rahng too-uh	parents
orang yang tidak dikenali	o-rahng yahng tee-dah(k) dee-ke-nah-lee	stranger
oren	o-rehn	orange (food, colour)
orgasma	or-gahs-mah	orgasm
orkestra	or-kehs-truh	orchestra
otak	o-tah(k)	brain
otot	o-tot	muscle

P

pada	pah-*duh*	at (time)
pada waktu tengahari	pah-*duh* wahk-too te-ngah-*hah*-ree	in the afternoon
padang pasir	pah-dahng pah-sir	desert
padang tenis	pah-dahng teh-*nis*	tennis court
paderi	pah-de-*ree*	priest (Catholic, Protestant)
(yang) paling	(yahng) pah-*ling*	most (the)
pagi	pah-gee	morning
pagi semalam	pah-gee se-*mah*-lahm	yesterday morning
paip	paip	pipe (plumbing)
pakar	pah-*kahr*	specialist
(kedai) pakaian	(ke-*dai*) pah-*kai*-ahn	clothing (store)
paku kayu	pah-*koo* kah-*yoo*	tent pegs
paling penting	pah-ling *pen*-ting	essential
pam	pahm	pump
pameran	pah-*meh*-rahn	exhibition
panas	pah-nahs	hot (temperature) • heat
pancang khemah	pahn-*chahng* kheh-*mah*(h)	tent pegs
panggang	pahng-gahng	roasted
panggung sandiwara	pahng-gung sahn-dee-*wah*-rah	theatre (play)
panggung wayang	pahng-gung *wai*-yahng	cinema
panjang	pahn-jahng	long (measurement) • length
pantai	pahn-tai	beach
pantas	pahn-*tahs*	quick • quickly
papan kekunci	pah-*pahn* ke-*koon*-chee	keyboard
papan markah	pah-*pahn* mahr-*kah*(h)	scoreboard
papan mata	pah-*pahn* mah-tuh	scoreboard
papan selancar	pah-*pahn* se-*lahn*-chahr	surfboard
parlimen	pahr-lee-men	parliament
parti	pahr-tee	party (political)
pas naik	pahs nai(k)	boarding pass
pasar (malam)	pah-sahr (*mah*-lahm)	(night) market
pasaraya	pah-sah-*rah*-yuh	supermarket
pasir	pah-sir	sand
(nombor) passport	(nom-bor) pahs-port	passport (number)
pasukan	pah-*su*(k)-kahn	team (sport)
patah	pah-*tah*(h)	broken
patung	pah-tung	statue
payung	pah-yung	umbrella
pecah	pe-*chah*	break (fracture)
pedang	pe-*dahng*	sword
pedas	pe-*dahs*	hot (spicy)
pegas	pe-*gahs*	spring (coil)

pegawai pengawas stesen keretapi	pe-gah-*wai* pe-*ngah*-wahs *steh*-sehn ke-reh-tah-*ah*-pee	stationmaster
peguam	pe-*gwahm*	lawyer
pejabat maklumat pelancong	pe-*jah*-baht *mah(k)*-loo-maht pe-*lahn*-chong	tourist information office
pejabat pos	pe-*jah*-baht pos	post office
pejabat tiket	pe-*jah*-baht tee-*keht*	ticket office
pejalan kaki	pe-*jah*-lahn *kah*-kee	pedestrian
pekak	pe-*kah(k)*	deaf
pekerja	pe-*ker*-juh	employee
pekerja pejabat	pe-*ker*-juh pe-*jah*-baht	office worker
pekerjaan	pe-ker-*jah*-ahn	job • occupation
pelabuhan	pe-lah-*bu*-hahn	port • harbour
pelacur	pe-*lah*-chur	prostitute
pelajar	pe-*lah*-jahr	student (school)
pelan	pe-*lahn*	plan
pelancong [lancong]	pe-lah-chong [*lahn*-chong]	tourist
pelarian	pe-lah-*ree*-ahn	refugee
pelayan	pe-*lah*-yahn	waiter
pelepasan	pe-le-*pah*-sahn	departure
pelik	pe-*li(k)*	strange
peluang	pe-loo-*ahng*	chance
peluk	pe-*lu(k)*	hug
pelukis	pe-*loo*-kis	painter (artist)
pelukis potret	pe-*loo*-kis po-*treht*	portrait sketcher
pemain	pe-*main*	player
pemain muzik	pe-*main* moo-zik	musician
pemain sukan	pe-*main* soo-*kahn*	sportsplayer
pemakaman	pe-*mah-kah*-mahn	funeral
pemenang	pe-me-*nahng*	winner
pemandangan [pandang]	pe-*mahn*-dah-ngahn [*pahn*-dahng]	scenery • view
pemandu	pe-*mahn*-doo	guide (person, audio)
pembasmi kuman	pem-*bahs*-mee koo-*mahn*	antiseptic
pemberian [beri]	pem-be-*ree*-ahn [be-*ree*]	present (gift)
pembuka botol	pem-*boo*-kuh bo-*tol*	bottle opener
pembuka tin	pem-*boo*-kuh tin	can opener
pemeriksaan kembali	pe-me-*rik*-sah-ahn kem-*bah*-lee	review
pemetik api	pe-me-*ti(k)* ah-pee	lighter
pemilik	pe-*mee*-li(k)	owner
pemimpin [pimpin]	pe-*meem*-pin [*peem*-pin]	leader
pemungut tiket	pe-moo-*ngut* tee-*keht*	ticket collector
pen	pehn	pen
(penagih) heroin	(pe-*nah*-gi(h)) heh-ro-in	heroin (addict)

penanaman hutan semula	pe-nah-*nah*-mahn hoo-*tahn* se-*moo*-luh	reforestation
penangguhan	pe-*nahng*-gu-hahn	delay
penat	pe-*naht*	tired
pencacaran	pen-chah-*chah*-rahn	vaccination
pencemaran	pen-che-*mah*-rahn	pollution
pencuri	pen-choo-*ree*	thief
(kaunter) pendaftaran	(*kown*-ter) pen-*dahf*-tah-rahn	check-in (desk)
pendakian tebing batu	pen-dah-*kee*-ahn te-*bing* bah-*too*	rock climbing
pendapat	pen-*dah*-paht	opinion
pendek	*pehn*-deh(k)	short (length, height)
pendidikan	pen-dee-*di(k)*-kahn	education
pendingin udara	pen-*dee*-ngin oo-*dah*-ruh	air-conditioner
penebangan hutan	pe-ne-*bah*-ngahn hoo-*tahn*	deforestation
penerbangan	pe-ner-*bah*-ngahn	flight
penerbit [terbit] (filem)	pe-*ner*-bit [*ter*-bit] (*fee*-lem)	producer (of film)
pengadil	pe-*ngah*-dil	referee
penganggur	pe-*ngahng*-gur	homeless • unemployed
penganut Buda	pe-*ngah*-nut boo-duh	Buddhist
pengarah (filem)	pe-*ngah*-rah(h) (*fee*-lem)	director (of film)
pengembalian wang	pe-ngem-*bah*-lee-ahn wahng	to refund
pengembaraan [kembara]	pe-ngem-*bah*-ruh-ahn [kem-*bah*-ruh]	to trek
pengemis	pe-*nge*-mis	beggar
pengenalan	pe-*nge*-nah-lahn	identification
pengguguran	peng-goo-*goo*-rahn	abortion
penggunting rambut	peng-*gun*-ting *rahm*-but	barber
penghibur jalanan	peng-hi-bur *jah*-lah-nahn	busker
penginapan	pe-*ngee*-nah-pahn	accommodation
pengsan	*pehng*-sahn	to faint
pengurus	pe-*ngoo*-rus	manager
pening	pe-*ning*	dizzy

Penipu! pe-nee-*poo!*		**Cheat!**

penjaga anak	pen-*jah*-guh ah-nah(k)	babysitter
penjaga gol	pen-*jah*-guh gol	goalkeeper
penjagaan anak	pen-jah-*gah*-ahn ah-nah(k)	childminding
penjara	pen-*jah*-ruh	prison
penjual dadah	pen-joo-*ahl* dah-*dah(h)*	drug dealer
penjuru	pen-joo-*roo*	corner
pensyarah	pen-shah-*rah(h)*	lecturer
pentas	pen-*tahs*	stage

penting	pen-ting	important • urgent
penuh	pe-nuh(h)	full
penuh sesak	pe-nuh(h) se-sa(k)	crowded
penulis	pe-noo-lis	writer
penumpang	pe-noom-pahng	passenger
penyakit	pe-nyah-kit	disease
penyakit berak darah	pe-nyah-kit beh-ra(k) dah-rah(h)	dysentery
penyakit kelamin	pe-nyah-kit ke-lah-min	venereal disease
penyakit sengal-sengal tulang	pe-nyah-kit se-ngahl-se-ngahl too-lahng	rheumatism
penyampai	pe-nyahm-pai	presenter (TV, etc)
penyampaian [sampai]	pe-nyahm-pai-ahn [sahm-pai]	presentation
penyanyi	pe-nyah-nyee	singer
penyeluk saku	pe-nye-lu(k) sah-koo	pickpocket
penyembahan	pe-nyem-bah(h)-hahn	worship
penyokong [sokong]	pe-nyo-kong [so-kong]	fan (of a team)
penyunting	pe-nyun-ting	editor
perak	peh-ra(k)	silver
perahu	pe-rah-hoo	boat
perang	pe-rahng	war
perasaan [rasa]	pe-rah-sah-ahn [rah-suh]	feelings
peraturan	pe-rah-tu-rahn	rules
perayaan	pe-rah-yah-ahn	festival
percaya	per-chah-yuh	to trust
percintaan	per-chin-tah-ahn	romance
percuma	per-choo-muh	free (of charge)
perdana menteri	per-dah-nuh men-te-ree	prime minister
perempuan	pe-rem-pwahn	female (human) • woman
pergaduhan	per-gah-du(h)-hahn	fight
pergi	per-gee	to go
(tiket) pergi balik	(tee-keht) per-gee bah-li(k)	return (ticket)

Pergilah!
per-gee-la(h)!

Get lost!

pergunungan	per-goo-nu-ngahn	mountain range
perhentian bas	per-hen-tee-ahn bahs	bus stop
perhimpunan	per-him-pu-nahn	rally (demonstration)
peribadi	pe-ree-bah-dee	personality • private
periuk	pe-ree-u(k)	pot (cooking)
perjalanan	per-jah-lah-nahn	trip • journey
perjalanan [jalan]	per-jah-lah-nahn [jah-lahn]	to trek
perkahwinan	per-kah(h)-wi-nahn	marriage
pernikahan	per-nee-kah(h)-hahn	wedding
perkataan	per-kah-tah-ahn	word

perlahan	per-*lah*-hahn	slow
perlu	per-*loo*	need
perlumbaan	per-*loom*-bah-ahn	race (sport)
permaidani	per-*mai*-dah-nee	rug
permainan	per-*mai*-nahn	game
		(board game, sport)
permainan komputer	per-*mai*-nahn kom-*piu*-ter	computer game
permit	per-*mit*	permit
permit kerja	per-*mit* ker-juh	work permit
pernah	per-*nah(h)*	already
perniagaan	per-nee-ah-*gah*-ahn	business
pernikahan	per-nee-*kah(h)*-hahn	wedding
perogolan [rogol]	pe-ro-go-lahn [ro-*gohl*]	rape
perpustakaan	per-poos-*tah*-kah-ohn	library
persatuan	per-sah-*too*-ahn se-*ker*-juh	unions
persendirian	per-sen-dee-*ree*-ahn	private
persimpangan	per-*sim*-pah-ngahn	intersection
pertama	per-*tah*-muh	first
pertanyaan	per-*tah*-nyuh-ahn	question
pertemuan	per-te-*moo*-ahn	meeting
pertolongan	per-*to*-lo-ngan	assistance
(kadar) pertukaran	(kah-*dahr*) per-too-*kah*-rahn	exchange (rate)
pertunjukan [tunjuk]	per-toon-*joo(k)*-kahn [toon-*joo(k)*]	performance • show
perut	pe-*rut*	stomach
pesanan	pe-*sah*-nahn	message
pesara	pe-*sah*-ruh	pensioner
pesta	pehs-tuh	party (fiesta)
peta	pe-tah	map
peta jalan	pe-tah jah-lahn	road map
petang	pe-*tahng*	afternoon
petang esok	pe-*tahng* eh-so(k)	tomorrow afternoon
petang ini	pe-*tahng* ee-nee	this afternoon
petang semalam	pe-*tahng* se-*mah*-lahm	yesterday afternoon
petani	pe-*tah*-nee	farmer
peti besi	pe-*tee* be-see	safe (vault)
peti sejuk	pe-*tee* se-*ju(k)*	refrigerator
petrol	peh-trol	petrol
Piala Dunia	pee-*ah*-luh doo-ni-*uh*	World Cup
pidato politik	pee-*dah*-to po-*lee*-tik	political speech
pil	pil	pill
pilihanraya	pee-lee-*hahn*-rah-yuh	elections
pinggan	*ping*-gahn	plate
pinggang	*ping*-gahng	back (of body)
pinggir bandar	*ping*-gir *bahn*-dahr	suburb
pinggir laut	*ping*-gir lowt	coast
ping-pong	ping-*pong*	table tennis
pintu	*peen*-too	door

pintu masuk	peen-too mah-su(k)	entrance
pisang	pee-sahng	banana
pisau	pee-sow	knife
pisau cukur	pee-sow choo-kur	razor
pisau lipat	pee-sow lee-paht	penknife
planet	plah-neht	planet
plastik	plahs-tik	plastic
plug	pluhg	plug (electricity)
PMS	pee em es	premenstrual tension
pohon	po-hon	tree
poker	po-ker	poker (the game)
poket	po-keht	pocket
pokok	po-ko(k)	tree
polis	po-lis	police
pondok	pon-do(k)	mountain hut
popular	po-piu-luhr	popular
poskad	pos-kahd	postcard
poskod	pos-kod	postcode
poster	pos-ter	poster
potong	po-tong	piece
presiden	preh-see-den	president
projektor	pro-jehk-tor	projector
Puan	pwahn	Mrs
puisi	poo-ee-see	poetry
pulang	poo-lahng	to go home
pulau	poo-low	island
pun	pun	also • too
puncak	poon-chah(k)	peak (of mountain)
purba	pur-buh	ancient
purse	puhrs	purse
pusat membeli-belah	poo-saht mem-be-lee-be-lah(h)	department stores
pusing	poo-sing	turn
pusingan	poo-si-ngahn	leg (of a race)
putih	poo-ti(h)	white

R

radiator	rah-dee-ah-tor	radiator
rakaman	rah-kah-mahn	recording
raket	rah-keht	racquet
ramah-tamah	rah-mah(h)-tah-mah(h)	outgoing
ramai	rah-mai	busy (place, party)
rambut	rahm-but	hair
rancangan	rahn-chah-ngahn	program (TV)
rantai	rahn-tai	necklace
rasa	rah-suh	taste
rasisme	rah-sis-muh	racism

rehat	reh-*haht*	rest (relaxation)
rendah	ren-*dah(h)*	low
rentak	ren-*tah(k)*	rhythm
republik	ree-*puhb*-lik	republic
resit	re-*sit*	receipt
restoran	rehs-*to*-rahn	restaurant
resume	reh-siu-*meh*	resumé
ribut	ree-*but*	storm
ringan	ri-*ngahn*	light (not heavy)
risau	ree-*sow*	worried
risiko	ree-*see*-ko	risk
roda	ro-*duh*	wheel
(kertas) rokok	(ker-*tahs*) ro-ko(k)	cigarette (papers)
rosak	ro-*sah(k)*	rotten
roti	ro-tee	bread
roti bakar	ro-tee *bah*-kahr	toast (bread)
ruam	roo-*ahm*	rash
ruam bayi	roo-*ahm bah*-yee	nappy rash
ruang	roo-*ahng*	space (area)
ruang tamu	roo-*ahng tah*-moo	lounge (room)
rumah	roo-mah(h)	house
rumput	room-put	grass
runtuhan	run-*tu*-hahn	ruins
runtuhan bersejarah	run-*tu*-hahn ber-se-*jah*-rah(h)	historical ruins
rusa	roo-suh	deer

S

saat	sah-*aht*	second (unit of time)
sabar	sah-*bahr*	patient (adj)
sabun	sah-*bun*	soap
sains	sains	science
saintis	sain-tis	scientist
saiz	saiz	size
sajak	sah-*jah(k)*	poetry
sakit	sah-kit	sick • pain
sakit gigi	sah-kit *gee*-gee	toothache
sakit haid	sah-kit haid	period pain
sakit kepala	sah-kit ke-*pah*-luh	headache
sakit lelah	sah-kit le-*lah(h)*	asthma
sakit perut	sah-kit pe-*rut*	indigestion • stomachache
saku	sah-*koo*	pocket
salah	sah-*lah(h)*	wrong
salah faham	sah-*lah(h)* fah-*hahm*	misunderstanding
sama	sah-muh	same

sambil	*sahm*-bil	while (currently)
sampah	*sahm*-pah(h)	rubbish
sampai	*sahm*-pai	to arrive
sampan	*sahm*-pahn	boat
sampul surat	*sahm*-pul soo-raht	envelope
sangat	sah-*ngaht*	very • intense
sangat baik	sah-*ngaht* bai(k)	excellent
sangat lemak	sah-*ngaht* le-*mah*(k)	rich (food)
sangat ulung	sah-*ngaht* oo-lung	excellent
sarapan pagi	sah-rah-*pahn* pah-gee	breakfast
sarung bantal	sah-*rung* bahn-tahl	pillowcase
satu saja	sah-too sah-juh	just one
sawan babi	sah-*wahn* bah-bee	epilepsy
saya	*sai*-yuh	I
sayang	sah-yahng	love
sayap	sah-*yahp*	wings
sayap kanan	sah-*yahp* kah-nahn	right-wing
sayap kiri	sah-*yahp* ki-ree	left-wing
sayuran saja	sai-yu-rahn sah-juh	vegetarian (food)
sayur-sayuran	sai-yur-sai-yu-rahn	vegetables
sebab	se-*bahb*	because
sebarang	se-*bah*-rahng	any
sebelum	se-be-*lum*	before
seberang	se-be-*rahng*	across
sedap	se-*dahp*	delicious
sederhana	se-der-*hah*-nuh	simple
sedia	se-dee-*uh*	ready
sedih	se-*di*(h)	sad
sedikit	se-dee-kit	little (amount)
segan	se-*gahn*	shy
segar	se-*gahr*	fresh
segiempat	se-gee-em-paht	square (shape)
(tiket) sehala	(tee-*keht*) se-*hah*-luh	one-way (ticket)
sehingga (Jun)	se-*hing*-guh (joon)	until (June)
sejak	se-*jah*(k)	since
sejarah	se-*jah*-rah(h)	history
sejuk	se-*ju*(k)	cold
sekali	se-*kah*-lee	once
sekali lagi	se-*kah*-lee *lah*-gee	once again
sekarang	se-*kah*-rahng	now • present
sekarang juga	se-*kah*-rahng joo-guh	right now
sekejap lagi	se-ke-*jahp lah*-gee	soon
sekolah	se-ko-*lah*(h)	school
sekolah menengah (SM)	se-ko-*lah*(h) me-ne-*ngah*(h)	high school
seks	sehks	sex
seks selamat	sehks se-*lah*-maht	safe sex
seksisme	sehk-*sis*-muh	sexism

selalu	se-*lah*-loo	always
selama	se-*lah*-muh	for (length of time)
selama-lamanya	se-*lah*-muh-*lah*-muh-nyuh	forever
selamat	se-*lah*-maht	safe (secure)

Selamat datang.
se-*lah*-maht dah-*tahng* — Welcome.

Selamat hari jadi!
se-*lah*-maht hah-ree jah-dee! — Happy Birthday!

Selamat jalan.
se-*lah*-maht jah-lahn — Goodbye. (speaker staying)

Selamat malam.
se-*lah*-maht mah-lahm — Good night.

Selamat pagi.
se-*lah*-maht pah-gee — Good morning.

Selamat petang.
se-*lah*-maht pe-tahng — Good afternoon.

Selamat tengahari.
se-*lah*-maht te-ngah-hah-ree — Good day.

Selamat tinggal.
se-*lah*-maht ting-gahl — Goodbye. (speaker leaving)

selatan	se-lah-*tahn*	south
selepas	se-le-*pahs*	after
selesa	se-*leh*-suh	comfortable
selimut	se-*lee*-mut	blanket
selipar	se-*lee*-pahr	sandals
seluar dalam	se-loo-*ahr* dah-*lahm*	underwear
seluar panjang	se-loo-*ahr* pahn-*jahng*	trousers
seluar pendek	se-loo-*ahr* pehn-*de(k)*	shorts (clothes)
seluruh	se-loo-*ru(h)*	whole (all)
semacam	se-*mah*-chahm	similar
semalam	se-*mah*-lahm	yesterday
sembahyang	sem-*bah*-yahng	prayer
sembelit	sem-be-lit	constipation
sempadan	sem-*pah*-dahn	border
sempit	sem-pit	tight
sempurna	sem-*pur*-nuh	perfect
semua	se-*moo*-uh	all
semua orang	se-*moo*-uh o-rahng	everyone
semuanya	se-*moo*-*uh*-nyuh	everything
semula	se-*moo*-luh	again
semut	se-*mut*	ant
senang	se-*nahng*	easy

seni	se-*nee*	art
seni prasejarah	se-*nee* prah-se-*jah*-rah(h)	prehistoric art
seni tembikar	se-*nee* tem-*bee*-kahr	pottery
seni ukir	se-*nee* oo-kir	sculpture
senibina	se-*nee*-*bee*-nuh	architecture
seni foto	se-*nee* fo-to	photography
seniman/seniwati	se-*nee*-mahn/ se-*nee*-wah-tee (m/f)	artist
sentiasa	*sen*-tee-ah-sah	always
senyap	se-*nyahp*	quiet
senyum	se-*nyum*	to smile
sepasang	se-*pah*-sahng	pair (a couple)
sepi	se-*pee*	quiet
serangan	se-*rah*-ngahn	assault
serangga	se-*rahng*-guh	bug • insect
seratus	se-*rah*-tus	a hundred
sering	se-*ring*	often
serius	see-*ree*-uhs	serious
seronok	se-ro-no(k)	fun
serupa	se-*roo*-puh	similar
seseorang	se-se-o-*rahng*	someone
sesuai	se-*soo*-ai	appropriate
sesuatu	se-soo-*ah*-too	something
sesudah	se-soo-*dah*(h)	after
setelah	se-te-*lah*(h)	after
setem	se-*tehm*	stamp
setengah	se-te-*ngah*(h)	half
setengah liter	se-te-*ngah*(h) lee-ter	half a litre
setia	se-*fee*-uh	loyal
setiap	se-*fee*-ahp	each • every
setiap hari	se-*fee*-ahp hah-ree	every day
setiausaha	se-*fee*-uh-oo-suh-huh	secretary

Setuju.	se-*too*-joo	Agreed.

siap	see-*ahp*	ready
siapa	see-*ah*-puh	who
siar-siar	see-*ahr*-see-*ahr*	stroll
sibuk	si-*bu(k)*	busy (time)
sihat	si-*haht*	healthy
sikap	see-*kahp*	bad (attitude)
silakan	see-*lah*-kahn	please
simpang jalan	sim-*pahng* jah-lahn	crossroad
sinseh	sin-seh(h)	herbalist (person)
sintetik	sin-*teh*-tik	synthetic

sisa	see-suh	rest (what's left)
sisa buangan toksik	see-suh boo-ah-ngahn tok-sik	toxic waste
smir	smir	pap smear
soalan	so-ah-lahn	question
sosialis	so-see-ah-lis	socialist
stadium	stah-dee-um	stadium
standard	stahn-dahrd	standard (usual)
stesen	steh-sehn	station
stesen bas	steh-sehn bahs	bus station
stesen keretapi	steh-sehn ke-reh-tuh-ah-pee	railway/train station
stoking	sto-king	socks
studio	stoo-dee-o	studio
suam	soo-ahm	warm
suami	soo-ah-mee	husband
suara	soo-ah-ruh	voice • volume (sound)
suasana	soo-ah-sah-nuh	environment • atmosphere
subang	soo-bahng	earrings
suci	soo-chee	pure
sudah	soo-dah(h)	already
sudu	soo-doo	spoon
sudut	soo-dut	corner
suhu badan	soo-hoo bah-dahn	temperature (fever)
suhu udara	soo-hoo oo-dah-ruh	temperature (weather)
suka	soo-kuh	to like
suka menerima rasuah	soo-kuh me-ne-ree-muh rah-soo-ah(h)	corrupt (adj)
sukan	soo-kahn	sport
sukar	soo-kahr	difficult
suku	soo-koo	quarter
sundal	soon-dahl	prostitute
sungai	soo-ngai	river
suntikan [suntik]	sun-ti(k)-kahn [sun-ti(k)]	injection
sunyi	soo-nyee	quiet
surat	soo-raht	letter
surat beranak	soo-raht be-rah-nah(k)	birth certificate
surat berdaftar	soo-raht ber-dahf-tahr	registered mail
surat khabar	soo-raht kah-bahr	newspaper
susah	soo-sah(h)	difficult
susu	soo-soo	milk
sutera	soo-te-ruh	silk
syarahan	shah-rah-hahn	lecture
syarikat	shah-ree-kaht	company (business)
syiling	shee-ling	coins

T

tadika	tah-*dee*-kah	kindergarten
tafakur	tah-*fah*-kur	meditation
tahi	tai(k)	shit
tambah	*tahm*-bah(h)	plus

Tahniah!	
tah(h)-nee-ah(h)!	Congratulations!

tahu	tah-hoo	to know (something)
tahun ini	tah-hoon ee-nee	this year
tahun depan	tah-hoon de-*pahn*	next year
tahun lepas	tah-hoon le-*pahs*	last year
tak apa	ta(k) *ah*-puh	never mind
takut	tah-*kut*	afraid
tali	tah-*lee*	rope • string
tali kasut	tah-*lee kah*-sut	shoelaces
tali pinggang keledar	tah-*lee peeng*-gahng ke-leh-*dahr*	seat belt
taman negara	tah-*mahn* ne-*gah*-ruh	national park
tampon	*tahm*-pon	tampon
tanah	tah-*nah(h)*	land (ground)
tanaman	tah-*nah*-mahn	plant
tanda	tahn-duh	sign
tanda lebam	tahn-duh le-*bahm*	bruise
tandas	tahn-duhs	toilet
tandas awam	tahn-duhs ah-*wahm*	public toilet
tandatangan	tahn-duh-*tah*-ngahn	signature
tangan	tah-*ngahn*	hand
tangga	*tahng*-guh	stairs
tanggungjawab	tang-gung-*jah*-wahb	responsibility
tanpa	*tahn*-puh	without
tanpa filter	*tahn*-puh *fil*-ter	without filter
taraf	tah-*rahf*	standard (adj)
taraf kehidupan	tah-*rahf* ke-hee-*du*-pahn	standard of living
tarikh	tah-*rikh*	date (time)
tarikh lahir	tah-*rikh* lah-*hir*	date of birth
taruhan	tah-*ru*-hahn	bet
tasik	tah-*si(k)*	lake
tatabahasa	tah-tah-bah-*hah*-suh	grammar
tawaran	tah-*wah*-rahn	offer
tawar-menawar [tawar]	tah-wahr-me-*nah*-wahr [*tah*-wahr]	to bargain
tayar	tai-yahr	tyre
tebing tinggi	te-*bing ting*-gee	cliff
teduh	te-*du(h)*	shade
teh	teh(h)	tea

telah	te-*lah(h)*	already
tekak	te-*kah(k)*	throat
tekanan	te-*kah*-nahn	pressure
tekanan darah	te-*kah*-nahn *dah*-rah(h)	blood pressure
teks	tehks	subtitles
telanjang	te-*lahn*-jahng	nude
telefon	teh-*leh*-fon	telephone
telefon awam	teh-*leh*-fon *ah*-wahm	phone box
telefon bimbit	teh-*leh*-fon *bim*-bit	mobile phone
telegram	teh-leh-*grahm*	telegram
teler (col)	teh-ler	teller
televisyen	teh-leh-*vee*-shen	television • TV
telinga	te-*lee*-nguh	ear
telur	te-*lur*	egg
teman	te-*mahn*	friend
teman lelaki	te-*mahn* le-*lah*-kee	boyfriend
teman wanita	te-*mahn* wah-*nee*-tah	girlfriend
tembakau	tem-*bah*-kow	tobacco
tembikai	tem-*bee*-kai	watermelon
tembok	tehm-*bo(k)*	wall (outside)
tempahan	tem-*pah(h)*-hahn	reservation
tempat	tem-*paht*	location • place
tempat duduk	tem-*paht doo*-du(k)	seat
tempat letak kereta	tem-*paht* le-*tah(k)* ke-*reh*-tuh	car park
tempat kelahiran	tem-*paht* ke-lah-*hi*-rahn	place of birth
tempat suci	tem-*paht* soo-*chee*	shrine
tempatan	tem-*pah*-tahn	local
temujanji	te-*moo*-jahn-jee	date (appointment)
tenaga nuklear	te-*nah*-guh noo-*klee*-er	nuclear energy
tenang	te-*nahng*	calm
tendangan [tendang]	ten-dah-ngahn [ten-dahng]	kick
tengah malam	te-*ngah(h)* mah-lahm	midnight
tengahari	te-*ngah*-hah-ree	noon
(padang) tenis	(pah-*dahng*) teh-*nis*	tennis (court)
tepat pada masanya	te-*paht* pah-*duh* mah-*sah*-nyuh	on time
tepi (jalan)	te-*pee* (*jah*-lahn)	side (of street)
tepi laut	te-*pee* lowt	seaside
terakhir	te-rah-*khir*	last (final)
terang	te-*rahng*	light (not dark)
terbaik	ter-*bai(k)*	best
terburu-buru	ter-boo-*roo*-boo-roo	in a hurry

Terima kasih.
te-*ree*-muh *kah*-si(h) — Thank you.

terkenal	ter-ke-*nahl*	famous
terlalu	ter-*lah*-loo	too (excessive)
terlalu banyak makan ubat	ter-*lah*-loo bah-nya(k) mah-kahn oo-baht	overdose
terlalu mahal	ter-*lah*-loo mah-*hahl*	rip-off
termasuk	ter-*mah*-su(k)	included
teropong	te-*ro*-pong	binoculars
terpencil	ter-pen-*chil*	remote
terseliuh	ter-se-*lee*-uh(h)	sprain
tersesat [sesat]	ter-se-saht [se-saht]	lost
terus ke hadapan	te-*rus* ke hah-dah-*pahn*	straight ahead
tetamu	te-*tah*-moo	guest
tetapi	te-*tah*-pee	but
tiada	tee-*ah*-duh	none
tiap-tiap	*tee*-ahp-*tee*-ahp	each • every
tiba	*tee*-buh	to come (arrive)
tidak	tee-dah(k)	no
tidak apa-apa	tee-dah(k) ah-puh-ah-puh	nothing
tidak kemas	tee-dah(k) ke-*mahs*	sleazy (person)
tidak pernah	tee-dah(k) per-*nah*(h)	never
tidak selamat	tee-dah(k) se-lah-*maht*	unsafe
tidur	tee-dur	to sleep • asleep
tifoid	tai-*foid*	typhoid
tikar	tee-kahr	mat
tiket	tee-*keht*	ticket
tikus	tee-kus	rat
tilam	tee-*lahm*	mattress
timun	tee-mun	cucumber
timur	tee-mur	east
tinggal	ting-gahl	to live (somewhere)
tinggi	ting-gee	tall • high
tingkap	ting-kahp	window
tingkat	ting-kaht	floor (storey)
tipis	ti-pis	thin
tisu	tee-soo	toilet paper • tissues
tokong Buda	to-kong boo-*dah*	temple (Buddhist)
tokong Cina	to-kong chee-nuh	temple (Chinese)
tolong	to-long	help • please
topeng	to-*pehng*	mask (face)
topi	to-pee	hat
topi keledar	to-pee ke-leh-*dahr*	helmet
trek perbandu	trehk ber-*pahn*-doo	guided trek
tua	*too*-uh	old (person)
tuala	too-*ah*-luh	towel
tuala wanita	too-*ah*-luh wah-*nee*-tah	sanitary napkins

Tuan	too-ahn	Mr
Tuhan	too-hahn	God (Muslim)
tukang jahit	too-kahng jah-hit	tailor
tukang tenung	too-kahng te-nung	fortune teller
tukang tilik	too-kahng tee-li(k)	fortune teller
tulang	too-lahng	bone
tulen	too-lehn	pure
tuli	too-lee	deaf
tumbuh-tumbuhan	toom-bu(h)-toom-bu(h)-hahn	vegetation
tunangan	too-nah-ngahn	fiance(e)
tunggu	toong-goo	wait
tunjuk perasaan	toon-ju(k) pe-rah-sah-ahn	demonstration
tuntutan bagasi	toon-tu-tahn bah-gah-see	baggage claim
tutup	too-tup	shut

U

ubat	oo-baht	medicine
(kedai) ubat Cina	(ke-dai) oo-baht chee-nuh	herbalist shop
ubat gigi	oo-baht gee-gee	toothpaste
ubat pencegah hamil	oo-baht pen-che-gah(h) hah-mil	the Pill
ubat pencuci perut	oo-baht pen-choo-chee pe-rut	laxatives
ubat tahan sakit	oo-baht tah-hahn sah-kit	painkillers
ubat tidur	oo-baht tee-dur	sleeping pills
ucapan politik	oo-chah-pahn po-lee-tik	political speech
udang	oo-dahng	shrimp
udara	oo-dah-ruh	air
ujian (peperiksaan)	oo-jee-ahn (pe-pe-rik-sah-ahn)	test (exam)
ujian darah	oo-jee-ahn dah-rah(h)	blood test
ujian nuklear	oo-jee-ahn noo-klee-er	nuclear testing
ukiran kayu	oo-ki-rahn kah-yoo	woodcarving
ular	oo-lahr	snake
umum	oo-mum	general
umur	oo-mur	age
undang-undang	oon-dahng-oon-dahng	law
ungu	oo-ngoo	purple
universiti	yu-ni-ver-si-tee	university
untuk	oon-tu(k)	for (purpose)
untuk berseronok	oon-tu(k) ber-se-ro-no(k)	to have fun
urat darah	oo-raht dah-rah(h)	vein
urutan	oo-ru-tahn	massage
utama	oo-tah-muh	main
utara	oo-tah-ruh	north

V

van	vahn	van
virus	vi-*rus*	virus
visa	*vee*-sah	visa
vitamin	vi-*tah*-min	vitamin

W

wain	wain	wine
waktu makan tengahari	*wak*-too *mah*-kahn te-ngah-*hah*-ree	lunchtime
wang	wahng	money
wang tunai	wahng *too*-nai	cash
wanita/perempuan	wah-*nee*-tah/ pe-*rem*-pwahn	woman
wap	wahp	steam
warung	wah-*rung*	food stall
warna	*wahr*-nuh	colour
wartawan	wahr-*tah*-wahn	journalist
wawancara	wah-wahn-*chah*-ruh	interview
wayar	wah-*yahr*	wire

Y

ya	yah	yes
yang	yahng	which
yang berikutnya	yahng be-ree-*kut*-nyah	next
yang lalu	yahng *lah*-loo	past (before)

Z

zakar	zah-*kahr*	penis
zebra	*zeh*-brah	zebra
zoo	zoo	zoo

SUSTAINABLE TRAVEL

As the climate change debate heats up, the matter of sustainability becomes an important part of the travel vernacular. In practical terms, this means assessing our impact on the environment and local cultures and economies – and acting to make that impact as positive as possible. Here are some basic phrases to get you on your way ...

COMMUNICATION & CULTURAL DIFFERENCES

I'd like to learn some of your local dialects.
sai-yuh *ee*-ngin mem-pe-*lah*-jah-ree
be-be-*rah*-puh *dee*-yuh-le(k)
tem-*pah*-tahn *ahn*-dah

Saya ingin mempelajari beberapa dialek tempatan anda.

Would you like me to teach you some English?
ah-duh-kah(h) *ahn*-dah mow
sai-yuh me-*ngah*-jahr *ahn*-dah
se-*dee*-kit bah-*hah*-suh *ing*-ge-ris?

Adakah anda mahu saya mengajar anda sedikit Bahasa Inggeris?

Is this a local or national custom?
ah-duh-kah(h) *ee*-nee *ah*-daht
tem-*pah*-tahn ah-*tow* ne-*gah*-ruh?

Adakah ini adat tempatan atau negara?

I respect your customs.
sai-yuh meng-hor-*mah*-ti
ah-daht *ahn*-dah

Saya menghormati adat anda.

COMMUNITY BENEFIT & INVOLVEMENT

What sorts of issues is this community facing?
ah-puh-kah(h) je-*nis* *ee*-soo
yahng dee-hah-*dah*-pee
mah-*shah*-rah-kaht dee *see*-nee?

Apakah jenis isu yang dihadapi masyarakat di sini?

drug abuse	sah-*lah(h)* *goo*-nah dah-*dah(h)*	salah guna dadah
environmental cleanliness	keh-ber-*si(h)*-ahn ah-*lahm* se-*kee*-tahr	kebersihan alam sekitar
social issues among the youth	ge-*jah*-lah so-see-*ahl* dee kah-*lah*-ngahn re-*mah*-jah	gejala sosial di kalangan remaja

I'd like to volunteer my skills.

sai-yuh *ee*-ngin me-nah-*wahr*-kahn   *Saya ingin menawarkan*
ke-mah-*hee*-rahn *sai*-yuh   *kemahiran saya*
se-*chah*-rah soo-kuh-*re*-lah   *secara sukarela.*

Are there any volunteer programs available in the area?

ah-duh-kah(h) se-*bah*-rahng   *Adakah sebarang*
pro-*grahm* soo-kuh-*re*-lah-wahn   *program sukarelawan*
yahng bo-*leh*(h) dee-dah-*pah*-tee   *yang boleh didapati*
dee kah-*wah*-sahn *ee*-nee?   *di kawasan ini?*

ENVIRONMENT

Where can I recycle this?

dee *mah*-nuh-kah(h) bo-*leh*(h)   *Di manakah boleh*
sai-yuh me-*ngee*-tahr   *saya mengitar*
se-*moo*-luh *bah*-rahng *ee*-nee?   *semula barang ini?*

TRANSPORT

Can we get there by public transport?

bo-*leh*(h)-kah(h) *kah*-mee ke   *Bolehkah kami ke*
sah-*nah* de-*ngan* me-*nai*-kee   *sana dengan menaiki*
peng-ang-*koo*-tan *ah*-wam?   *pengangkutan awam?*

Can we get there by bike?

bo-*leh*(h)-kah(h) *kah*-mee ke   *Bolehkah kami ke*
sah-*nuh* de-*ngahn*   *sana dengan*
me-*noong*-gahng bah-*see*-kahl?   *menunggang basikal?*

I'd prefer to walk there.

sai-yuh le-*bih*(h) soo-kuh   *Saya lebih suka*
ber-*jah*-lahn ke *sah*-nuh   *berjalan ke sana.*

ACCOMMODATION

I'd like to stay at a locally-run hotel.

sai-yuh *ee*-ngin meng-*hee*-nahp dee   *Saya ingin menghinap di*
ho-*tehl* yahng dee-ken-*dah*-lee-kuhn   *hotel yang dikendalikan*
o-*leh*(h) o-rahng tem-*pah*-tahn   *oleh orang tempatan.*

Are there any ecolodges here?
  ah-puh-kah(h) ter-*dah*-paht
  se-*bah*-rahng *roo*-mah(h)
  toom-*pah*-ngahn dee *see*-nee?

*Apakah terdapat
sebarang rumah
tumpangan di sini?*

Can I turn the air conditioning off and open the window?
  bo-*leh(h)*-kah(h) *sai*-yuh
  me-mah-*tee*-kahn pe-*nyah*-mahn
  oo-*dah*-ruh dan mem-*boo*-kuh
  ting-kahp?

*Bolehkah saya
mematikan penyaman
udara dan membuka
tingkap?*

There's no need to change my sheets.
  tee-dah(k) per-*loo* me-*nyah*-leen
  chah-dahr *sai*-yuh

*Tidak perlu menyalin
cadar saya.*

SHOPPING

Where can I buy locally produced goods/souvenirs?
  dee *mah*-nuh-kah(h) bo-*leh(h)*
  sai-yuh mem-be-*lee bah*-rahng-ahn/
  chen-de-ruh-*hah*-ti
  ke-loo-*ah*-ruhn tem-*pah*-tahn?

*Di manakah boleh
saya membeli barangan/
cenderahati
keluaran tempatan?*

Is this made from …?	*ah*-duh-kah(h) *ee*-nee dee-per-*boo*-aht dah-ree-*pah*-duh …?	*Adakah ini diperbuat daripada …?*
Ramin	kah-*yoo* ke-*rahs*	*kayu keras*
hardwood	*rah*-meen	*Ramin*
turtle shell	*koo*-lit *pe*-nyu	*kulit penyu*

FOOD

Do you sell …?	*ahn*-dah men-joo-*ahl* …?	*Anda menjual …?*
locally	mah-*kahn*-nahn	*makanan*
produced	ke-loo-*ah*-ruhn	*keluaran*
food	tem-*pah*-tahn	*tempatan*
organic	*hah*-sil	*hasil*
produce	or-*gah*-nee(k)	*organik*

Can you tell me which traditional foods I should try?

bo-*leh(h)*-kah(h) *ah*-dah	*Bolehkah anda*
be-ree-*tah*-hoo *sai*-yuh	*beritahu saya*
mah-*kah*-nahn trah-dee-see-*o*-nahl	*makanan tradisional*
ah-puh-kah(h) yahng pah-*toot*	*apakah yang patut*
sai-yuh *choo*-bah?	*saya cuba?*

SIGHTSEEING

Are cultural tours available?

ah-duh-kah(h) lah-*wah*-tahn	*Adakah lawatan*
boo-*dah*-yah yahng bo-*leh(h)*	*budaya yang boleh*
dee-dah-*pah*-tee?	*didapati?*

Does your company ...?	*ah*-duh-kah(h) *shah*-ree-kaht *ah*-dah ...?	*Adakah syarikat anda ...?*
donate money to charity	men-der-*mah*-kahn wahng ke-*pah*-duh *bah*-dahn-*bah*-dahn ah-*mahl*	*mendermakan wang kepada badan-badan amal*
hire local guides	me-*ngahm*-bil be-*ker*-juh pe-*mahn*-doo pe-*lahn*-chong tem-*pah*-tahn	*mengambil bekerja pemandu pelancong tempatan*
visit local businesses	meh-lah-*wah*-tee per-nee-ah-*gah*-ahn tem-*pah*-tahn	*melawati perniagaan tempatan*

Does the guide speak ...?	*ah*-duh-kah(h) pe-*mahn*-doo pe-*lahn*-chong ee-too ber-bah-*hah*-suh ...?	*Adakah pemandu pelancong itu berbahasa ...?*
Iban	*ee*-bahn	*Iban*
Kadazan	kah-*dah*-zahn	*Kadazan*
Kelantan	ke-*lahn*-tahn	*Kelantan*

don't just stand there,
say something!

To see the full range of our language products, go to:

lonelyplanet.com

What kind of traveller are you?

A. You're eating chicken for dinner *again* because it's the only word you know.

B. When no one understands what you say, you step closer and shout louder.

C. When the barman doesn't understand your order, you point frantically at the beer.

D. You're surrounded by locals, swapping jokes, email addresses and experiences – other travellers want to borrow your phrasebook or audio guide.

If you answered A, B, or C, you NEED Lonely Planet's language products ...

- **Lonely Planet Phrasebooks** – for every phrase you need in every language you want
- **Lonely Planet Language & Culture** – get behind the scenes of English as it's spoken around the world – learn and laugh
- **Lonely Planet Fast Talk & Fast Talk Audio** – essential phrases for short trips and weekends away – read, listen and talk like a local
- **Lonely Planet Small Talk** – 10 essential languages for city breaks
- **Lonely Planet Real Talk** – downloadable language audio guides from lonelyplanet.com to your MP3 player

... and this is why

- **Talk to everyone everywhere**
  Over 120 languages, more than any other publisher
- **The right words at the right time**
  Quick-reference colour sections, two-way dictionary, easy pronunciation, every possible subject – and audio to support it

Lonely Planet Offices

Australia
90 Maribyrnong St, Footscray,
Victoria 3011
☎ 03 8379 8000
fax 03 8379 8111
✉ talk2us@lonelyplanet.com.au

USA
150 Linden St, Oakland,
CA 94607
☎ 510 893 8555
fax 510 893 8572
✉ info@lonelyplanet.com

UK
2nd floor, 186 City Rd
London EC1V 2NT
☎ 020 7106 2100
fax 020 7106 2101
✉ go@lonelyplanet.co.uk

lonelyplanet.com